Blockchain:

Discover the Technology behind Smart Contracts, Wallets, Mining and Cryptocurrency (including Bitcoin, Ethereum, Ripple, Digibyte and Others)

herein is also presented without contract or any type of guarantee assurance.

The trademarks presented are done so without any consent, and this publication of the trademarks is without permission or backing by the trademark owners. All trademarks and brands within this book are thus for clarifying purposes only and are the owned by the owners themselves, and not affiliated otherwise with this document.

Table of Contents

Chapter 9: Blockchain Technology and the Ledger of Things 103

Chapter 14: Understanding the Ripple Blockchain   157

Chapter 15: Understanding the Factom Blockchain   170

Chapter 16: DigiByte Blockchain   186

Chapter 17: Hyperledger   195

Chapter 18: Blockchain Technology and Financial Services 219

Chapter 19: Blockchain and Global Financial Products 228

Conclusion   309

Author's Note

Thank you for purchasing this book!

I hope you will benefit from this book. A lot of time was put into researching, writing, editing and compiling it.

If you do find it useful, would you be kind enough to write a positive review on Amazon? I would greatly appreciate it.

Introduction

Whenever business is discussed today, two of the most important terms that arise are *Bitcoin* and *cryptocurrency*. Many have heard of Bitcoin because of the rapidly-growing interest in cryptocurrencies. However, they are still unfamiliar with the *blockchain* technology behind Bitcoin and cryptocurrencies, or they have diverse opinions about exactly what blockchain technology is and how it works. While some may have an idea of what blockchain means, they often still hold the opinion that blockchain is a difficult concept, one that is only meant to be understood by Computer or Economics geeks, or both. Therefore, the goal of this book is to make blockchain technology understandable to all.

In contrast to popular belief, blockchain technology is actually a simple concept that can be easily understood. Even without a background in Economics, Computer Programming, or Business-related fields, most everyone can gain a comprehensive understanding of blockchain technology, its applications, and its potential for the future.

In addition to the basics of blockchain technology, this book also explains the *Internet of Things*, *smart contracts*, the *Ledger of Things*, as well as the application of these technologies. After delving into the conceptual analysis of how these technologies work, this book provides guided, practical instruction on working with blockchain and cryptocurrencies, such as creating and executing a smart contract and opening an *Ethereum wallet*, with steps that are designed to help readers get started investing in cryptocurrencies.

This book further considers the future of these technologies, such as the potential impact of blockchain on the world's economy, pointing toward the employment opportunities that global acceptance of blockchain and cryptocurrencies can bring for billions people around the world.

If a reader is interested in investing in cryptocurrency, yet is unsure of the best digital currencies to invest in, this book importantly provides a list of the most credible digital coins, with the reasonable assurance that your money will be invested wisely.

However, it is also important to note that scammers abound in cyberspace and many will attempt to leverage the popularity of cryptocurrency in order to lure investors and scam them of their hard-earned money. Therefore, finally, this book recommends some practical tips to prevent readers from falling victim to such scams.

Chapter 1: About Cryptocurrency

A *cryptocurrency* is a virtual or digital currency that was designed to serve as a medium of exchange. To make these digital assets secure, written *codes* known as *cryptography* are used. Cryptography is also used for verifying *digital currency transactions*, as well as controlling the creation of more cryptocurrencies. Cryptocurrencies are also known as *alternative currencies, digital currencies,* or *virtual currencies.*

History of Cryptocurrencies

The first cryptocurrency, Bitcoin, was created in 2009 by Satoshi Nakamoto, a pseudonym for an anonymous programmer, or a group of programmers. Although Bitcoin's inventors originally wanted to create a *peer-to-peer* cash system, they ended up instead with what is currently regarded as the leading cryptocurrency in the world, *Bitcoin.*

Since the creation of Bitcoin, an estimated one thousand different cryptocurrencies have been created. Some notable cryptocurrencies include:

- Ethereum
- Dogecoin
- Litecoin
- Zcash
- Ethereum Classic
- Ripple
- Monero

The cryptocurrencies listed above, as well as others not listed here, are collectively known as *altcoin* or *alternative coins*. These alternative coins were created in response to the huge success of the world's number one cryptocurrency, Bitcoin, mentioned above. (The best cryptocurrencies will be discussed in detail later.)

Features of Cryptocurrencies

Cryptocurrencies have some distinct, appealing features that are responsible for their huge acceptance and global recognition. These features have given cryptocurrencies a huge potential for becoming the first generally accepted international currencies, and are thereby positioned to replace traditional (as well as national) hard currencies.

Some distinct features of digital currencies are:

Cryptocurrencies are *decentralized*: Traditional currencies are under the control of their respective governments, central banks, and the financial branches of their federal governments. In contrast to traditional hard currencies, cryptocurrencies are designed to be independent of any government authority. Instead, cryptocurrencies are under the control of the *miners* that are located all around the world. For instance, a miner may be working in a local café in Africa, while another one may be mining from his patio in London. Miners work hand-in-hand to ensure the continued functioning of the cryptocurrency network, a network that includes the miners and the machines they use for operating. For this reason, it becomes impossible for a central government, or an individual, to alter the content of a Blockchain *public ledger*, as it has been updated by the miners after a transaction is completed. This decentralized network of miners works to ensure trust in cryptocurrency transactions and functions.

Cryptocurrency holders are *anonymous*: Anonymity is an important feature of cryptocurrency. The identities of cryptocurrency holders are kept as secret as possible. Therefore, no account can be traced back to its owner because all the personal information that can lead to the connection, such as addresses, names, or any other valuable piece of information that can be used for identification, are neither requested, nor provided, when creating a wallet for holding a cryptocurrency.

Cryptocurrencies are *transparent*: A public ledger, blockchain contains a complete history of all the completed transactions that have ever been entered. Since each cryptocurrency keeps its own ledger of transactions, all the miners for each cryptocurrency can easily connect a transaction to a particular wallet at any time. This ensures that transactions remain transparent, therefore preventing any potential scammers from altering a transaction because they can easily be caught.

Cryptocurrencies are *widely accepted*: Although cryptocurrencies were initially rejected by many, they now enjoy global acceptance from many big corporations and countries. For example, Bitcoin is widely accepted by many companies and organizations, such as Wikipedia, Virgin Galatic, Tesla, Microsoft, Overstock, Namecheap, and others.

It is important to note that cryptocurrencies have their own peculiar attributes that distinguish them from fiat currencies. Many of these attributes have made cryptocurrencies popular, thereby spurring their impressive appreciation in value in recent years.

How Cryptocurrency Works

Many have wondered exactly how cryptocurrency works. As mentioned earlier, cryptocurrency is synonymous with digital currency. It is a decentralized digital coin that functions as a medium of exchange. However, since cryptocurrency is also very different from fiat currency, there is much more to how it works.

A number of the ways cryptocurrencies work are mentioned below:

Transactions: A transaction occurs whenever a cryptocurrency is transferred from a cryptocurrency owner to another via their respective digital wallets. Whenever a transaction occurs, it is automatically submitted to the blockchain, which is a decentralized public ledger where the transaction will be confirmed. After the successful completion of a transaction, it is verified with a *cryptographic signature*, which is an *encrypted cryptography* (security code) for ensuring that the transaction was initiated from a credible source.

The confirmation for a transaction processes within ten minutes. Confirmations are usually accomplished by miners. Once a transaction has been fully confirmed, it will then be added to the public ledger, where it remains for as long as the program exists. A confirmed transaction is thus permanent and can never be altered or deleted from the public ledger.

Public Ledgers: A public ledger is a list of all the transactions that have ever been confirmed and entered into a blockchain. In essence, it is a complete history of a cryptocurrency ever since its creation up to the current moment. The information stored in the public ledger is not limited to a history of transactions alone; it also includes encrypted information about the cryptocurrency owners.

Cryptographic techniques are used to ensure the accuracy of the records that are confirmed and stored in a ledger. One of the benefits of the ledger is the ease for which it can be used to check new transactions to ensure that a digital currency holder does not attempt to spend beyond the number of digital coins he or she possesses. The public ledger is considered synonymous with the term, *transactions*, in blockchain.

Mining: Each transaction must undergo a *confirmation* process before the transaction can be considered to a completed transaction that will then be recorded on a blockchain. This confirmation process is called *mining*. A transaction that has not yet been confirmed can never be recorded in a blockchain, and is thus not considered valid until it is confirmed. It is only after the confirmation of a completed transaction that the transaction can be added to the public ledger. Once the transaction is added to the blockchain, it becomes an irrevocable.

It is important to note that the confirmation process is not easy. It requires that the miners solve difficult computational problems or a mathematical puzzle. Each successful solution the miner makes signals that a transaction has been fully completed.

The confirmation of transactions, however, is not exclusively assigned only to some particular miners. Instead, mining is *open source*, and thus this offers all miners equal opportunities to solve the mathematical puzzles, and therefore confirm transactions.

When a miner has successfully solved a puzzle, he or she then updates the public ledger with a block of transactions. These updated transactions will now be kept permanently in the ledger. The miner receives a fraction of the cryptocurrency as a reward for his or her efforts. This mining process is called a *proof-of-work* system. This is what is responsible for a digital currency's security. The connection between the confirmed transactions, blocks, and the public ledger increases the overall security of the digital currency, thereby making it virtually impossible for an individual to alter the content of the public ledger.

Digital Wallets: Unlike the traditional hard currencies, cryptocurrencies are digital. Cryptocurrencies are thus stored in software programs, known as *digital wallets*, which are digital equivalents of a bank account. Transactions are made when there is a transfer of digital currency from one digital wallet to another. Without digital wallets, no transaction can occur. The recent growth of a vast majority of these coins points to the potential future value they have for everyone's lives.

Cryptocurrency's Use

The changing perception of cryptocurrency has led to the increased application of these currencies and their use in different aspects of life. A cryptocurrency investor can perform several different kinds of transactions with their coins. Some of these transactions are:

Make a donation: If one wishes to make a donation to a worthy cause or charity organization, this can be accomplished with cryptocurrency. TampaBay.com is the number one platform for cryptocurrency donations.

Finance an education: Some universities around the world accept Bitcoin for tuition. The first university that accepted Bitcoin for tuition was the University of Nicosia, Cyprus. Tuition can also be paid through Bitpay, which is a payment processor with a reputation for excellence. As other universities increasingly begin accepting cryptocurrencies for tuition, it will make this process more convenient for students.

Crowdfunding: When contemplating raising funds for a project, many cryptocurrency investors have now turned to cryptocurrency. Also, as an investor, one can contribute to a project by making a contribution with cryptocurrency. There are several successful projects that have been exclusively funded with digital currencies. For example, the Jamaican Bobsled team was exclusively sponsored by Dogecoin. Another project that was financed exclusively with cryptocurrency is Lighthouse. Cryptocurrency has a bright future as a dependable source of crowdfunding.

Vehicle Purchase: Tesla made the decision to accept payment with Bitcoin and sold the Tesla Model S for a whopping 91.4 Bitcoin. After this successful transaction, another car, a Lamborghini Gallardo, followed suit and was sold for an incredible 216.8 Bitcoin.

House Purchase: The first home bought with digital currency was a villa sold in February, 2014, for 1,000 BTC, in Indonesia. Another home was sold in Las Vegas, Nevada, for a whopping $157,000 BTC.

These are only some of the transactions that can be made with digital currencies. As the number of cryptocurrency enthusiasts grow, the types of transactions that can be made will also increase.

Chapter 2: Reasons to Invest in Cryptocurrency

The current rise in the popularity of cryptocurrencies is caused by several important factors. For instance, the continued growth of cryptocurrencies makes these a good investment for investors. The allure of gaining financial freedom through investment in cryptocurrencies, of course, also appeals to many. One of the most important reasons, however, to invest in cryptocurrencies is that cryptocurrencies, and the technology behind them, are the wave of the future. What follows are a few reasons for considering investing in cryptocurrencies:

High rate of appreciation: In 2018 alone, the price of Bitcoin has increased several times and currently sells at over $14,500 per coin, up from a little less than $800 per coin a year ago. This means that investing in Bitcoin only a year ago would have reaped a profit of over $13,000 per coin. Bitcoin is not the only cryptocurrency where the value has increased so dramatically over the past few years. Cryptocurrencies, such as Litecoin, Ethereum, and Ripple, have also experienced rapid increases in values as well. These dramatic increases in values are only one of the reasons to consider investing in cryptocurrencies.

Security: Cryptocurrencies enjoy a unique security system, known as cryptography encryption, that is proven to be secure and one of the factors responsible for the astronomical rise in the values of digital currencies. Through encrypting all the information about cryptocurrency transactions, developers created a safe platform, where investors need not fear losing their investments to scammers. These high-security measures have spurred increased interest in cryptocurrencies. Most all exchange websites have security measures in place to drastically reduce the risk of investors losing any coins.

Inflation-proof: The fact that cryptocurrencies are invulnerable to inflation due to governmental interest rate hikes is one of the most important distinctions between digital coins and hard currencies. Wise investors thus view cryptocurrencies as a way to avoid the effects of inflation, which have been a perennial problem and the bane of hard currencies for centuries. While hard currencies will usually be affected by inflation at some point, if kept in banks, digital currencies are immune to inflation because they are kept in *digital wallets*. Rather than depreciate in value due to inflation, cryptocurrencies will instead continue to appreciate, and investors will thus also rewarded in this manner for investing in cryptocurrency.

Where to Buy Cryptocurrency

The rapid growth and acceptance of cryptocurrency has made digital currencies the target of cybercriminals. This underscores the necessity for investors to use reputable exchanges when buying a digital currency, as a preventive measure against losing money to cybercriminals. For this reason, it is important for investors to take into consideration the credibility and reputation of the exchange before investing. The website security, as well as that of the server, should also be considered to prevent being scammed when attempting to purchase a digital currency.

When considering these safety factors, an investor needs to seek out the best exchange from which to purchase a digital currency. Over the years, some exchanges have built a reputation for honesty and credibility. These exchanges have usually been in business for several years. Some exchanges that have proven safe and reliable over time include:

Coinbase.com

Coinbase.com has been around for several years and is one of the few reputable names and leading exchanges. Coinbase's interface is both attractive and easy to navigate, designed to make an investor feel comfortable in its use. Purchases can be made with a debit card. After purchase, an investor can also create a personal wallet on the platform, in which to store the digital currency. Coinbase.com has over 5,000,000 active subscribers, making it a popular site, and it also provides thousands of different apps. Coinbase.com is an especially good site for investors based in America, Europe, or Canada.

Bitmex.com

Bitmex.com is considered to be the best margin trading site for Bitcoin. On its platform investors can trade different cryptocurrency derivatives, with about 100x leverage, for example, Yen, Ripple, BTC/USD, Ethereum, or Dash. The Bitmex cryptocurrency exchange was designed by Bitmex CEO, Arthur Hayes, to meet the rising need of cryptocurrency investors. Hayes leveraged his experience as a former equity derivatives trader from his previous employment at Deutsche Bank. However, beginners should probably avoid this exchange because the platform is primarily designed for seasoned and experienced traders.

LocalBitcoins.com

To compare the best trading platform for cryptocurrency deals, LocalBitcoins.com is another reputable name in the in the crypto-trading industry. When trading on LocalBitcoins, investors are not limited to a single trading option. Instead, the platform offers multiple options to choose from. One of the highlights of this exchange is the privacy it offers its users. Moreover, the platform provides different payment options. Therefore, regardless of the payment options available in your country, traders will find one that is appropriate. In some countries, it is impossible to purchase any cryptocurrency without using LocalBitcoins because it is the only available trading platform in those countries for cryptocurrencies.

Bittrex.com

Bittrex.com is considered by many crypto-investors as the largest crypto- exchange in the world. This exchange achieved landmark success through years of dedication to the services it offers its growing user base. The sudden disappearance of some exchanges, such as Poloniex, BTC-e, and Cryptsy, also helped Bitrex to gain more users who are looking for a dedicated exchange offering them the best service. Bittrex is currently the altcoin exchange with the highest number of visitors, where investors carry out huge volumes of transactions.

Bisq.io

Bisq.io is not a site to be missed. While it does not have the technical advances of some of the more established exchanges, it does offer a decentralized platform where peer-to-peer trading is possible. With more than 60 different cryptocurrencies available for transaction, there are a lot of options on this site. One can trade here with their coin of choice through escrow, bank transfer, or a credible third party. Bisq has also has trusted escrow system for bank transfers.

CoinATMradar.com

A unique cryptocurrency exchange platform, CoinATMradar.com is an exchange that provides a list of all the Bitcoin ATMs in the world. This makes it easy for Bitcoin enthusiasts or investors to make purchases with hard currency at a physical ATM machine. This exchange does not require users to submit their personal information because it does not carry out verification exercises on users' ID's. This practice allows users to stay anonymous when conducting business transactions over CoinATMradar.com's hundreds of ATM machines that are spread across all the continents.

Poloniex.com

Poloniex's exchange once had the reputation as the best cryptocurrency exchange in the world. It also had the now extinct Cryptsy as its main competitor; however, Poloniex managed to survive the stiff competition offered by Cryptsy, and that led to an impressive growth for this crypto-exchange. Since the arrival of many different altcoins, Poloniex has continued to experience drastic growth. Between February and May 2017, its user base increased from 7 million monthly visits, to 30 million.

Poloniex has a user interface that is second to none in the industry. Whether trading on a desktop computer, or mobile device, its user interface allows for the best user experience. To begin trading on this platform, a trader must first buy Bitcoin from another platform, and then deposit it in Poloniex.

Poloniex currently ranks as the second-best exchange platform, after Bittrex; however, it still has the future potential to reclaim its spot as the world's leading cryptocurrency exchange platform.

As an investor, there are several excellent exchanges available for trading in cryptocurrency. A comprehensive study of available exchanges will allow an investor to join other cryptocurrency investors across the globe without worrying about centralized services or custodial accounts.

It is important to note, however, that when dealing with many exchanges, an investor gives absolute control of their investments to the exchanges. As a result, there exists the risk of losing coins if an exchange is shut down. However, in contrast, the Poliniex exchange allows investors to always be in control of their investments because their personal funds are stored in smart contracts. The *private keys* remain in the possession of investors, and in this manner, investors remain in control of their money.

Poliniex runs on a decentralized exchange platform, which is proof of its security. Registration on the site is also easy because name and ID's are not needed, since no registration is required on the platform.

Blockchaininfo.com

Blockchaininfo.com is a large exchange where an investor can easily purchase digital currency and make payments. A leading name in the cryptocurrency business, Blockchain.info has offered stress-free transactions for its growing number of customers for several years.

If the security of the currency is a concern, Blockchain.info has one of the best security measures in the industry. This is accomplished, in part, by the fact that a wallet address is comprised of an alphanumeric and a 2-factor authentication that ensures confirmation of an owner of an account before allowing access to the account. This security measure is designed to prevent criminals from gaining access to the account because they would not be able to pass the security test. Therefore, accounts are protected against hacking, while coins are held safe in wallets.

Opening an account on one of these platforms and starting to investment on the platform of your choice is easy. Blockchain.info is recommended first for cryptocurrency investments. The following steps explain how to set up an account and start investing:

Step 1: Enter the website address (www.blockchain.info) into the address bar. This will show a page with different options.

Step 2: Next, click on "Wallet" at the top left-hand corner of the home page.

Step 3: Click on "Sign Up." This will load a page where a personal account can be created.

Step 4: After clicking the "Sign Up" menu, a page will be displayed with a registration form that asks for an email address and a password for the creation of the account.

Note: Be extremely careful here. All the information supplied must be accurate. The email address provided will be needed for the confirmation of the account, as well as for verification of login attempts whenever checking a wallet. Be certain as well to ensure against the loss of any of the information supplied because there is no way to change a password, or to retrieve it, as can be done on other sites. This security measure was built into the platform to ensure that users do not lose their hard-earned currencies to scammers.

After entering an email address and password, and taking steps to guard these against loss, accept the Terms of Service. Then, click "Continue."

Step 5: A confirmation will be sent to the email address for verification of identity, so check the email at the address provided for the verification link. Click the verification link in the email as a proof of ownership, which will automatically reroute to the registration page to complete registration.

Step 6: After completing registration, an account page will load. What follows are explanations of some of the page's functions.

Send: Use this option for transferring a coin from the user's account to create a transaction with another user's account, whether that transaction is to raise money for an important project, auction some coins to pay for a service or product, or to purchase from an online store. When sending, there is a request to provide the address for the user to transact with. After providing all the relevant information, the transaction can be made.

Receive: This option is, of course, the opposite of the option discussed above. The "Receive" option is for receiving payment from another wallet holder, such as making a request for payment for products or services rendered to a client.

Your Balances: This function displays the user's account balances and the cryptocurrencies held. After conducting a transaction, this section will be automatically updated to reflect the current status of your account.

Recent activity: This section contains the transactions history, such as all payments and funds received. For example:

BTC = $12,020.67: This is the current price of Bitcoin, at the time of writing this book. This figure is not a constant, but instead always changes to reflect the real-time price of Bitcoin. If creating a personal account now, the price will, of course, be different from what that shown in the screenshot here.

ETH = $664.21: This section functions in a similar way to the BTC section. It also reflects the real-time value of Ethereum, as of the time of login into the account. The price also changes to reflect the value of the currency at any given time.

Graph: The graph displays the different prices of the currency as it rises and falls. A comparison of the graphs for two different time periods will demonstrate much the coin has lost or gained within a given time period.

How to Store Digital Currencies

Storing cryptocurrency safely is one of the many things investors need to know before deciding to invest. There are two ways to store cryptocurrencies:

Online: Storing digital coins online involves keeping them on a computer, an exchange, or a mobile device that is connected to the Internet. The online storage can be accomplished in a number of ways. Some ways to store digital currencies online include:

An exchange: It is best to purchase cryptocurrencies from an exchange, such as Coinbase, Blockchain.info, and/or others. If purchased from an exchange, the private key is not held in the investor's possession but by the exchange. In this case, the exchange is in absolute control of an investor's digital currency, although an investor can conduct a transaction any time they wish. This method of storing digital currency with an exchange is one of the easiest ways to store cryptocurrencies. (The only risk here is that hackers could break into the exchange's server and steal investors' currencies.)

Online wallet: Most of the exchanges offer an online wallet to each investor. When purchasing a cryptocurrency from an exchange, an investor can just keep their currency in the wallet with that exchange. Similar to how digital coins are kept on the exchange, an investor's private key is also kept with platform that offers the wallet service. (This method shares a similar risk with just the exchange option above.)

Offline: When storing digital coins offline, they are kept on a computer, without an Internet network or a hardware wallet. To complete the storage, an investor keeps their private key in the wallet, thereby avoiding exposing it to the Internet. There are a few ways to store digital currency offline:

A software wallet: There are a couple of software wallets available where the software can be downloaded to a PC. A couple of these software wallets are Ethereum wallet, for keeping Ethereum, and Armory, for storing Bitcoin. When using software wallets, the private key is the investor's responsibility, not the platforms. That provides an investor with absolute access and control over their coins. However, this method also involves risk. In the event that an investor loses their PC or forgot their password, they run the risk of losing their digital currency. The same problem can occur if a private key is stolen; this may lead to a cyber-thief stealing the coins.

<u>Hardware</u>: Storing coins in a hardware wallet is probably the safest method for keeping digital currencies safe. There are two hardware wallets to choose from, Trezor wallet, or the Ledger. The latter is one of the best, most reliable hardware wallets brands and is known as Ledger Nano S, or Ledger Blue.

If choosing the hardware wallet option, an investor, of course, cannot access their wallet in the absence of the hardware. Without the hardware, approving or conducting transactions is impossible. This can be a bonus for wallet holders, however, because it prevents hackers from gaining access to your digital currencies. Without the wallet, any hacker who has access to your account cannot tamper with it.

If the hardware is ever lost, all hope is not lost. An investor would only need to provide their recovery phrases for the cryptocurrency to be restored. This underlines the importance of keeping the recovery phases where they cannot be lost.

<u>Paper</u>: One can print a private key and address on a piece of paper and keep the paper in a safe place.

These are just some of the ways to store cryptocurrency safely. Since any of these options have their risks, it is best for investors to choose the one they are most comfortable with.

Investing in Cryptocurrency

Investing in cryptocurrency need not be a chore; it should be viewed instead as an opportunity to see an investment grow. The following tips are designed to help investors make the best decisions when choosing which cryptocurrency to invest in and which platform, or exchange, to use:

- Never invest more than what one can afford to lose. Cryptocurrencies are volatile, fluctuate rapidly, and an investor must be ready for the risks involved. Therefore, to minimize the impact of any loss, one should only invest amounts that will not overly affect their overall finances.
- Make certain that coins are safe. An investor should choose a method of storage they trust and are comfortable with. Many investors prefer the hardware wallet option because of the freedom it offers them to be in absolute control of their currencies.
- Buy cryptocurrencies only from exchanges with excellent reputations. There are many scammers are out there who are ready to prey on the ignorance of newbie investors. Search the ratings of the exchanges first before using them, or use the list of credible exchange platforms above.
- Understand how cryptocurrencies work before investing. This means performing due diligence on these currencies before investing.

How to Invest

While one does not need to understand all the technicalities behind the operation of a cryptocurrency before becoming an investor, this does not mean it is fine just to go ahead and invest in any currency. Before investing in a cryptocurrency, one *must* perform the following:

Due diligence: It is imperative to research the top cryptocurrencies to understand the investment pattern. Research should include the history, current price, rate of appreciation in recent times, and the potential for growth. One can start by researching the top cryptocurrencies discussed above.

Visit an exchange: Pick one of the cryptocurrency exchange platforms from those provided above. Visit the official website of the exchange and create a personal wallet.

Determine how much to invest: Despite the allure of cryptocurrencies and the hype surrounding them, many financial experts have suggested that investors in digital currencies should invest only what they can afford to lose, in the event of circumstances that cause a loss of the investment. In this case, an investor would not lose all their savings but only a portion of it.

Make a purchase: After deciding on an amount to invest, go ahead and buy the currency. There are tons of trusted sellers to buy from. Contact a credible exchange where the chances of getting legitimate coins for purchase are high. Buy the coins and keep them until they appreciate. Later, if desired, sell them for a profit.

If one implements these tips to invest in a cryptocurrency, the investment process should be easy.

Chapter 3: Qualities of a Good Digital Currency

There are many different opinions about what makes a good digital currency. However, there are some qualities that are universally accepted investors should consider:

Acceptability: Before investing in a cryptocurrency, one should consider the number of countries that recognize and accept that currency as a means of legal exchange. Since international transactions have become more frequent, this is an important consideration.

Portability: A digital coin must be portable. An investor should be able to carry it from one place to another without problem. Any digital currency that does not offer portability should not be considered as an investment.

Security: A cryptocurrency must be secure. This is an inherent characteristic of any legal currency.

Durability: A cryptocurrency must be durable, meaning that it will not lose value or disappear over time. Similar to how hard currencies have been in existence for centuries, cryptocurrencies should also offer the same assurance.

Divisibility: Divisibility is the ability to divide a currency into smaller parts. For example, dividing a $100 bill into two means each half is 50% of the whole, or $50. A divisible cryptocurrency must also offer that ability.

Transportable: The ability to transport a digital currency from one place to another makes it so it is fully usable. For example, if transfer of a digital currency cannot be made from one account to another, then it is not transportable.

Impossible to duplicate: This is one of the many reasons why Bitcoin and other cryptocurrencies are considered to be more secure than conventional hard currencies. While hard currencies can easily been duplicated, the same cannot be said of such digital currencies. The mining process of digital currencies is very complex, and thus prevents duplication.

Elasticity: The rising demand for Bitcoin and other cryptocurrencies, such as Ethereum, Litecoin, Ripple, and others, has recently led to an increase in the number of currencies that are mined each day. This increase thus provides the coins with a reasonable degree of elasticity.

Economical: It should be cheaper to mine the coins than their actual value. For this reason, cryptocurrencies are reasonably economical.

Inherent Value: From decentralized applications to smart contracts, cryptocurrencies promise to be more than just a medium of exchange, and thus should also be viewed as important tools that will change the future of currency and technology.

If a cryptocurrency meets all of these major characteristics, it makes it a credible digital currency that offers both current value and future benefits.

How to Detect Cryptocurrency Scams

Cryptocurrencies are in high demand as millions of people around the world become a part of the Cryptocurrency era. Of course, scammers are also taking advantage of digital currencies in attempts to lure unsuspecting victims into purchasing fake cryptocurrencies. Therefore, it is imperative to understand how to detect cryptocurrency scams. This section will share some practical tips that can help identify cryptocurrency scams.

When considering a cryptocurrency, watch out for the following concerns:

Check the blockchain: Every cryptocurrency is built on a blockchain technology. Knowing this can help to determine the authenticity of a cryptocurrency by asking what blockchain the digital currency is built on. For example, is it built on Bitcoin, or Ethereum, blockchain? If so, rest assured that the digital currency has some degree of legitimacy.

Liquidity: If a digital currency is legitimate, it should be easy to liquidate, in other words, have the ability to be able to turn a digital currency's commodity asset into other cryptocurrencies, or back to hard currency. A digital currency that lacks this attribute is far from legitimate.

Function: The function of a digital currency also determines its legitimacy. The company behind a legitimate cryptocurrency will have a functional business plan, or model, through which the currency can be used to address a real-life problem and/or solve it. The Bitcoin and Ethereum blockchains have many uses for the creation of decentralized applications and smart contracts. Thus, these two important blockchain technologies are currently used to solve some real-life problems and have the potential to be used for solving even greater problems in the future. Digital currencies such as these that meet this requirement are therefore legitimate.

The people behind it: This is another factor not to overlook. The people behind the creation of a cryptocurrency also determine the legitimacy of a digital currency. One should perform research to see if the people behind the currency have a track record of honesty, as well as flawless personal and economic records. They should never have been involved in any illegal businesses, such as Penny Auctions and Ponzi Schemes, and are both conservative and transparent in their dealings.

Phishing impersonators: The cryptocurrency world is filled with impostors. Most of these impostors use social media to lure unsuspecting prey with offers that are intended to defraud them. Such impostors may offer a service, and then ask their potential target to give them their private keys to confirm the authenticity of their wallet. Once such confidential information has been released, these impostors will phish the private key and use that information to eventually scam an investor, even after gaining their coins. Under no circumstances reveal your private keys to anyone. A credible cryptocurrency company will never ask for private keys, unless the actual investor needs it to access their own account.

Cryptocurrency-flipping scams

This is another common cryptocurrency scam investors should guard against. If a cryptocurrency company asks to exchange your digital currency for money after an investor has paid the initial start-up fee for the currency, or if an investor is promised that an initial investment will be doubled overnight, caution is needed.

Cryptocurrency pyramid schemes: This cryptocurrency scam is more difficult to identify than some of the other scams listed here. This difficulty in detection has made it more successful than the other scams.

Scammers who use this technique often present themselves as cryptocurrency creators and promise high yields on investments, within a short period of time. They encourage investing in the digital currency as a multi-level business idea. They lure with the promise of turning a small investment into a goldmine by signing up more members for the business through referral links. In a short time, hundreds, or thousands, are lured into the scheme. The scammer then walks out on investors after fleecing them of their money.

Detecting a cryptocurrency scam can be done by comparing any digital currency with the qualities listed above. If the digital currency meets these requirements, one can be reasonably certain it is a safe investment. It is always advisable to trade with care when investing in cryptocurrency.

Ways to Protect Yourself

As the saying goes, prevention is better than the cure. Here are some further warnings to heed to when considering investing in cryptocurrency:

1. Social media and the Internet in general have scammers on the prowl. Exercise caution when presented with any cryptocurrency investment offer. Do not be tempted to jump at any offer. Instead, perform due diligence to arrive at a wise investment decision.
2. If a website offers you too-good-to-be-true cryptocurrency offers, do not be in a hurry to accept such offers. Remember, if it sounds too good to be true, it is probably not true.
3. Even when dealing with a credible cryptocurrency broker online, be on guard. Make certain it is both the right broker and an authentic one. A proliferation of imposters and fake websites are run by scammers.
4. When redirected to a website and asked to provide confidential information, such as a wallet address or private keys, this is, of course, a red flag. Instead of

supplying such information, log out of the website and do not return.

5. Do not engage in any financial transactions involving cryptocurrency on social networks. If your gut tells you that you are dealing with a potential scammer, follow your instincts. That decision alone may prevent becoming a victim of an online scam.

Cryptocurrency investors can ward off potential scammers by implementing these tips. Ignoring these can lead to being scammed. An informed investor will avoid financial loss by playing it safe.

Chapter 4: Top Ten Cryptocurrencies

Cryptocurrency is an Internet invention that is quickly becoming an international sensation. While Bitcoin continues to be the front runner, thousands of other cryptocurrencies have been created to serve different purposes. Cryptocurrencies, however, are not created equal and each one can have many different features designed to make them stand out from the pack. What follows is a list of the Top Ten Cryptocurrencies that are changing the world:

1. Bitcoin

Bitcoin is the first decentralized digital currency. It is responsible for starting the cryptocurrency revolution that eventually led to the creation of thousands of other currencies designed to meet the growing demand for digital coins. Created by Satoshi Nakamoto in 2009, Bitcoin currently has the biggest capitalization of all the digital currencies in existence. With a market value of approximately $250 billion at the time of this writing, Bitcoin dwarfs other currencies in the digital currency world.

Thus Bitcoin is considered to be the reference point, when discussing cryptocurrencies, because of its importance in relation to other cryptocurrencies. The coin has such a large reputation and value that, in relation to Bitcoin, all other coins are collectively referred to as "altcoins," in other words, alternative coins to Bitcoin. For this reason, Bitcoin always comes up whenever a list of the top cryptocurrencies is compiled.

2. Ether

Just as Bitcoin is the official digital coin of the Bitcoin blockchain, Ether is the digital currency of the Ethereum blockchain. If Bitcoin is the king of the cryptocurrency world, Ether is arguably the queen.

Created by a 21-year-old programmer, Vitalik Buterin, Ethereum is a decentralized platform that can be used for the execution of smart contracts. First launched in 2015, it was sold to the general public as the "next generation cryptocurrency and decentralized application platform." Currently, as of this writing, Ethereum has an impressive market capitalization of over $73 billion.

Ethereum is known in particular for its peer-to-peer smart contracts that have enabled developers to develop applications that can be used for signing contracts, while making obeisance to the terms of the contract, without a third-party in the middle.

3. Litecoin

In 2011, a former Google employee, Charles Lee, invented Litecoin. He released the digital currency in October 2011 as another alternative to Bitcoin. Litecoin possesses some of the outstanding qualities of Bitcoin, as it can be used both as currency and a medium of exchange. As of this writing, it currently has an estimated market capitialization of $180 million and is gradually working its way to becoming one of the digital currencies that will shape the future.

4. Monero

In 2014, Monero, an open-source digital currency was created. Monero focuses on decentralization, privacy, and scalability. This cryptocurrency can run on a wide range of Operating Systems, such as Linux, Windows, Android, and MacOS. While Monero functions on similar principles as other cryptocurrencies, this digital currency was created with the goal of improving existing digital coins by creating a more egalitarian mining process.

In 2016, the cryptocurrency experienced an unprecedented surge in its market capitalization. Its transaction volume for that year also increased tremendously as a result of the adoption of the currency by some major organizations, such as AlphaBay.

5. Ripple

Ripple is simply one of the best cryptocurrencies on the market. Released to the cryptocurrency market in 2012 as a currency exchange, Ripple is a real-time gross settlement system and remittance network. As of this writing, Ripple currently has a market capitalization estimated to be over $76 million, after it overtook Ethereum to become one of the most sought-after cryptocurrencies. This year alone, Ripple has experienced an astounding 20,000 percent appreciation in value.

Ripple is built on a consensus ledger, internet protocol, and native cryptocurrency. It was designed to make it possible for cryptocurrency users to conduct instant and secure financial transactions with another party anywhere in the world. According to Brad Garlinghouse, Ripple Chief Executive Officer, during an interview with Bloomberg Television, "within the year of crypto, Ripple has outperformed every other digital asset out there."

As a leading cryptocurrency, some banks have integrated the cryptocurrency into their system to make payment easy for their customers. Some of the notable companies that are using Ripple are UBS, UniCredit, and Santander. Many banks and other financial institutions are increasingly adopting Ripple as a credible payment network. Two of the features of this coin that makes it acceptable for use in the banking industry are its affordable price and peerless security.

6. Dogecoin

Dogecoin was not created as a digital currency given the potential to have any impact on people. Instead, it was created as a "joke currency," in the likeness of an Internet meme, Doge. However, the coin took off and gradually triggered the creation of an online community of users. From December 6, 2013, to January 2014, Dogecoin reached an estimated market capitalization of approximately $60 million. Currently, its capitalization is estimated to be $1 billion.

When compared with other digital currencies, the initial production schedule of Dogecoin was rapid. By mid-2015, Dogecoin had 100 billion coins in circulation. Every year since 2015, over 5.2 billion coins have been added. Dogecoin has proven useful in social media, where it is often used for tipping users that contribute noteworthy content to the Internet. Users of this digital currency believe the coin will soon experience a great increase in value, an overall rise in value of the coin that is referred to with the expression "To the moon!"

Dogecoin is also frequently used for fund raising. For instance, during the Doge4Water campaign, it raised thousands of dollars. The campaign was so successful that over 4,000 donors made donations with the coin, including an anonymous donator, who donated some 14 million Dogecoin, worth approximately $11,000 at the time of the donation.

7. Dash

Dash is a cryptocurrency used for making instant, anonymous payments when shopping online. With Dash, purchases from office or home can be made with a direct payment from a Dash wallet. Dash can save time while shopping because the platform makes payments easy and stress-free. While the Dash platform makes payments easy, it also offers a practical way to protect financial information while shopping online. It does this by ensuring that account balances and transaction activities are all kept private. This privacy additionally helps thwart potential scammers.

Apart from the privacy offered by the platform, Dash also provides maximum security. All the transactions conducted on the platform are confirmed by a very powerful computing power, a 200 TerraHash, and the more than 4,500 servers hosted in strategic locations around the world. All these features make Dash one of the Top Ten Cryptocurrencies to consider investing in to reap many financial benefits from the cryptocurrency world. As of this writing, Dash currently has a market capitalization of approximately $4 billion.

8. MaidSafeCoin

MaidSafeCoin is also known as Safecoin. This cryptocurrency was created by the Secure Access for Everyone (SAFE) network. SAFE is a security-oriented data platform and was created to loan out a space on your personal computer in return for coin. Safecoin is designed to ensure that at there will always be only 4.3 billion coins in circulation. These coins will also never be identical, as the coin has its own unique features and identity. A couple of decentralized apps currently depend on the SAFE network for their data storage because of the security it offers them. As of this writing, the coin has a market capitalization of approximately $40 million.

9. Lisk

Lisk is a unique cryptocurrency, in that it is a crowdfunded digital currency and prides itself as "the first modular cryptocurrency utilizing sidechains." Lisk shares some similarities with Ethereum, such as it can also be used for developing decentralized apps. This is available for developers that are good at Javascript. The currency is useful for creating e-commerce stores, social media platforms, and other decentralized applications. Recognized as the first cryptocurrency built on sidechains technology, as of this writing, it has an estimated market capitalization of $25 million.

10. Zcash

Zcash is another cryptocurrency that is a decentralized and open-sourced. Therefore, it offers privacy protections that cannot be easily breached. This makes it one of the most secure cryptocurrencies. The identities of parties involved in Zcash transactions are carefully concealed when transacting with Zcash, thus hiding information about the recipient, sender, as well as the value of the Zcash held on the blockchain. While Bitcoin remains the undisputed top digital currency, these other nine cryptocurrencies are important competitors in terms of both security and privacy.

Defining Cryptography

Cryptography is the security measure behind the success of cryptocurrencies. While conventional hard currency is vulnerable to theft and fraud, cryptocurrencies are protected through this unique security measure. Cryptography is defined as "the practice and study of techniques for secure communication in the presence of third parties called adversaries. More generally, cryptography is about constructing and analyzing protocols that prevent third parties of or the public from reading private messages."

Prior to the current application of cryptography, it was formerly synonymous with *encryption*, which involves the conversion of valuable information into a non-readable format. The sender of a encrypted message shares the technique for decoding an encrypted message with the intended recipients. The goal was to prevent unauthorized access to confidential information, and thus preserve the confidentiality of sensitive information.

However, the development of advanced machines, such as computers, during the World War II, and the rotor cipher machines during World War I, also led to the development of more complex cryptology methods. These methods eventually led to an increased application of the technology in different sectors of the economy, to be used as effective security measures.

Today's cryptographic methods have proven to be more effective than previous ones because they are based on Computer Science practices and mathematical theory. The underlying principles of cryptographic algorithms are computational hardness assumptions. These have succeeded in making cryptography extremely difficult for hackers to break into. Theoretically, today's cryptography method can still be broken into; however, it has been found to reliable against attempts at breaking into it. As the security measure behind cryptocurrencies, investors have little cause for security concerns because these have been taken care of through the security measures.

When considering a list of the Top Ten Cryptocurrencies, it is important to note that most digital coins are designed with an ultimate cap that limits the number of a particular digital currency that can ever be in circulation. Cryptocurrencies also have several distinct qualities that separate them from hard currencies, thus making digital coins more flexible in their use. Finally, the technology of cryptography makes cryptocurrencies more secure than banks and other financial institutions. These reasons, in part, are behind the rapidly increasing popularity of the cryptocurrencies.

Chapter 5: Unraveling Blockchain Technology

The advent of the Internet was greeted with excitement, as it brought about many changes in daily human life, such as communication, business and personal interactions, and financial transactions. Among the many important changes Internet technology has brought to modern civilization are social media, e-mail, online job opportunities, and globalization. The achievements of the Internet are, in fact, too numerous to list here but have, in the main, arguably turned our world into a better place.

A recent, rapidly-developing technological innovation, known as the Internet of Things (IoT), will greatly affect the future. IoT will eventually change how our homes, assets, and other valuables are protected. A concept with a promising future, IoT will be discussed in more detail later in this book.

Information exchange, research, and other crucial activities are rapidly growing and are carried out on much larger scales than ever before. Leveraging the power of Internet research has proven not only to lower the costs of such activities, but also makes valuable information instantly available at one's fingertips. The outstanding benefits the Internet offers have also spread across the global economy, thereby benefiting many sectors and their economies as well. In addition, the impact of the Internet has been realized in such areas as insurance, politics, education, and social sectors.

However, in spite of all of the benefits it offers, the Internet also has limitations, especially in the areas of the economy and business. One of these limitations is that some people find it increasingly difficult to trust one another completely, especially when engaging in online business transactions.

Potential business partners, clients, or customers in an online environment are even less ready to part with their money, without any form of validation or assurance from a third-party, such as a bank.

In addition, third-parties, such as banks, often take their customers for granted. Third-parties also collect vital information about individuals, under the guise of verifying the identities of the parties in a transaction, and they sometimes use this information for personal gain, such as sharing private customer information with others, such as advertisers and data mining companies, without the owners' consent.

For the most part, however, technology has arguably impacted the world in positive ways. For instance, one can argue that introduction of the Internet has succeeded in turning the world into a global village. The Internet has inspired numerous online entrepreneurs and opened up employment opportunities for millions across the globe. In spite of increasing job opportunities and other infrastructural development brought by its technology, the Internet has not yet succeeded in creating the promised prosperity at its beginning.

As aforementioned, however, a lack of trust can pervade internet interactions. For instance, many would agree that the internet has eliminated individual's privacy and security, especially as it often seems most everything in the world today revolves around technology. The internet has often been used as a force for both good and bad. With the use of the Internet, there also is the risk of identity theft and invasion of privacy. Using credit cards online can lead to financial loss.

Technology has also caused an unprecedented explosion in electronic communication, and has equally triggered cybercrime at an unprecedented rate. Just waiting to exploit the weaknesses in online security, scammers, cyber bullies, spammers, spies, and con artists hide under the umbrella of technology as a way to perpetrate their evil acts. Internet technology has proven to be an invaluable tool for cybercriminals. For example, note the damage that can be done when ransomware is unleashed on your personal computer or mobile devices. In 2017, the world witnessed the damage done by the dreaded WannaCryransomware virus that wreaked havoc on many personal computers around the world, leading to the loss of valuable data and money for thousands of its victims.

Scientists and inventors of technology, however, have not just waited and watched, of course, as the Internet continues to be used as a tool for invading individual's privacy and stealing their valuable confidential data and information. For decades, inventors have been working on finding a permanent solution to the problems of security and privacy, as well as the many other challenges that are part of using the Internet.

One of the most important problems in terms of trust in using the Internet has been the existence of third-parties that persist in functioning between users and the Internet in ways that make users less secure. For instance, most online registration involves divulging one's personal information to a website, often without giving a second thought to the potential implication of such a decision. This confidential information may later be stolen by cyber criminals, accidentally revealed to unauthorized personnel, or even made public on the web. For years, security experts have tried to address this issue and find a lasting solution to both security and stopping privacy being breached, regardless of the cause. However, even their best efforts have been mostly futile.

In 2008, a Developer, working under the pseudonym, Satoshi Nakamoto, created a new protocol that powered a Bitcoin-based peer-to-peer electronic cash system. Sakamoto's goal was to use the protocol to eliminate the issues that the current technology was not capable of handling. This important development has made blockchain and cryptocurrency the driving force behind future technology, thereby having a huge impact on the global economy.

The protocol proposed by Nakamoto has a set of rules, whereby the integrity of any data exchanged by two parties in an agreement will not be violated. This protocol eliminates the need for a third-party, which was a much needed, revolutionary breakthrough. Over the past few years, this protocol has taken the world by storm. It has influenced the business world and other areas, such as privacy advocates, media theorists, and governments, just to name a few. There is now finally a technology that is designed to truly address security and privacy issues.

The impact of Sakamoto's work is so important that Marc Andreessen, Co-Creator of Netscape, could only say: "They're like, 'Oh my God, this is it. This is the big breakthrough. This is the thing we've been waiting for. He solved all the problems. Whoever he is should get the Nobel Prize-he's a genius.' This is the thing! This is the distributed trust network that the Internet always needed and never had."

At first consideration, this protocol seems to be a strange idea for some. The realization that third-parties could be totally eliminated by a protocol that ensures a degree of trust between two parties through technology is beyond the imagination of many people. The protocol, in fact, makes the collective interest reign supreme, thereby leading to a mutual trust that is both encouraged and enforced by a simple code.

Many still, however, have reservations. Nevertheless, it is important to note that this protocol has completely changed how things are done, such as how transactions are processed, or how records are stored and secured, and has also had a positive impact in many other areas. Most importantly, the protocol has fostered trust between people who have never met or conducted any online business transactions, something previously considered unthinkable.

The protocol has also opened the door to many other innovations that have impacted people's lives in important ways. The most important of these innovations is the blockchain. There are currently thousands of blockchains that are used by digital currencies. Notably, the first digital currency, Bitcoin blockchain, stands out from other blockchains in terms of its mode of operation and its potential.

Blockchains have fundamentally changed the way people conduct transactions and pay for goods or services. They have simplified the process by allowing business partners, or clients, to send money safely and directly from one person to another, thereby bypassing a credit card company, bank, or any other financial institution in the process. The elimination of these third-parties has given people new, vibrant business transaction techniques that are also secure enough to protect them from fraud. The previous practice of intermediaries capitalizing on user's ignorance, taking them for granted, and ripping them off, will, in the future, be completely eliminated and replaced with a better, more transparent alternative. In the meantime, direct transactions between two or more parties can now easily be conducted without trust issues.

One of the most important features of blockchain is its open source code. This offers anyone the ability to download the code and build on it in order to develop new innovations for a variety of uses. Blockchains have so many yet untapped potentials that will prove useful in the future. Once even more developers start to explore the potential of blockchains, the world will see it transform many things.

Defining Blockchain

A blockchain is "a ledger of records arranged in data batches called blocks that use cryptographic validation to link themselves together." It is a decentralized, digitized, and public record of all cryptocurrency transactions. Blockchain constantly grows, as the most recent transactions are added to the blockchain. Blockchain works much like a data structure, where the creation of a ledger of records is possible, and where the ledger can also be shared for use among different people.

The data stored on a blockchain is foolproof, and all the transaction processes will readily be available for verification and confirmation to all those who are connected to the network (nodes). Each node automatically receives a copy of the blockchain and downloads it automatically. The diverse uses of blockchains have given rise to an increasing array of types of blockchains:

Public blockchains: Public blockchains refer to a huge, distributed network under control of a native token. These blockchains are available for anyone who is interested in participating in them. As a result, whoever is interested in reading and writing the data that is stored on the blockchain can do so because the data is accessible to people around the globe, regardless of their location.

Anyone can also join a public blockchain network and send, store, and receive data, the same as any other person on the network. This is because the network is decentralized, and all those on the network have equal rights and permission to write data on the blockchain, or to read from it. In public blockchains, no one has exclusive power over a blockchain. Public blockchains also have open-source code incorporated in them that makes it possible for the community to continue. Bitcoin and Ethereum are two cryptocurrencies that are built on the principle of public blockchains. Investors in these coins have the privilege of making direct transactions without the need for a third-party due to the public nature of the blockchain technology behind them.

Private blockchains: These blockchains are smaller than the rest and do not make use of a token. Membership in a private blockchain is limited, as is suggested by the name. These are the preferred blockchains of consortiums composed of trustworthy members.

In private blockchains, the organization or consortium controls the permission to write data onto this blockchain. This restriction provides private blockchain with more privacy than is possible in public blockchains. Since the company is in charge of the blockchain, the organization may decide at any time to change the rules governing the blockchain. It may also decline some transactions if these do not meet the company's rules and regulations. Transaction verifications are also easier than in public blockchains because only a handful of people are needed for the verification.

Permissioned blockchains: In this type of blockchain, each individual is under the control of the blockchain. A user cannot have a role in the blockchain without authorization from the blockchain. Similar to the public blockchains, permissioned blockchains also still make an extensive use of native tokens, while their code may either be open source, or not. A typical example of a permissioned blockchain is Ripple.

Permissioned blockchains are the middle ground between public and private blockchains. The verification process is not handled by all the members of the network, as is practiced in the public blockchain, and neither is it controlled by a single organization, as is done in private blockchain. Instead, predetermined nodes are allowed to conduct the verification. A common factor among all these blockchain types is that they are all driven by cryptography. They use this cryptography to give permission to anybody using any network, thereby ensuring that the ledger is well-managed and secure, without being forced to do so by a higher authority. The absence of a higher, or central, authority is called decentralization, and this is what makes blockchains considered to be *thick*.

Blockchain has gradually carved a niche for itself as one of the most important elements of computing, as well as an important element of the Internet. Any information written into a blockchain is permanent. It is nearly impossible to alter such information. This is an unprecedented feature for a database of information. This permanence of information also ensures the reliability of such information, and as such open ways for other business transactions to be made with the blockchain. For instance, many banks and other financial institutions now carry out safe transactions on these blockchains.

Blockchain Structure

Blockchains maintain back-linked, ordered lists of transactions in blocks as a data structure. Blockchains can be stored in a database, or as a *flat file*. Each block in a blockchain refers to the previous block in a chain; this is to say they are *connected back*. Under ideal conditions, blockchains are blocks that are placed one after the other. The first stack of the blockchain is known as the *basis* of each stack. Because blocks are considered to be placed on each other, the terms, *top* and *tip* refer to the last item added to a stack. The distance between other blocks in a stack and the first block in the same stack, is known as *height*.

In a blockchain, each of the blocks has a *hash* for identification. This is generated by making use of the SHA256 cryptographic hash algorithm present in the *header* of each of the blocks. Each block also has reference to a previous block that is known as the *parent block*. This means that the header of each of the blocks has its parent's hash. As each block is linked to its parent through a hash, a *genesis block* is formed, a chain that goes all the way back to the first block that was created.

Despite the fact that a block is limited to a single parent, it has the ability to temporarily have multiple *children*. All the blocks contained within a block refer to the block as their *parent*, as they contain the same hash, or parent, in the field considered the *previous block hash*. The issue of multiple children can occur when a *blockchain fork* occurs. However, it is only one of the children that will form a member of a blockchain.

The *previous block hash* is a field that can only be found in the block header, which therefore impacts the hash of the current block. Whatever happens to the parent will have a corresponding impact on the child. For instance, if there is an alteration to the parent's identity, the identity of the child will change, too. Any modification of the parent will also cause a change in the parent's hash. When the parent's hash is changed, it will cause the previous block hash that leads to the child to change as well, so the child's hash will also change. That same change will also necessitate a change in the hash of a grandchild, and so on.

The importance of these changes is that whenever a block is followed by many generations, any changes made to any of these will trigger the recalculation of all the blocks before it. Since the process of the recalculation will require a huge amount of computation, the existence of a long chain of blocks is what contributes to the immutability of blockchains, a valuable feature that guarantees the security of Bitcoin.

Blockchain technology can be compared to geological layers. As the seasons pass, there may be some small changes to the surface, and perhaps before the surface even has time to settle it may be blown away by the elements. However, the deeper into the layers one goes, the less the impact of external forces, therefore making the structure more stable. Hundreds of feet down, the layers will remain stable for centuries.

This is similar to blockchain. Although recent blocks are prone to sudden changes, the deeper into a blockchain, the more stable it becomes, and thus the more difficult it is to change. Beyond a hundred blocks in, the blockchain becomes permanent. While there is still a possibility any block can be changed, as time passes, the likelihood of a change significantly decreases.

Therefore, blockchain has a built-in structure that makes it extremely difficult for anyone to remove or change a block of date. If someone decides to remove or make a change to a block, all the members of the network can evaluate the proposed transaction and see whether they can verify it or not. This process ensures the accuracy and transparency of each transaction.

Blockchains are divided into three combined structures: *block, chain, and network*:

1. **Block**--A block refers to a list of transactions that are recorded into a ledger within a specific period of time. Each blockchain has a distinct period, size, and event that will

trigger the block. A block will automatically record any transaction that has not been previously entered into any block. For this reason, a block can be compared to a page in a record book, or ledger. The completion of a block opens the door for the subsequent block in the same blockchain. A block thus contains records that cannot be removed or altered once they are written.

When comparing transactions conducted over Bitcoin network to brick-and-mortar banking transactions, a blockchain represents a record of all the bank transactions carried out at within a given period. A block itself can be compared to a confirmation of a single transaction that is carried out by a customer of the bank, by providing an ATM printout, after the transaction has been conducted at the ATM.

A block stands for the *present* and contains information about the past and future of the block. Whenever a block is completed, it automatically belongs to the past, and then allows a new block to take its place in the blockchain. The completed block now represents a record of transactions conducted in the past that are permanently recorded. The new block will hold current records.

The continuing replacement of an old block with a new one makes it so the whole process is a cycle where data is permanently stored. Each of the blocks contains either records of all recent transactions, or some of the transactions. It also contains a reference to the preceding block.

2. **Chain**--A chain is a hash that mathematically "chains" two blocks together. It is also the principle behind the gluing together of blockchains, and thus makes the creation of mathematical trust possible for the blockchain.

3. Network--A network is made up of full nodes. They work together to ensure the security of the network. Each of the nodes contains all the information about every transaction that has been recorded in a blockchain.

Nodes are location independent because they are located in different parts of the world and can be operated by anyone is interested in that responsibility. Operating a node can be expensive, difficult, and time-consuming. This has made operating a node a process that involves costs. However, node operators are mainly motivated by the allure of earning cryptocurrency as a reward for their efforts.

How Blockchain Technology Works

Some governments and banks are taking advantage of blockchains to change the way people and organizations store information, as well as the way people conduct transactions. Governments and banks that have adopted blockchain technology have admirable goals: lower cost, speed, security, and the elimination of intermediaries.

Bitcoin blockchain is the most influential of the blockchains. Satoshi Nakamoto created a technology that has changed how businesses and transactions are conducted. Blockchain contains several appealing qualities that make it popular among its users as an efficient technology:

Distributed: Blockchain is distributed, meaning that it runs on the computers of volunteers from all walks of life. This distributed quality ensures that there is no central database for potential hackers to hack.

Public: Blockchain is an open-source technology that is accessible to anyone. Since the blockchain network does not reside at a single institution, anyone who is interested in it can view it at their convenience.

Encrypted: Blockchain technology is heavily encrypted. A multiple encryption system that combines both private and public keys is used to ensure the security of the blockchain. For this reason, one need not fear the loss of any stored information to identity thieves, weak firewalls, and other potential security concerns.

All transactions conducted on a blockchain are cleared, verified, and stored every ten minutes. Transactions are stored in a storage block that is connected to the preceding block that creates a chain; this is the reason it is called a blockchain. It is a mandatory procedure that each block must make reference to the preceding block for its validity to be determined. As a result, information and records can be safely stored, without giving anyone a loophole to exploit, or alter, the ledger.

Security measures implemented by the blockchain make it nearly impossible for anyone to steal the coin. Anyone who wanted to steal the coin must be prepared to rewrite the entire history of all the coins stored on the blockchain. This would be is an impossible task, even for the most skilled developer.

The digital ledger known as blockchain can also be used for storing valuable information and records, such as marriage licenses, birth certificates, deeds, titles of ownership, death certificates, financial accounts, and others. In the future, many things will be easier due to all the potential of blockchain technology. In the meantime, developers are currently working to design applications with a universal appeal and acceptance that can be used in all areas of our lives. This is just the beginning of a blockchain world.

Blockchain technology has also generated excitement in the business world. For both investors and other professionals, blockchain presents a new way of doing things. Attitudes towards blockchain in the business world are rapidly changing for the better, as businesses begin embracing the changes and innovations brought about by the technology. For instance, influential people, such as Laura Shin, of *Forbes*, Daniel Roberts, and Ben Lawsky, a former New York State's Superintendent, who quit his job to build a business around blockchain, as well as a host of other influential investors in blockchain, are proof of the power of this technology and its future promise.

In the political arena, many US politicians support blockchain. In the U.K., Gulnar Hasnain, a politician, and a Green Party candidate, was the first politician in the U.K. to accept Bitcoin for her campaign. She believes blockchain has several appealing attributes: "Surprisingly, the Green Party is vocal on the same issues as the Bitcoin movement – more decentralized power, smaller government, a need for a shift in the concentration of power in the banking system and a more inclusive society."

Several media houses have run advertisements that support blockchain innovation. In October 2015, *The Economist* ran a cover story entitled, "The Trust Machine." The article asserts that blockchain has the potential to change how things are done in the future, and especially the potential to change the economy.

It is no wonder that banks, and other financial institutions, are taking advantage of blockchain technology to improve their services. Bankers are especially enamoured of the security of transaction brought about by blockchain. They are also awed by the ease and promptness of blockchain transactions. The widespread acceptance of blockchain technology has, in fact, led to a rebranding of the financial services industry. The industry has privatized and rebranded blockchain technology, considering it to be *the distributed ledger* technology, one that consolidates the speed, security, and cost of blockchain with the traditional ledger system. The financial industry considers blockchain technology to provide better, more trustworthy databases that allow sellers, buyers, regulators, custodians, and other stakeholders in the financial industry to keep indelible records and to be able to share these records with others when needed. This move to blockchain has thus reduced costs as well as eliminated transaction failures.

While the 1990s saw a huge leap in investments in dot.com innovation, something similar can be said about investments in the blockchain industry today, however, on a much larger scale. Blockchain technology, in fact, offers much more than what the Dot.com era delivered, and investors from all walks of life are taking advantage of what is a rare opportunity.

Proof of the promise that blockchain technology holds for the future can be measured, in part, by the high turnout of investors in cryptocurrencies. In 2014 and 2105 alone, millions of investors across the world invested over $1 billion in cryptocurrencies. This amount of money invested is unprecedented. The Dot.com era never even came close to this amount. In the future, cryptocurrency will be the main topic in technology, in ways similar to how the Internet is today.

Chapter 6: Trusting Blockchain Technology

Trust is one of the most important qualities that people look for when making business investments or conducting transactions. For a business to be trustworthy, it must meet some basic qualities, generally known as the four basic principles of integrity: *consideration, honesty, transparency, and accountability*:

Consideration: A trustworthy business should be exemplary in being considerate of others. This means giving the other party the benefit of the doubt that it will be fair in its operations and interactions with you. However, true trust requires that each party respects the desires, interests, and feelings of the other party. It also means that both parties can operate towards one another in good faith with one another. Being considerate is an important element of trust, and every business should strive to have a good reputation in that aspect.

Honesty: No savvy businessperson, or investor, would invest in a business where honesty is not a value. Today, honesty in not just an ethical issue, it is an economic issue as well. To establish a trusted relationship with business partners, customers, clients, shareholders, and the rest, honesty is essential. **Transparency:** Transparency means there is nothing to hide from others. A lack of transparency reduces the degree of trust people have and will possibly make them see a business as dishonest.

Accountability: Having accountability means being committed to a course and abiding by the terms of the course. Both institutions and individuals must therefore recognize the importance of accountability by honoring their commitments and agreements. Doing so means never giving excuses for a failure to live up to promises to others, including during business transactions. A strong sense of accountability, means accepting full responsibility for mistakes, and to make any necessary amendments.

From academics to government officials, to CEOs and industry experts, most professionals, as well as members of the general public, share the same mind-set. When trust has been compromised, individuals cannot conduct business transactions smoothly, without the input of a third-party, or intermediary, to vouch for the integrity of the parties. Prior to the introduction of blockchain, intermediaries, either individuals, or organizations, helped people resolve their trust issues. Most relied on third-parties to vouch for potential business partners or clients, and also to help with business transactions. Notable intermediaries primarily include governments, banks, and others.

However, in the world of blockchain, trust is no longer a concern because blockchain technology ensures that trust is already built-in to anything composed on blockchain, from new devices, to business transactions. The rationale behind this built-in trust is expressed by Carlos Moreira: After working for WISeKey, a cryptographic security company for years, he opined that blockchain technology has delegated trust to everything, including physical things, stating, "If an object, whether it be a sensor on a communications tower, a light bulb, or a heart monitor, is not trusted to perform well or pay for services, it will be rejected by the other objects automatically." Therefore, a blockchain ledger is itself a custodian of trust.

There are many current and future benefits that individuals and organizations stand to derive from blockchain technology and its effort to address the issue of trust. In blockchain, they will find a convenient and cost-effective way to ensure that people can deal with each other with complete trust. The increased transparency offered by blockchain will make investors expect more from CEO's. Investors will now be able to determine easily whether a CEO's actions justify their position and pay or not. Shareholders will also be able to increase their expectations of financial firms and organizations that are run on blockchain, as blockchain calls for both more trust and accountability.

Another innovation in blockchain technology is that it has made it possible for business transactions to occur without each party being unduly concerned about trust issues through the use of *smart contracts.* Thw blockchain-based smart contract application forces parties to abide by their terms of agreements. (There are many other areas for the application of smart contracts that will be discussed in detail in subsequent chapters.)

Another important issue that blockchain technology will address is the abuse of technology. For years, many governments and corporations have abused technology for their own selfish ends. They have, in fact, used technology to gather information about their opponents and used that information to intimidate and spy on their citizens, undermine individual's rights and freedoms, as well as to change public opinion, without the proper consultation of all the parties involved.

The Internet has also been used to support the rise and ambition of authoritative governments. A typical example is in China, where Bitcoin is banned, and the government vows to punish anyone who trades in ICO's. Some countries have also banned the use of social media platforms, thereby preventing their citizens to enjoy the freedom of having a beneficial social relationship with people from the other parts of the world.

These are only some of the issues that have been plaguing technology for years, without a practical solution until now. Everything will change once blockchain technology becomes the mainstream technology. It will open more opportunities for everyone. When blockchain technology closes the loopholes currently being exploited by governments and big organizations that take an undue advantage of individuals, all will benefit.

Blockchain has both the mechanisms and human support to gradually, but progressively, address all of these aforementioned issues and more. Miners are always working around the clock to ensure its security. Its peer-to-peer platform promises many more positive changes and innovations. Some of these have been discussed earlier, while others will be covered later in more detail.

Protecting personal information and privacy is now possible without fear of breaches of privacy and security, while transactions can be conducted without the assistance of intermediaries. These are already huge benefits. The future prospects of blockchain technology are exciting and encouraging for all. It is truly causing a revolution in the way things are done.

Creating and Storing Your Identity

The use of social and other types of media often brings up the question of our identity. Social media and others, in many ways, seeks to define our identity for us, and we often change to fit these media's views of who we are. However, blockchain technology solves this problem. Now, personal data can be permanently stored in a blockchain and referred to whenever needed.

The ability to store aspects of personal identity in blockchain has many benefits. For example, blockchain storage can keep one's identity safe for more important uses in the future, such as for a college fund that is linked to it. Family and friends can then contribute to the education fund. This can offer free access to funding education, without having to take student loan from the government, a bank, or other financial institutions.

When creating and storing one's personal identity in blockchain, valuable information, such as financial accounts, birth certificates, service accounts, medical information, and so on, can be included. A user can then choose which information to make public, thereby shifting the monetization of the value of one's personal information to themselves, and not to third-parties that may exploit it. For example, one can send a different subset of personal information to their dentist and another subset to their banker. Users who have control over their own stored records and reputation, as stored by blockchain technology, shift the power and control from third-parties to themselves in ways that benefit users.

Protecting Economic Rights

Not many would argue that there exists widespread inequality, in terms of the economic rights of the world's citizens. While developed countries enjoy a measured degree of economic rights, the same cannot be said of the developing world, where billions of people are still denied basic economic rights.

For example, in some countries, citizens are not allowed to own property because of government restrictions. And, in some other countries, if you own land or a home, it is possible to lose one's property without a prior warning from the government. It can be impossible to get property back without providing proof of ownership. Without proof of ownership, it can also be impossible to gain a building permit, or to secure a loan for your building project. Selling the property may be restricted by many local and national government rules and regulations that prohibit such a transaction without due authorization from a centralized government.

Blockchain offers a practical solution to these problems. It can eliminate the restrictions placed by government on properties, therefore making it easy for a property owner to do whatever they wish with their property, without any undue interference by the government or other regulatory body.

An Economist explained that "The central idea to blockchain is that the rights to goods can be transacted, whether they are financial, hard assets or ideas. The goal is not merely to record the plot of land but rather to record the rights involved so that the rights holder cannot be violated." This kind of policy would empower property owners to have absolute authority on their own property, beyond the control of the government, through a decentralized technology.

Eliminate Corruption of Foreign Aid

The objective of foreign aid for most countries is to provide a palliative measure to the financial challenges and economic hardships suffered by the recipient countries. However, there is currently no reliable measure of the performance of some non-profit organizations that are used as a channel for the distribution of foreign aid, especially during disasters. This has allowed some distributors to misappropriate the funds they received for providing aid to victims of natural disasters, such as cyclones, earthquakes, and tsunamis.

In a paper entitled, "Aid Abuse and Mismanagement in Africa: Problems of Accountability, Transparency, and Ethical Leadership," Gervase S. Maipose notes that "unfortunately, the impact of aid has been largely disappointing both in terms of the degree of dependency on air resources and economic growth performance."

Africa is not the only country that contends with this issue. The distribution of much-needed aid is a global issue, especially in developing countries. For example, take the actions of the Red Cross during the recent earthquake in Haiti: During the devastating earthquake in Haiti that led to the loss of thousands of lives, as well as the destruction of millions of dollars of property, many alleged that the custodian of foreign aid, the Red Cross, misappropriated the funds.

When ProPublica and NPR conducted an investigation into how the funds were sent as foreign aid and used by the Red Cross, the investigation revealed that the Red Cross only delivered a small percentage of the relief it received, thereby highlighting the problems of monitoring the use of foreign aid funds by non-profits. In the words of Daniel Borochoff, of Charity Watch, "There's a lot of waste and abuse that's allowed to go on just because there is no accountability." The beauty of blockchain technology in this case is that it eliminates the middlemen, or the charities themselves, that are responsible for the mismanagement of foreign aid funds. In some cases, just a fraction of the aid gets to the intended recipients, therefore making it so the beneficiaries do not ever receive the true value of the aid.

Blockchain will now make it possible for each individual to track the progress of a foreign aid funds. Even if middlemen are somehow not entirely eliminated, they can still be held accountable for how funds are used. If it now becomes possible for everyone to track how funds for foreign aid are used by a charity on their mobile devices, these charities will now have to be more cautious of misappropriating such aid.

This actual accountability will thus lead to a more judicious use of foreign aid.

As mentioned earlier, trust is an integral part of a successful business, or at least a business with the potential for success. For example, when taking a student loan, the lender needs some assurance that the borrower can pay it back. The same goes for a loan taken as a start-up capital for a business. Any entity that lends money demands a high degree of trust and assurance that it will be repaid.

Aside from all the areas covered here, everyone should have the rights to good health care, security, education, as well as the right to succeed economically. All of these rights require that everyone have access to services that will support these efforts, and that will create an environment to help them achieve their dreams. In addition, free access to transactional tools that will ensure that a smooth connection to the global economy is another important factor. Blockchain brings the promise of all this and more.

Blockchain Entrepreneurship

It goes without saying that the global economy cannot succeed without entrepreneurship and entrepreneurs. However, entrepreneurship still remains the unfulfilled dream of billions of aspiring entrepreneurs around the globe. Granted, the Internet has opened a floodgate of opportunities for many entrepreneurs; however, most of the beneficiaries of these opportunities exist in developed countries. Those entrepreneurs also have better chances of leveraging technology to advance their cause than their counterparts in developing countries.

In contrast, in the developing world the Internet has not really yet had a significant impact on aspiring entrepreneurs. It has not yet given them the financial tools they need to launch businesses that billions of people can benefit from. It has also not given them immunity from the bureaucracies of governments. These conditions call for a location-independent technology that will boost the chances of any aspiring entrepreneur and give them access to the tools that will ease their journey into entrepreneurship.

It appears blockchain also has an answer to this challenge by overcoming the obstacles that have made it difficult for aspiring entrepreneurs in developing countries to have access to all the tools they need. This means improved access to funding, investment opportunities, business partners, and so on, when all the obstacles have been successfully removed. Regardless of how seemingly small an entrepreneur's talent may be, blockchain can help them monetize it.

Make Governments Accountable

Blockchain can also have an impact on government. The technology can effectively be deployed in ways to ensure that governments give their electorates the best service. Blockchain can also be used to effect a permanent change in terms of democracy because it also calls for accountability on the part of the political leaders. If one is interested in government or the political process, they can participate by voting and other electoral processes, regardless of their political affiliation, through the blockchain technology. The technology can also be used to hold political leaders accountable for their electoral promises, in ways that may be considered revolutionary in politics and government. The use of Blockchain technology in the political process can have both direct and indirect impacts.

It is possible to state that Blockchain can offer a rewarding and promising future where everyone will have a chance at prosperity, a future where interfering intermediaries will disappear. The potential of blockchain, then, is better than most could have ever imagined.

Chapter 7: Blockchain Economy

When Satoshi Nakamoto came up with blockchain theory, he had certain ideas in mind, in in terms of the principles of blockchain. If properly implemented, blockchain would change how things are done. With the assistance of talented individuals who could see the future in blockchain technology, Satoshi worked to create significant achievements based on blockchain principles.

Satoshi's vision does, in fact, have the potential to change the world. Although the ideas for the technology informing Bitcoin in the paper Satoshi delivered about the Bitcoin blockchain project in 2008 appeared simple, these have nevertheless proven to be a key to a better future, as well as the beginning of a new era in the digital industry. In the paper, Satoshi described a future that will be controlled by a combination of mathematics, computer engineering, cryptography, and technology.

Although Satoshi himself did not define a specific set of principles, an analysis of blockchain and its numerous applications for different areas of life reveal certain principles that can be applied in many different areas, such as services, software, business, markets, and so on. These principles are further based on the importance making such processes more trustworthy. What follows offers the basic principles behind blockchain and underscores its potential to become the template on which almost every facet of human life in the future will be built on.

Networked integrity

One of the most fundamental principles of blockchain is integrity. The integrity of blockchain is built on the principle that it eliminates intermediaries, thereby allowing individuals to carry out any transaction with mutual trust. This is because the blockchain process is decentralized, which makes processing a transaction to be distributed process, rather than being controlled by a single individual. In this manner, through decentralization, trust between parties is enforced by the blockchain technology.

All operations that are carried out on blockchain are done by taking into consideration the need for accountability on the part of all of the individuals involved, so that everything will go smoothly. Accountability involves taking responsibility for ones' decisions and actions, being transparent in dealing with others, and doing everything within to ensure honesty. Blockchain technology, in fact, helps to enforce this integrity by ensuring that it is both easier and cost-effective.

Potential Problems

Conducting online transactions has never been without problems. There is still often an element of distrust, which can be mutual among potential business partners, or customers. Practically no one is ever willing to release their product or money, without any assurance of getting real value for their money. Stories abound about those who have been scammed online because they were too trusting.

To thwart scams, blockchain importantly protects individuals from being defrauded through its *double spend problem*. When making online payments, this problem is solved by using the databases of a couple of third-parties, in order to clear transactions. Sometimes, clearing transactions may take a couple of days, or even weeks, due to the different stages of clearance the transaction goes through.

Significant Breakthroughs

Prior to Satoshi's introduction of blockchain technology, there was a peer-to-peer system that was not as effective as that ultimately offered by blockchain. Satoshi took advantage of this pre-existing system and created instead a consensus mechanism by combining the peer-to-peer system with an existing cryptography system. His new design is thus able to overcome the double-spend issue as effectively as a third-party.

To prevent double-spending, blockchain stamps a coin whenever it is used to make a transaction. This makes it so that if an attempt is made to use a stamped coin for another transaction, it gets flagged and rejected automatically. This stamp thus eliminates spending a particular coin twice and, in general, works to prevent scams.

Blockchain technology additionally is designed to encourage transparency. Transparency in blockchain works so that a transaction cannot be hidden because all the miners can see any transaction that is in progress. Therefore, a potential scammer cannot hide their identity, or present any false information during a transaction, without being penalized. A transaction cannot be confirmed, unless a valid document or information is presented. This is because a blockchain is an open-source, and therefore a public ledger. Satoshi, in fact, designed blockchain in a way that its network takes advantage of its algorithm to reach consensus on any transaction before recording it in a cryptographic form on the blockchain.

The blockchain network achieves consensus through a *proof-of-work* system. This simple idea requires a miner to solve a difficult puzzle; however, it is one that can easily be verified. When a miner finds the right hash, he has solved the puzzle. The rule is that permission to create the subsequent block will be given to the miner that solves the puzzle. Miners work hard to solve these puzzles, expending significant resources, such as electricity and computing hardware.

Whenever a miner solves puzzle and gains a block, he or she is given a Bitcoin as the reward for his or her efforts. Considering that the puzzles are difficult to solve, and there is no shortcut to solving them, this is a good reward. In terms of mining 350 million trillion attempts have been made since November 2015, demonstrating the significant work that miners do to create hash blocks through proof of work.

Impact on Blockchain Economy

Currently, most depend on governments and companies for the verification of our identities. They also often vouch for our reputations. However, they have just as often failed to live up to their billings. Avoiding such disappointments from third-parties is the idea that blockchain that will provide the same service, in a way that can be trusted; this is a welcome development.

For the first time, there is now a trusted platform to turn to for assistance during transactions. This development, will, in fact, have a huge impact on the world's economy, as well as politics and society in general. Blockchain can be deployed most anywhere trust is a prerequisite, as well as wherever there is a need to ensure smooth transactions.

Distribution of Power

Blockchain ensures that power is distributed across a peer-to-peer network, without any centralized authority or control. This means, of course, a central authority cannot decide to shut it down. If, for example, more than half of the network decides to take over the system, their efforts will be seen by all of the stakeholders in the blockchain network.

Problem

For as long as online technology has been in existence, there has also existed the problem of large institutions giving little thought to the social contract of their user base. Instead, major corporations often maintain their indifference and decide to override their users whenever they feel a need to do so.

Solution

While those companies have achieved a high level of success with overriding its users, these practices are rapidly changing with the advent of Bitcoin blockchain technology. Today, it is becoming increasingly impossible for companies to continue with such previous practices. For instance, the cost of running a system that can overpower the Bitcoin blockchain would be enormous, and thus not an option for most companies. Most would consider it a waste of time and resources to embark on a project where cost is does not meet benefit. Satoshi's proof-of-work system provides a much better alternative to a system that consumes tons of computing power and electricity. This effectively means that the security of information has never been more guaranteed than now.

Implications

One of the implications for a platform with all of the above-mentioned attributes is its potential for leading to the creation and distribution of many different models that can lead to wealth creation. For example, a new form of peer-to-peer relationship can be used to address some of the most challenging social problems that humanity faces; it can trigger a shift of power to the citizens, and it can potentially liberate people from abuse by the government and political leaders. Finally, it can resolve issues of trust, leading to an increase in confidence in both interactions and transactions. When this blockchain power shift fully occurs, individuals will be empowered to have the opportunity for prosperity, as well as the ability to freely participate in society with free access whenever they desire.

Value as Incentive

Blockchain is designed in ways that stakeholders will always have the right incentive to place their confidence in the system. Whether you are a miner, or an investor in tokens, the system will reward your efforts.

Solution

Because of the constant exploitation of individuals by large corporations, Satoshi decided to design a system where, instead, all participants come first. He built the system in such a way that an individual's actions will always have a positive impact on society, regardless of how selfish their actions may be. Since users are rewarded with Bitcoin for their efforts, the large amount of obtainable resources have succeeded in encouraging users to be honest and to do what is expected. For this reason, miners have a built-in motive to be trustworthy.

When addressing the impact of these incentives on users, Satoshi stated: "By convention, the first transaction in a block is a special transaction that starts a new coin owned by the creator of the block. This adds an incentive for nodes to support the network." This has turned out to be an effective idea. The allure of earning Bitcoin has encouraged many participants to do what is expected of them, without any resistance. This has also earned the system the support of the nodes because they are satisfied with the incentives. As a result, the system works well. To protect their earned Bitcoin, miners see themselves as a part of the network and will do anything possible to ensure that the platform succeeds. If there is a need to replace equipment, miners will not hesitate to do so. They will also go out of their way to exert more energy in order to maintain the ledger and ensure the overall success of the network.

Blockchain's monetary policy is another measure that has been put in place for preserving the value of the blockchain. Since the first conventional currency was introduced, humankind has always had to deal with the insecurity of such currencies. Some of the challenges have included inflation and theft.

Satoshi was, of course, aware of these problems, so he made a provision that would eliminate them: he capped Bitcoin supply at 21 million. However, he did not release all of the 21 million Bitcoin into the global economy at once; instead, this will be a gradual process that is expected to be completed by 2040. This move was taken by Satoshi to address one of the most challenging problems with other currencies: inflation. Thus the Bitcoin system has been fortified against both currency devaluations and inflation, which are often caused by corrupt and/or incompetent financial systems and governments.

Another solution will be the coming Internet of Things (IoT). IoT will allow users to connect their devices to the Internet, while assigning an identity to each one, thereby giving users more secured control over them. (IoT will be discussed in more detail later.)

Implications for Bitcoin Economy

Blockchain provides a platform to create new things, as well as to work with others on those ideas. One of the hidden potentials in blockchain is the ability for a group of people to use their friendship constructively for the good of their community. This is a huge potential that will obviously have a positive impact on Bitcoin's economy.

Security

Importantly, Satoshi did not leave the security of the network to chance. He also did not take it for granted and leave the security in the hands of government instead, or other authorities. Rather, he ensured that he embedded security measures into the system that have a zero chance of failure. In addition to those security measures, authentic privacy and confidentiality are also built into the system. The goal was to make blockchain impossible for potential hackers who may try to breach its security. For this reason, it is mandatory that users go through the process of cryptography.

Solving Problems

There are several security issues that blockchain can address to give online users peace of mind. Some of the security issues that people have had to contend with in the online space include cyberbullying, hacking, theft, identity theft, ransomware, fraud, and malware. Despite advancements in technology, these issues continue to be a constant menace. The Internet has done little to address these issues and has had little to no impact on such security challenges.

Security practices, such as using passwords for protecting online accounts, mobile devices, apps, and email have been insufficient in addressing these problems. Financial institutions that use passwords overestimate their power in thwarting cybercriminals.

In 2008, several large data breaches occurred in many organizations around the world. Companies, such as Countrywide, BNY Melon, and many others, were subjected to the identity theft of their customers (Identity Theft Resource Center). Other sectors, such as health care, also witnessed high-level breaches of an unprecedented 42% for the same year. Billions of dollars of data were stolen in just the two years spanning 2008 and 2009. Many individuals also lost on average $13,500 to medical identity fraud, as well. In contrast to how these aforementioned institutions handled their customers' data, blockchain offers the secure ability to conducting direct transactions without involving a third-party. This means that these transactions are well-secured and hack proof.

Solution

For all of the previous concerns mentioned above, blockchain has an answer. For example, stakeholders secure the platform with a *public key infrastructure* (PKI.) based on *asymmetric cryptography*. Asymmetric cryptography requires a user to use two keys that perform different tasks for securing the platform. While one of the keys is used for encryption, the second key is automatically used for decryption. This practice boosts the security of the system and makes it difficult for potential intruders to gain access. This practice is so effective that Bitcoin blockchain ranks second only to the U.S. Department of Defense in the use of PKI throughout the world. This makes blockchain the largest civilian user of this form of security measure.

Some past security schemes did not work because, according to Andreas Antonopoulos, "Past schemes failed because they lacked incentive, and people never appreciated privacy as incentive enough to secure those systems." Most of those problems were solved, however, by Bitcoin blockchain encouraging users to adopt PKI through incentives. If PKI is adequately practiced by all, there is less to worry about when it comes to corrupt employees, inefficient firewalls, or hackers. If everyone eventually uses Bitcoin, it will be easier for them to exchange confidential information without worrying about it. Digital assets can also be safely stored on blockchain.

Implications for the Blockchain economy

In a digital age where security is connected to technology, the technology is a determining factor in how secure an individual's information may be. Our reliance on technology for security has come at a price: the more one thinks they are secure, the more exposed to security breaches they actually become. Despite advancements in technological security measures, users are still exposed to scams, cyberattacks, identity theft, and more. The more completely individuals have relied on modern technology for security, the more disappointed they have become. As in other areas, blockchain technology provides a solution to this problem. The transparency and security embedded in blockchain technology guarantee the security of digital assets.

Privacy

Another important issue addressed by blockchain technology is privacy. Most would agree that it would be ideal if each individual were the custodian of his or her data. Each individual would have the freedom to determine the volume of data they wanted to make public, who to share the data with, and when to do so. In this manner, personal information would not be for public consumption but carefully protected by each individual. While this ability to control our own data does not currently exist, blockchain technology has succeeded in putting measures in place that compels users to demonstrate mutual trust for each other. This has successfully eliminated the need to have to release personal information about someone before conducting business with them, or interacting with them based on what we know.

Problem

A truly free society cannot exist without each individual being responsible for his or her own privacy. This is because privacy should be a fundamental human right and a necessary ingredient in the quest for a free society. The advent of the Internet has led to the extensive and ongoing collection of data and confidential information about individuals and organizations, increasingly without their knowledge and consent. This has raised serious security concerns among many who assert that their privacy has been breached. In addition, many of these collectors of data do not protect their databases of information, which frequently leads to repeated hacking and identity theft. However, blockchain technology, with its amazing security features, ensures that an individual's privacy will not breached, especially because the individual is control of that confidential information.

Solution

There are no conventional means of identity on blockchain. Users do not supply their names, email addresses, or other personal information that can be traced back to them when using Bitcoin technology. No individual's personal data is captured because the program does not need it. There also exists a separation between the verification and identification processes.

Even during a transaction, the identities of both parties involved are not required. The network only confirms that both parties meet the requirements for the transaction--that the seller has the amount of Bitcoin requested and has authorized its transfer to the other party. During the process, the sender still owns the digital currency, until when the other party starts to spend it, after the network has changed the ownership to the second party.

The distinction between blockchain technology and the use of credit cards is that with a card's use identification is required. This emphasis placed on identification by credit cards is one of the many reasons why individuals' information gets appropriated and stolen. Since millions of people are registered with different credit card dealers, hacking those databases will lead to the identity theft of the victims. Some big companies, such as Anthem Blue Cross Blue Shield, Home Depot, Sony, JPMorgan Chase, eBay, and others, have millions of names and personal information in their databases, where breaches often lead to identity theft.

With blockchain, there is no need to store any aspects of identity information in any database, and therefore users can retain a large degree of anonymity, if desired. Without a database of information and personal data, hackers do not have an unrestricted access to individuals' personal and confidential information. And Blockchain protocol offers even more than that by allowing users to determine the degree of privacy they are comfortable with as well as how much information they care to release during a transaction.

Thus blockchain offers individuals the opportunity to manage both their own privacy and identity. Austin Hill explains the anonymity of blockchain:

A TCP/IP address is not identified to a public ID. The network layer itself doesn't know. Anyone can join the Internet, get an IP address, and start sending and receiving packets freely around the world. As a society, we've seen an incredible benefit allowing that level of pseudonymity... Bitcoin operates almost exactly like this. The network itself does not enforce identity. That's a good thing for society and for proper network design.

While the blockchain network is open-source available to the public, the identities of the users are not. They remain as anonymous as possible. With decentralization, information about the users is never in the possession of a single entity, thereby eliminating the chance of information theft. The result is privacy and security.

Rights Reserved

Most democratic societies believe that humans have fundamental rights, while also expecting that everyone should have their rights respected. One of the most important rights those that live in a free society demand is to have our privacy respected.

Problem

When the Internet came on the horizon, it was considered one of the best innovations ever, as it had a positive impact on nearly all the sectors of the human economy. Sadly, however, it was not able to address the issue of human rights efficiently. This continued the need to use some form of middleman, a practice that leads to these intermediaries reaping profits and proliferating abuses at users' expense.

Solution

Blockchain solves the issue of intermediaries by combining two features: *proof-of-work* and *PKI keys*. Proof-of-work requires that a miner mints coins and stamps transactions to make certain that only the first coin is settled. In contrast, PKI involves using verification keys to ensure the security of information. By combining both, blockchain ensures there are no issues of double-spending, or confirming who owns what.

Moreover, transactions are irreversible. Satoshi ensured that no one can spend anything that does not belong to them, whether an asset, property, or anything else. Individuals' freedom of assembly, expression, and religion are also recognized in order to create a free world. No one can carry out a transaction on behalf of someone else, in any capacity, without his or her full authorization. Another effective way blockchain achieves this is through the use of *smart contracts*. (These will be discussed in more detail later.)

Implications for Blockchain Economy

Individual rights have to be clarified before being able to enforce them. Blockchain clarifies such rights. For instance, smart contracts can be used, together with blockchain, to plan a goal, work towards it, and to achieve it, all with transparency. A consensus for agreements can be created as well through the use of management systems, such as for property and voting rights. All of these can be clarified within the blockchain network.

Inclusivity

The ideal economy is one where everyone has an equal opportunity both to participate and prosper.

The problem

Despite the introduction of the Internet, when it comes to prosperity, in this regard, billions of people still experience unfilled dreams. A large percentage of the world's population still does not have access to the Internet, the right technology, or other tools they need to improve their economic conditions. Although technology has its shortcomings, it has often succeeded as a force for good in developing countries, where millions of jobs have been created. Aspiring entrepreneurs have also been given a platform to showcase their skills and work towards achieving their goals.

However, much still needs to be done to meet the growing needs of developing countries, where there is often a gradual decline, or lack, in prosperity, issues that still need to be addressed. Many economic opportunities are still far beyond the reach of the many. Millions of people still depend on their cell phones as the only means of connecting to the outside world. Even so, subscription rates are beyond the means of many others. Something drastic must be done to bring both access and affordability of technology to areas of the world that still desperately need these.

Solution

Satoshi designed the blockchain system to work both on the Internet and without it, if necessary. The blockchain program is so easy to access that a user only needs a *simplified payment verification* to be able to interact with the blockchain. Therefore, users can participate in the global economy with only a mobile phone. To make it easy for users, they are not required to have a bank account. They can also participate without their birth certificate or proof of citizenship. They do not even need to have a local currency to participate in blockchain network. This is good news for all, especially those who may face some challenges that the current Internet technology cannot handle.

Implications for Blockchain Economy

Inclusivity is one of the most important ingredients for prosperity. The ability to have equal access to and to be able to participate in economic activities can lead to the elimination of all forms of dominance, whether economic, social, or racial. The ability for an inclusive economy can further spur the elimination of issues of gender, health, and/or sexual discrimination. Everyone deserves an equal opportunity to enjoy the good things of life, regardless of who they are. This is the future that is possible with blockchain technology. The blockchain economy reveals only some of the prospective benefits that blockchains have for the future.

Chapter 8: World-Changing Blockchain Applications

Due to the rapidly increasing popularity of blockchain, its use has moved beyond just recording transactions and storing coins. Blockchain technology is also rapidly branching out into many other applications, in several sectors.

Financial Services

Traditional financial systems are error-prone, cumbersome, and can be frustratingly slow. In addition, a third-party is often needed to speed up the process, as well as to resolve any ensuing conflicts. All of these processes can be time-consuming, stressful, and expensive. Existing financial services use outdated tools and technology that are prone to error. They are also regulated by rules and regulations, some of which are over a century old. This exposes these financial services to serious problems. One cannot always be guaranteed of a secure transaction with the old technology many financial institutions still use.

For these reasons, many financial services have turned to using blockchain-inspired innovations, such as *smart contracts* and *smart bonds*. The former are digital contracts that have the ability to self-execute when necessary and are self-maintaining, when certain terms are met. The latter automatically makes coupon payments to bondholders, also upon the fulfilment of certain requirements.

The turn to blockchain technology in the financial sector has led to increased competition among these services, with users becoming the beneficiaries. Users, who have previously been thwarted by the earlier rules from using these services, now have increased freedom to participate in ways that can help them succeed. Blockchain technology can be used to borrow money for a business, to sell products or services, or to engage in other financial activities that give everyone a better chance at prosperity.

Thus blockchain technology is revolutionizing the financial industry in several areas, such as stock exchanges, brokerages, accounting firms, credit card networks, insurance companies, micro-lenders, and others. The changes in all of these areas because of blockchain technology will be beneficial to billions of people around the world, as well as lead to the future empowerment of more entrepreneurs in different sectors of the world economy.

Some outstanding blockchain financial services include:

Trade Processing and Settlement

Trade processes that are carried out within asset management are known to be risky and expensive. The risk is even more pronounced when conducting cross-border transactions. In this case, each party, such as the custodian, broker, or settlement manager often has a personal record filled with inefficiencies that can ultimately create room for errors. However, this problem can be avoided with the use of the blockchain ledger. Because of the encryption of all records by blockchain, the vulnerability to error is thus eliminated. Blockchain also simplifies trade processing and settlement, without the need for third-parties, or other intermediaries.

Cross-Border Payments

Every day, flaws in the payment sector are exposed. Aside from being error-prone, the payment sector is expensive and has been an easy tool for money launderers. In addition, it often takes a long period of time to complete an international transaction. Therefore, many financial organizations have looked for an alternative to conventional payment systems to avoid errors. Today, many leading financial organizations, such as banks, insurance, and other payment companies have turned to using blockchain technology for their services:

Tradel

This start-up company has leveraged blockchain technology for storing personal data. Since insurance companies are always in need of accurate personal data, they can now partner with Tradel to have access to secure data.

R3

This start-up company works in the banking sector, using the power of blockchain technology to sell transaction security to banks. Thus far, the company has addressed the security needs of over 70 of the world's largest banks. R3 also has an impressive list of clients, including J.P. Morgan, Barclays, UBS, Goldman, and many others. 11 of these banks are already connected to R3's peer-to-peer ledger system. This has helped banks to share valuable information between banks, and thus reduce costs in the process.

Abra

This U.S.-based remittance service provider has also taken advantage of blockchain technology to make international money transfer easy. Since blockchain technology enables the company to offer more secure transactions than other payment services, such as Skrill, PayPal, and Payoneer, it has gradually grown to become one of the most credible avenues of money transfer across borders.

As blockchain becomes more acceptable across the globe, it is expected that the number of businesses and organizations that will take advantage of the technology behind it will skyrocket. The benefits of blockchain technology, and its advantage over other payment methods, will ensure that this soon becomes a reality.

Insurance Claims Processing

Claims processing is one of the most difficult and frustrating procedures in the insurance industry. Insurance processors are tasked with the responsibility of going through data sources, fraudulent claims, or previously-abandoned policies for insurance holders. This creates much room for error. However, errors in these processes can be avoided with blockchain technology because it provides users a perfect system that eliminates risk, while promoting transparency. With the encryption feature of blockchain, insurers can securely and efficiently conduct business.

Smart Property

Smart technology can be embedded into both tangible and intangible property, such as houses, cars, pressure cookers, property titles, patents, company shares, and so on. The registration for property can be stored on a ledger, along with the detail of others who can claim ownership of the property. Those who have access to the property can only do so with smart keys. Once the contract has been verified, the ledger will store the contract and make it possible to exchange the smart keys.

Since the ledger is decentralized, it can be used for managing and recording property rights. It can also be used for duplicating small contracts, in the case of accidental loss of a smart key. Turning to smart functions for property reduces the chances of paying heavy mediation fees, being defrauded, as well as protects from questionable business transactions. Instead, business is conducted with increased trust and efficiency. A couple of uses of smart technology are listed below:

Hard money lending

The existing lending system can be revolutionized with smart contracts. Unscrupulous money lenders will often take the property of people with poor credit history, who also need a loan, as collateral for their loan when they default in their payments. When borrowers are hit with bankruptcy, sometimes they can lose their homes. These unfortunate outcomes can be avoided with the introduction of smart property. With blockchain technology, a user can get a loan from a stranger, while offering smart property to the lender as collateral. This importantly eliminates the need for a lender to know where a borrower works or their credit history. All the information that the lender needs would already exist on the blockchain.

Internet of Things (IoT)

IoT refers to objects that are connected to the Internet as well as each other. This connection makes it possible for these objects to be remotely-controlled. It is estimated that more than 26 billion devices will be connected by 2020. This massive connection of billions of devices exposes these devices to cybersecurity risks. However, the security of these devices can be strengthened with blockchain security. The blockchain ledger system will ensure that only trusted parties will have access to information about these devices, and in this manner, the security of the devices is guaranteed.

Smart Contracts

When individuals enter into a conventional contract, a third-party, or intermediary, is sometimes needed to ensure that both parties obey the terms of their agreement. This can be time-consuming and costly. In contrast, smart contracts have what is known as *if-this-then-that (IFTTT) code* attached. The code allows self-execution to take place based on certain conditions. With blockchain, third-parties are completely eliminated because both parties are aware of the contract details. They also know that the contract will be implemented only if the conditions of the contract are met. This spares either party the problems of having to force the other party to uphold their part of the agreement.

Smart contracts have been found to be useful in many applications: insurance premiums, financial derivatives, crowdfunding, and property law. In addition to defining the rules and penalties that govern an agreement, similar to a traditional contract, smart contracts also enforce those rules and penalties when appropriate.

Smart contracts have a wide array of applications for individuals, businesses, and IoT devices:

Insurance

One of the biggest problems common to insurance policies is the time it takes for insurance claims processing. In some cases, this can take weeks, or even a couple of months, before the insurance payment is made. In addition, the manual processing of insurance makes it susceptible to a certain degree of human error.

As a result, administrative costs have increased, causing insurance holders to pay higher premiums. However, these processes can be automated by turning them into smart contracts. If any of the conditions changes, then there will be an automatic trigger of the claims process. In that case, the insurance policy holder will be paid accordingly, without any human input or intervention. This reduces administrative costs as well as enables trust and transparency in the claims process, so that the regulatory bodies and stakeholders will all have the correct information about the process simultaneously.

Internet of Things (IoT)

The Internet of Things promises a future where all devices will be connected to the Internet, and by extension, to Blockchain technology. This will eliminate some of the challenges that people face today with their devices. For instance, snail mail can be lost, or stolen, in transit, and vehicles can also be stolen. With the Internet of Things, a user is guaranteed maximum protection for their assets, since everything is connected to the Internet, making it so an owner's approval is needed for anyone to have access to their assets. IoT will thus ensure that all possessions are closely monitored and will not be lost or stolen. In the case of an item in transit, the location of the package will be encrypted into the blockchain technology in a specific order, so that tracking the package will be reasonably easy.

Copyrighted content

In some industries, such as the music industry, the copyright to content is owned by the publishing company, or the artists themselves. The copyright allows the owner of the content to receive a royalty fee whenever the content is put to commercial use. With current practice, it is sometimes challenging to identify who owns the copyright, so that the right person receives payment. This problem, however, can easily be solved with smart contracts. If a smart contract is built on blockchain technology, it will keep track of all the existing ownership rights. This will eliminate the issue of who owns what, as well as who gets paid the royalty fees. Since an individual cannot alter the data stored on the blockchain, without the consent of the other parties, the data always remains valid. This will ensure that there is prompt payment of royalties to the right person.

Mortgages

Another area where smart contracts are useful is mortgage contracts. If used in mortgage contracts, smart contracts will be automated, so that both parties can be connected automatically to ensure a smooth mortgage process. When loan payments are made, these can also be automatically-processed and the records updated. Record visibility will also be improved, so that payment can easily be tracked and verified. This reduces the kinds of costs and errors that are common in a manual process.

Digital Identity

As an individual, with smart contracts, a user will be able to have absolute control of their digital identity, such as reputation, data, and digital assets. It will further allow users to decide what information they wish to disclose to other people, or counterparties. This reduces the chances of counterparties holding sensitive information for verification purposes, as well as also increases resiliency, compliance, and interoperability.

Government

Recent concerns about the hacking of the U.S.'s and other voting systems, reinforce the fact that smart contracts can make voting systems become more secure. To hack a blockchain voting system, it would be necessary to decode ledger-protected votes, and that would require a high degree of computing power; however, this computing power is beyond the reach of a single individual.

Smart contracts also have the potential to drive voter turnout. Most indifference to voting is often triggered by the flaws in the system, with its long lines, the need for showing ID's, and completing a long list of forms. If the voting system were replaced with smart contracts, then voters can easily transfer their voting online, which would especially appeal to younger voters.

Another area where smart contracts can be useful in government is in the security of the voting system. The 2016 election in the U.S. is a case study. After the election, both the Republicans and Democrats raised questions about the security of the voting system. In some areas, such as Pennsylvania, Wisconsin, and Michigan, the Green Party was not satisfied with the result of the elections and asked for a recount in those areas. Additionally, computer scientists have determined that professional hackers can hack and rig an electronic voting system, with a view to manipulating votes for their preferred candidate.

All of these concerns, however, can easily be put to rest with blockchain technology. Since all votes can be recorded in a ledger in an encrypted form, manipulating the votes will become nearly impossible. This will serve to give more credibility to the results of an election. Private individuals, who are interested in confirming that their votes are counted, can also do so from their smartphones or personal computers. They can also confirm which candidate they voted for, and perhaps change their vote, if they have changed their mind about a candidate they have previously voted for. By incorporating blockchain technology into the voting system, governments can also save money, while avoiding error, as well as assuring an electorate of accountability.

Blockchain Identity

Personal online identity can be protected with blockchain technology, thereby offering protection against identity theft. Victims of identity theft can lose their money and other valuable assets if hackers steal their login information, financial history, bank and other personal information. Areas where blockchain can prevent identity theft include:

Personal identification

Each day, many people carry with them a wide range of identification, such as computer passwords, driver's license, keys, identity cards, Social Security ID, and others. Losing any of this identification can create financial disaster. Blockchain ID, however, is the perfect solution to this problem. With this digital ID, all physical identifications can be replaced with a more reliable, secure digital ID. Digital ID is an open-source code that banks on blockchain technology use for its security. It is also protected by the transparency of the ledger. Fintech scientists are even of the opinion that in the future, everyone can use their digital ID to sign up anywhere.

Healthcare

The inability of the healthcare sector to share data across platforms, without security breaches, is one of its greatest challenges. When healthcare providers can easily share data with each other, this will have a positive impact on both their diagnoses and the effectiveness of their treatments. This will also make more cost-effective treatment possible.

These are only some of the current, outstanding applications of blockchain technology. Many more areas of applications are expected to be explored in the future.

Chapter 9: Blockchain Technology and the Ledger of Things

The Ledger of Things will have a huge impact on the world. The Ledger of Things is built on the same technology and software that powers the Internet of Things (IoT). However, this technology and software will now be used to animate physical things, so that they can become more efficient.

In an article, entitled, "The Internet of Things Needs a Ledger of Things," Alex Tapscott, a *Forbes* contributor, defines how this will function, in that by "using emerging software and technologies, we can instill intelligence into existing infrastructure, such as a power grid, by adding smart devices that can communicate with one another, reconfigure themselves depending upon availability of bandwidth, storage, or other capacity and therefore resist interruption."

For the Internet of Things to function at maximum capacity, it needs a Ledger of Things. This Ledger of Things will help in tracking whatever is connected to the IoT, to ensure that it is absolutely reliable. Paul McNeil, in a *Huffington Post* article, states that the expansion of the Internet of Things requires a technology that will able to accommodate and support it. According to Neil, the answer to that problem may be distributed ledgers. These will make the world of things connect seamlessly.

Imagine the possibility of instilling intelligence into our infrastructure through the incorporation of smart devices that are designed to communicate effectively with one another. This will lead to the creation of a secure and flexible network that is both time and cost-effective, and thus provide people with more efficient and economical services.

The Ledger of Things has a wide scope of applications in several different sectors of the global economy:

Transportation

The application of the Ledger of Things has already been made in the transportation sector with the introduction of autonomous, or self-driving, vehicles. These vehicles offer benefits that a manually-driven vehicle cannot. For instance, autonomous vehicles offer more safety as well as a guarantee of getting to a destination. Seemingly intuitively, the vehicle avoids obstacles, such as construction, and takes the fastest and best route, while avoiding traffic lights, all designed to ensure safe arrival at a designated destination. The vehicle deals with traffic congestion by using a passing rate to avoid heavy traffic, and to arrive at a destination, without missing deadlines or appointments.

Freight managers will also be able to take full advantage of this opportunity as well. By installing IoT on cargo vehicles, it will be easier for them to pass required inspection, including clearing customs, faster than before.

Infrastructure Management

Infrastructure develops weaknesses and damage, with repeated use over time. Sometimes, this damage is unexpected, and thus unprepared for. Rail lines, runways, bridges, ports, and pipelines, as well as other both private and public infrastructure need to be constantly monitored to quickly identify problems and find quick solutions. Imagine how beneficial it will be if power lines can give detailed analysis of problems, without technicians spending days or weeks identifying them.

The same can be said of telephone, and other, poles. If a pole can always provide a real-time situation, report its condition, and trigger an alert when it is about to fall, or if it catches fire, then this would be much safer, easier, and less expensive to maintain than having to replace a pole completely after it has been destroyed. This would be possible due to a technology that is referred to as *mesh network,* which ensures the connection of computers with other devices. To ensure there is no failure, the devices can also self-configure, for instance, if storage, bandwidth, and other resources are available.

Mesh networks can be used by communities to provide services that are usually either unaffordable, or non-existing. To maximize the opportunities offered by mesh networks, many corporations are now building these networks into blockchain technology, thereby finding permanent solutions infrastructure problems that have caused problems for years. Devices that are connected with the mesh network can also have direct communication with each other, up to a distance of 16 km, or 10 miles. Backed by blockchain technology, such devices have a wide range of applications.

Retail Operations and Sales

Retail operations can also benefit from the Ledger of Things. When shopping offline, shoppers will no longer have to worry about trying on several clothes before finally getting the right size dress. Instead, they will be able to walk into any store and find the right size because the information is always available, and the right size dress, too, will become available. After trying on the dress, there is no worry about payment. Just scan the dress to make the payment.

Shoppers will also be able to be notified about the right dress, say, on their way to the cinema. A message on their smartphone mobile can alert that a favorite brand of shoes is available in a nearby offline store. In addition to the simplicity of the transaction process, the dress can even be sent home before the buyer arrives.

Retailers will also derive benefits. If customers make their information available for use, retailers can gain this information from the blockchain. They will then be able to personalize their products or services to meet the needs of their customers based on their demographics, purchasing history, known interests, and more.

Household management

Home management is being taken to a new level since IoT took over the technological landscape of smart devices. With the Ledger of Things, however, many products and services have been developed that can increase the automation of homes. These include automatic temperature adjustment, nanny cams, lighting, and access controls. A smart home, fully automated via the Ledger of Things, will be energy efficient, and even make it both possible and convenient to communicate with your house.

Although building up smart homes has been slow, many notable companies are currently working to simplify the installation process. They have the same goal for operations. BBC research made this stunning revelation: "The U.S. home automation market is estimated to go from almost $6.9 in 2014 to $10.3 billion in 2019." This means most homes will be fully automated in the future based on blockchain technology and the Ledger of Things.

Energy, Water, and Waste management

Some utilities will be able to use blockchain technology for tracking distribution, production, collection, and consumption. A typical example would be the proposed neighborhood energy micro-grid. This will be a complete deviation from current energy infrastructures and their numerous flaws. An overflowing waste bin will be able to send signals to the waste management team to come and empty it. A leaky pipe will be able to send a similar message and request immediate repair. There are other areas where the introduction of the Ledger of Things will impact waste management, while increasing its efficiency.

Farming and Resource Extraction

Blockchain technology can also be incorporated into the farming industry to simplify the work, while ensuring maximum result for the effort. For instance, it will be possible to monitor livestock with blockchain technology, such as tracking their medication, what they eat, health history, and other variables that will provide a complete overview.

There is also the possibility of using this technology for tracking specialized, expensive equipment that can be readily available for use by farmers at affordable prices. This tracking can also be used for improving farmworker and miner's safety by tagging their automated checklists and safety equipment, monitoring crop conditions, soil, irrigation, or to carry out other operations that will lead to improved farming.

Sensors can be placed on trees or in the soil to make it convenient for environmental protection agencies to oversee the activities of farmers and how they use the land. This can help to ensure the proper management of land.

Health Care

Professionals in the health care sector already manage assets with digitization. They use the same method for managing their medical records, ordering, keeping inventory, and making payments for pharmaceuticals and equipment. Some hospitals, too, also have smart devices that oversee the services provided at these hospitals. However, currently, only a handful of them communicate effectively with each other or manage to properly treat the importance of security and privacy protection when dealing with patients. However, all of these services can now be linked with IoT built on blockchain.

Some applications include wearable devices and smart pills that can be used for disease management and monitoring. Others improve quality control. A typical example would be an artificial knee or hip that is equipped with the ability to self-monitor, and to send a score sheet of performance to the manufacturer, so that they can come up with better designs and communicate directly with the physician treating a patient.

 The introduction of blockchain-enabled hospitals and health care centers will improve the quality as well as make disease management easier. This can be achieved when the hospitals use blockchain technology to connect devices that are used for inventory, medical records management, and others. During clinical trials, smart drugs, with the ability to track, will be able to relay to the medical team their effectiveness, as well as any potential side effects.

Environmental Monitoring and Emergency Services

Today, serious environmental challenges are threatening the existence of humanity: cyclones, hurricanes, earthquakes, and other natural disasters. Blockchain can increase preparation and monitoring of these disasters. It can also flag radioactivity, or dangerous chemicals, when emergency workers are at work. It can be used for monitoring forest fires and lightning strikes. Blockchain can be applied to tsunami and earthquake alert systems. Weather sensors can be created for selling tremor data, air quality, and providing timely warnings for people in advance of natural disasters. The Ledger of Things can help make accurate predictions a possibility, and thereby increase our response time during emergencies.

Smart Documents

The previous chapter discussed smart contracts in detail. Smart documents work on the same principle as smart contracts. Documents related to registration, patents, insurance, warranty, and so on, are coded, giving them the ability to control whatever object a document is attached to. For instance, an item that is displayed on a shelf for sale can notify the store managers when it has reached its expiration date. To fully use the technology to the maximum, such items can be programmed to automatically reduce their price. In this manner, shoppers can be notified of the reduced price. Some similar functions can work with a vehicle attached to a smart document; if it has expired insurance, or has previously has not passed a safety inspection, the vehicle simply will not start. The same can occur for a vehicle where the owner still owes parking tickets, or is guilty of some moving violation, or has a suspended driver's license.

Other material assets can also undergo a transformation to digital assets as well. In the future, all necessary information about all *things* may be able to be digitized, becoming more objects on the blockchain. This may include documentation, such as ownership, patents, inspection certifications, warranties, replacement dates, approvals, insurance, and so on. This will make data more readily available and credible, thereby gradually reducing the need to handle paper at all, while not having to worry about loss, storage, and other related documentation-related processes.

Building and Property Management

The real estate sector will be another beneficiary of blockchain technology. With the Ledger of Things, property management will be easier. For instance, rather than people moving from one real estate company to another to find a place to live, information about vacant properties can be made more readily available to the public through the use of digital sensors with the capability to create better marketplaces for real estate assets. These sensors will allow real-time usability, discovery, and will also be able to accept payments.

Many real estate vendors are gradually working towards taking full advantage of this opportunity to increase coverage and performance. They can much more easily rent a vacant space within a couple of hours with the new technology. For instance, rather than having a conference room unused for days, these can temporarily be converted into office space for companies or organizations that need an office for emergency use. The implication is that properties will no longer be vacant for days on end. Since the property itself will send out a signal that it is vacant, potential users will be contacted, thereby increasing the chances of getting the space filled quickly.

The same can be said for residential spaces that will be able to advertise themselves up for lease, using the Ledger of Everything to negotiate prices with students on vacation, tourists, and others, who are in need of a home, whether temporary or permanent. Other potential benefactors include hotels, factories, commercial real estate, and so on.

Other applications that will be useful in the property management sector include heating and cooling, lighting, access control, water and waste management, security, and many more.

Insurance and Financial Services

Financial institutions can also find other good uses for the Ledger of Things. They can also use it to track, tag, or trace any physical assets, such as jewelry, antiques, or other precious assets. The fact that digital currencies can be used for storing and transferring value securely and rapidly also make them an efficient tool for risk management and assessment. Tagged objects can easily be traced as well as identify their own location. The insurance rate for each object can be calculated based on location. For example, a piece of jewelry worn by Rihanna will attract higher insurance rates if it is worn in public versus the home. Devices will also be to handle and settle their insurance claims on the spot, with the assistance of their sensor data.

Industrial operations

The Ledger of Things will be valuable for use industries. Factory managers will be able to take advantage of smart devices to monitor production lines, distribution, performance data, warehouse inventory, maintenance, and the rest. A whole plant or industry may adopt this technology to increase its efficiency for use in other areas, such as chain management. Complex machines, such as locomotives, airplanes, and other large machines, are made up of a huge number of parts, sometimes running into millions. Maintaining these mammoth engines is always challenging but can be managed more effectively with blockchain.

When there are a millions of parts to deal with, it is obviously not easy to identify a non-working component when a machine fails. This is one of the reasons it can take days, or even weeks, to fix complex machines when they break down. With the Ledger of Things, however, individual components of these machines will each have sensors for sending out alerts when they need to be fixed. By sending alerts in advance, before a part is completely worn out, it can be replaced in time to prevent accidents that may result from a missing or malfunctioning part. With the right programming, a part can not only send out an alert for replacement, but can also consider bids, accept bids, as well as notify the vendor of its present location, or destination, for immediate delivery. This will save repair time and improve operating efficiency.

The application of blockchain technology is not exclusively reserved for complex machines. Other manufacturers will also be able to take full advantage of the technology as well, such as manufacturers of motorcycles, light bulbs, cars, and small appliances. Manufacturers will also be able make their products fully- equipped with smart chips, or even parts of the products, so that they can monitor those products, collect performance data from them, and analyze the data. The result of the analysis will allow manufacturers to anticipate the numerous needs of their clients, make automatic upgrades to their products, as well as offer them a new line of new services. This will lead to a complete transition from supplier-based services, to software-based ones.

Retail

The retail industry will also feel the impact of the Ledger of Things. For a retailer with a high number of customers, attending to such customers becomes easier when the retailer has all the necessary information to render personalized services or products. This personalized information will be based on customer interests, demographics, purchasing history, and so on. The market can thus be conveniently changed by leveraging the values of companies, individuals, and societies. These values can be coded into the blockchain and used as criteria for determine larger values. The Ledger of Things will eventually animate material things and make life easier.

Benefits of the Ledger of Things

Some of the benefits offered by the Ledger of Things include:

Speed: Getting work done at a faster rate than was previously possible is one of a long list of benefits inherent in this technology. Since the speed is connected to its end-to-end automation, that makes it easy for devices to connect and communicate with themselves.

Cost-effective: In most cases, intermediaries, or third-parties, are responsible for the high cost of products and services. By eliminating these intermediaries, the technology helps customers to reduce the prices they pay for goods and services.

Increased efficiency: Increased efficiency, revenue, and overall productivity will result. Excess capacity can later be reused in other ways to further increase overall performance.

Increased integrity and security: This is possible as a result of the mutual trust that is already built into the system. This trust eliminates bottlenecks and other challenges that may threaten to reduce the integrity of a system.

System durability: Durability is another important benefit of this technology. While there may be potential for failure in a conventional system, the introduction of this new technology will drastically reduce failures.

Reduced energy consumption: the need for an energy-efficient technology also makes this technology ideal. The increased efficiency of the technology makes it to naturally consume less energy. This is supplemented by its dynamic pricing and the appreciable reduction in waste.

Better privacy protection: Privacy is another important benefit of the technology. Third-parties will no longer have the ability to interfere between two or more parties. They will no longer be able to ignore, or override specific rules because these will now be in the blockchain.

Improved predictive ability: The technology will improve predictive abilities, such as more accurate predictions about natural disasters and severe weather, best planting periods, and so on.

All of the aforementioned benefits derived from blockchain technology would not be possible without the concepts of a decentralized, or distributed, network. Blockchain decentralization makes it possible to eliminate third-parties, such as management, or clearinghouse apps. Speaking on the value of decentralization, Eric Jennings notes,

People will do the things they'll do to minimize their own discomfort, leading to silos and concentration and centralization. What's a short-term gain for those particular people is a long-term loss for everyone else. The Internet of Things should be completely decentralized where devices can be autonomous, discover each other directly, establish secure communication with each other directly, and eventually pay each other in value, directly between machines.

The Success of the Internet of Things

The introduction of the Internet of Things has already led to a significant improvement in how our homes are run. The Ledger of Things takes these advances even further, and in part, contributes to the ongoing success of blockchain technology. Some experts have conducted research to identify the driving force behind the amazing success of blockchain technology. Some of the most important factors are that with the use of blockchain, it is easier for users to search for whatever products or services they want, to access these, and to easily make payment on the spot.

The possibility of making an online assessment of risk and credit in real time also makes the technology more appealing. For this reason, operational efficiency will receive improve when devices and systems become fully automated. The automation of some devices already has proven that automation offers long-term benefits to users. Another important aspect of IoT is the ease of crowdsourcing, or collaborating with business partners, via value chains in real time. In other words, blockchain provides a platform to make better markets. Previously inaccessible assets will now become easily available at the click of a button. The price of assets can be determined in real time and used to guard against unnecessary risk.

The Ledger of Things offers even more value than previously discussed. Unleashing the full potential of the technology will significantly change the way things are done. Since distributed capitalism is possible with this technology, the markets can be controlled according to preference. Companies, individuals, or societies can express their values and make them an integral part of the blockchain technology.

For instance, using some services requires hiring these for a fee. In some cases, one may need to download a company, or an organization's, app and create an account on the company's website in order to gain access to the company's services. For example, to hire a car one first has to request a car of their choice from a list of cars available for hire. In order to process the fee, a users' location must also be indicated, or located on a map. With the assistance of the app on a mobile device, a user will be charged a fee for hiring the vehicle. This is how current car hiring services work; however, there are several risks involved in this process, since there have been reports of passengers who have made false allegations against drivers, wrongly accused them of theft, sexual assault, and more. A recent sexual assault allegation was levelled against an Uber driver; however, the allegation was later proved to be false. Of course, drivers are not the only ones being accused. Some drivers have sexually harassed their passengers, robbed them, and worse.

In some developing countries, drivers have been kidnapped, robbed, and beaten up. Sometimes, car-hire companies exploit their drivers by underpaying them, despite the huge fees they charge their passengers. In 2017, some drivers in Nigeria went on strike, protesting against their poor remuneration, despite the fact that the company that hired them is notorious for its exorbitant fees.

Blockchain technology, however, can help remove some of the challenges that are particular to vehicle owners in developed countries, for example, parking problems, huge traffic jams, and other related challenges. Blockchain technology can also back the further development of autonomous, or self-driving, vehicles, in ways designed to prevent such problems.

Self-driving vehicles are here to stay. Developers in the auto and technology industries are working on incorporating an impressive database of information that will contain comprehensive information about the general parking rules a vehicle can use to sort out such issues. Smart cars will also be able to handle their payments for repairs, fuel, and other expenses, negotiate liability in accidents, or activate auto insurance without the input of a third-party.

Through leveraging blockchain technology, a vehicle's protocol can be programmed into the technology, so the vehicle can perform all of these functions on its own, as well as outperform human drivers. This will make both the transport business and traffic conditions much better overall.

Vehicle maintenance will be covered as well. Sensors that are built into a vehicle will also handle its maintenance, both preventive and corrective. The sensors will have the responsibility of carrying out a comprehensive monitoring of the vehicle, and to monitor for potential signals that indicate a dire need for immediate repairs. Without waiting for the owner, the vehicle will look for the nearest repair shop and make an appointment with a technician. If some parts need to be replaced, the vehicle will automatically place an order for all the parts. For this reason, a driver cannot be deceived into replacing a part that is in good condition.

To effect the changes necessary for self-driving cars, corresponding changes to the infrastructure will also be needed to be made, so that the vehicles can communicate to work together for their overall success. Most of the infrastructure that will support self-driving cars must be automated. This will include the automation of traffic signal management, using traffic flow as criteria for determining signals.

Safety control for vehicles will also be incorporated into the blockchain technology as well. For example, warnings supported by automated braking will protect vehicles against accidents. Since many accidents are often caused by human error, such as by bad drivers and/or driving under the influence, unqualified, or impaired, drivers will automatically be prevented from driving. These preventive measures will lead to a gradual reduction in accident rates caused by both human and other factors. The sensors can also assist cities in the management of their infrastructure, in ways that will make the operation of vehicles smooth.

Since self-driving vehicles will become more readily available, they will gradually reduce the number of private vehicles on the streets, which will improve traffic congestion as well as lessen pollution and the impact of emissions on the environment. These transport systems will appeal to investors, whether as an individual, a group, or a large organization, and investing in these new developments will pave the way to global acceptance of the blockchain technology and its promises for the future.

In fact, in the near future, blockchain technology will soon be readily accepted and implemented to solve the world's transportation problems, especially in cities where traffic congestion is at its worst. Car thefts can be prevented with the use of the technology because antitheft systems can be incorporated into the blockchain.

With self-driving vehicles, more cars will be shared, rather than individuals having a personal vehicle. When in need of a car, a request can be placed with a car company. This request will trigger all the vehicles that are vacant to post offers automatically because they are all on the same blockchain. This will give clients a wide array of options to choose that will meet their budgets and other requirements. Since it will be a self-driving vehicle, the risk of sexual assault, beatings, robbery, and other crimes will be eliminated completely.

Chapter 10: Blockchain Lifecycle

As discussed earlier, the creation of Bitcoin led to the creation of blockchain technology. This invention demonstrated to the whole world that individuals who have never met can work together online, within a system that can be trusted, because the members of the system cooperate on the network.

The need to provide adequate security for Bitcoin cryptocurrency necessitated the building of the first Bitcoin network. With about 5,000 nodes, the Bitcoin network is distributed around the globe. It was primarily used as a means of exchanging value and trading Bitcoin, but the creators eventually saw the potential to put the network to better use. Because of its huge size and the credibility of its security, blockchain can also be used for the security of other, smaller, blockchain applications and blockchains.

The Blockchain network was followed closely by the development of the Ethereum network. The blockchain structure is the template for Ethereum and is complemented by a built-in programming language. The Ethereum network shares the same number of nodes with Bitcoin, and also enjoys global distribution. The uses of Ethereum include trading Ether, making smart contracts, and creating decentralized autonomous organizations (DAOs). The Ethereum network is also used for securing smaller blockchains and blockchain applications.

The third blockchain technology evolution led to the creation of the Factom network. This network has voting incorporated in the network, and its consensus system is lighter than the rest. It also has more information storing capacity than the other two. The primary goals of building the Factom network were system and data security. Behind the operation of this small network are limitless auditing and federated nodes. To maintain its status, the Factom network finds a way to connect itself with other networks, and thus builds bridges that will make connection with other blockchains easy.

The Driving Force of Blockchains

The features and areas of application of blockchains have contributed greatly to their reputations as very powerful tools. They have importantly created honest systems that do not need the input of a third-party to be corrected. Without anyone enforcing the rules, blockchains depend on built-in consensus algorithms to enforce the rules.

Consensus refers to the development of an agreement between individuals who do not naturally trust each other in the blockchain world. These agreements form the full nodes on each network. These nodes are responsible for the validation of transactions entered in the network before they are recorded in the ledger. Each blockchain has an independent algorithm that can be used for creating agreement on all the data that is entered into the network. Consensus can be created by using a wide variety of models because each blockchain has the responsibility of creating an array of entries. Some blockchains are for data storage, while some are used for trading value, contracts, and system security.

A typical example of consensus agreement is Bitcoin. This leading cryptocurrency trades the value of its token among members of the Bitcoin network. Some of its attributes, such as consistency, performance, threat model, scalability, and failure model are a bit higher due to the market value of its tokens. The operation of this coin relies on the assumption that the tokens may be stolen, if a hacker is determined to render the history of trades useless by corrupting it. However, Bitcoin has a mechanism in place to prevent such events from happening. It uses a consensus model known as *proof of work*. This model is used to solve the problem of knowing that the information a user is looking at has not been changed internally or externally. This susceptibility of data to manipulation makes its reliability has been a huge challenge for Computer Science.

The common fear among most blockchain users is the potential attack from other users or outside forces. The trust housed in the nodes behind the operation of the blockchains, and the expected threat of being hacked, played a significant role in choosing the right algorithm for settling ledgers. Bitcoin and Ethereum thus use the proof of work consensus algorithm because they expect an equal degree of threat from both users and external forces. In contrast, a faster and lighter consensus is needed for blockchains that are designed for recording financial transactions between parties that know and trust each other. This is because they need high-speed transactions, while proof of work does not offer these. Since the users of financial blockchains are fewer than those using other blockchains, it is expensive to operate proof of work there.

In view of the growing list of blockchains and their applications, making the right decision when choosing a blockchain for ones' needs can be quite challenging. The following chapter offers tips on how to choose the right one.

Chapter 11: Choosing the Right Blockchain

The blockchain industry is rapidly growing, while also increasing its complexity and capabilities. Therefore it is necessary to gain a good understanding of the fundamental types of blockchains, and their weaknesses and limitations, as well as to reveal even more future potential for this technology.

How Blockchains Add Life Value

Blockchains and their cryptocurrencies have been a major focus of attention in recent years. The rapid fluctuations in the prices of digital currencies, as well as the fear that the technology may eventually have a negative impact on governments and industries, are responsible for the negative reception that governments, and some financial organizations, have had about cryptocurrencies and blockchain technology. This rapid increase in interest has also led to widespread desire for the development of cryptocurrencies and blockchain technology and digital currencies to prevent investors from losing money. Entrepreneurs see great opportunities to explore many potential business models.

As a unique type of database, blockchains can be used anywhere, in lieu of a traditional database. All the operations that can be performed on a normal database can also be performed on blockchains; however, it is generally preferable to use a normal database unless further conditions apply. Blockchain should be used instead if dealing with unknown parties, especially when sharing sensitive information. Blockchains are also the databases of choice to audit data, or to prevent your data from being compromised by either external, or internal forces. One should determine if a normal database is capable of handling an operation efficiently before moving to blockchain technology.

Determine Need

As previously discussed, blockchains come in different forms. The key to finding the most appropriate one is first to determine need. This can be accomplished with the use of a weighted decision matrix.

Weighted Decision Matrix

A weighted decision matrix is defined as "a tool used to compare alternatives with respect to multiple criteria of different levels of importance. It can be used to rank all the alternatives relative to a 'fixed' reference and thus create a partial order for the alternatives." With this tool, it is possible to quantify project needs, and to do so accordingly, thereby making decisions easier.

To create a weighted decision matrix, follow the steps below:

1. Consider the goals and criteria the team wants to achieve, such as the following:

Speed and latency: Consider the speed of the technology and how fast it can get your project completed without delay.

Scale and volume: The sheer volume of the project is another fundamental factor not to overlook. Consider whether the technology has the capacity to handle a project of such huge volume.

Structural needs and storage capacity: Ask if the technology can satisfy the structural needs or not. Its ability to meet that need will go a long way to determine whether it is the ideal technology for the project, or whether to look for a better alternative. Do not forget to consider its storage capacity, too, such as whether it can easily accommodate the project, or not. If not, a change of technology should be considered.

Immutability and security: How secure is the technology? Can it guarantee the security of your project?

2. Reduce criteria to the shortest list possible.

A long list of criteria will complicate things and make decision-making a challenge. Reducing the criteria to the barest minimum will help speed up decision-making. If needs cannot be reduced easily, a comparison matrix tool will prove useful.

3. Assign a weight to each criterion.

Rate the criteria from 1 to 10 according to their order of importance. If working with a team, assign the responsibility of weighing the criteria to all members of the team.

4. Find the average value.

By assigning the responsibility to all the members of the team, it will make it so they each come up with different results, as different figures will be assigned to the criteria. Add up the numbers and divide the result with the number of your team members to gain a composite weight.

5. Make the necessary adjustments.

Review the result and find out whether it works for the project. If not, make any necessary adjustments, and ensure that each criterion is assigned the right order of importance.

Upon completion, a list of criteria will be generated that must be met for the blockchain project to be successful.

Determine the Goal

Efforts at building a blockchain project may turn out to be a total loss if it does not have a specific goal or purpose. It is therefore imperative to take the time to consider the needs and determine the goals before settling on a specific blockchain. One cannot achieve success by just randomly picking a blockchain.

How to Obtain Blockchains

From this book's discussion so far, most will have realized that blockchains are powerful tools, with the potential to have a positive impact on all facets of the human economy. It thus has the potential to change the world, such as how systems are secured, money is moved, and digital identities are built.

While one may not have an in-depth knowledge of blockchain if not a developer, but wants to contribute to its development in the future, it is still important to have at least a fundamental knowledge of how blockchains work. Decisions will need to be made, such as the use of blockchain, and knowledge of the technology will prove an invaluable tool that will help guide this decision-making. There is also a need to understand the core limitations of blockchains in terms of their potential widespread applications in the future. Some of the current areas of application of blockchain have already been discussed, while the technology is expected to have many more areas of application in the future. Therefore, increasing one's knowledge that includes vital aspects of working with cryptocurrencies and blockchains, as well as the tools needed, is imperative.

Chapter 12: Understanding the Bitcoin Blockchain

Among all the existing blockchain, none is as powerful and large as Bitcoin blockchain. This blockchain was designed primarily for sending and receiving Bitcoin, the world's most important cryptocurrency. The principle behind the technology requires that a transaction must take place between two Bitcoin holders before the creation of a message in Bitcoin blockchain is possible.

Whenever a Bitcoin is sent, or a fraction of the digital currency, from one account to another, the transaction will be recorded in the Bitcoin blockchain. Once that transaction has been recorded, it is permanent and cannot be removed. The transaction history will be permanently recorded in the blockchain for as long as it exists. Although this seems to be a very simple operation in a blockchain, it is one of the most powerful attributes of a blockchain. It is the principle behind the high security that the blockchain technology offers users. Before one can send Bitcoin from one account to another, they must already have a Bitcoin account.

How to Create a Bitcoin Wallet

A Bitcoin wallet address consists of 32 characters. The wallet allows users to conduct Bitcoin transactions. A user can both send and receive Bitcoin. The Bitcoin wallet address works as a bank account through which users can send money to other account holders as well as receive payment from them.

Each Bitcoin wallet holder is assigned a private key. This is a unique secret code that is associated with each Bitcoin address. If one has a Bitcoin wallet, they will have a private key. Other owners will have their unique private keys as well.

A private key is a proof of ownership of the coins in a specific Bitcoin wallet address. Remember that a private key gives access to the content of a user's wallet. Therefore, never share a private key with anyone because anyone that knows it will have unrestricted access to a user's coins and may spend it. It is also mandatory that a user link their first Bitcoin wallet to their bank account or credit card.

There are different platforms where one can create a Bitcoin address. The following platforms are recommended:

Coinbase

Over the years, Coinbase has created an enviable reputation as one of the best platforms for creating a Bitcoin wallet. The site combines an attractive interface with multiple online wallets, to make investing in any digital currency of choice easy. One can also use any of the available wallets for saving digital currency. With almost 5 million registered users, and some 46,000 merchants, Coinbase has carved a niche for itself in the industry.

The platform is very easy to use and offers one of the best services in the cryptocurrency world, as evidenced by its thousands of dedicated subscribers. One can visit the official website to create a personal wallet address.

To create a wallet address on Coinbase, follow these steps:

1. Enter www.coinbase.com in the browser address bar.
2. Click on "Sign Up." A sign-up form will be displayed.
3. Fill in the form, and check "I'm not a robot."
4. Check the age confirmation box. This will indicate that you are age 18 years or above. It is also a sign of acceptance of Coinbase's User Agreement and Privacy Policy.

5. Click "Create Account."

6. An email-verification message will be displayed. Proceed to email address and click the "Verify Email Address" link to complete registration.

7. Complete a captcha form after clicking the "I'm not a robot" box.

After the successful creation of an account, add a little amount of money to experiment.

How to Create a Second Wallet Address

One will need a second wallet address to carry out this experiment. Without a second address, one cannot send and receive Bitcoin, unless carrying out the experiment with someone that already has a Bitcoin wallet address.

For the second address, use **Blockchain.info wallet**. It has all the features of a formidable wallet address platform.

Follow the steps below to create a wallet on this platform:

1. Type www.blockchain.info in the browser address bar.

2. Click "Wallet."

3. Click on "Sign up." This allows the creation of a personal account.

4. Click "Create Your Wallet."

5. Provide a valid email address.

6. Create a strong password.

7. Click "Continue."

8. An email verification request will be sent to the email address provided. Open the email and click on the verification request to confirm the validity of the email.

A wallet address will not be created and displayed with the account balance and other information that can be used to initiate or complete a transaction.

How to Make an Entry in Bitcoin Blockchain

Data entry into a blockchain has been discussed earlier. However, to enter data on Bitcoin blockchain, a transaction must be made on the blockchain. This requires a fund transfer between the two wallet addresses.

Although the process differs a bit from one wallet to another, this is a general idea of how to make an entry into a Bitcoin blockchain:

1. Login to either of the two wallet addresses where there are funds.
2. Enter the recipient.
3. Copy and paste vanity address into the recipient's address field.
4. Enter the desired amount to send.
5. Click "Send."

When clicking "Send," the first message is entered into the Bitcoin blockchain and will also be permanently kept in the blockchain. Bitcoin transactions are not immediately confirmed. It may take up to 10 minutes or more before a transaction will be confirmed. The duration depends on the value of the transaction. Huge transactions take longer periods of time to be confirmed, compared to smaller transactions. The larger the transaction, then the longer the wait will be for its confirmation to take place. During the waiting period, the transaction will not be entered into the blockchain. This is only done when a transaction has been confirmed. This also means that an unconfirmed transaction is still reversible.

How to Use Bitcoin with Smart Contracts

A smart contract is software that is designed for making autonomous financial decisions. Recently, Bitcoin and smart contracts have been synonymous because of their contribution to the world economy. A smart contract can automatically carry out a verification process to determine whether the condition for a particular agreement has been met, so that the contract can be automatically executed. It can also self-execute on the confirmation of an agreement. It will automatically release payment data after the confirmation.

In an earlier chapter, I outlined some of the benefits and areas of application of smart contracts. From the information included there, it is easy to deduce that the applications of smart contracts go far beyond finances to most other sectors of the human economy. The revolutionary roles played by smart contracts have replaced services that were previously manually conducted, written on ink and paper, to now being digitally carried out via credible and secure platforms. Thus, smart contracts have changed the whole outlook of business transactions, as well as eliminated the need for a third-party involvement during a business transaction. It thus acts as the intermediary between the parties involved in a contract, equally enforcing the terms of agreement between the two parties. Any operation handled with smart contract is mostly irreversible. Also, since it controls data and conducts verification, it automatically controls the contract.

As aforementioned, Bitcoin is the world's leading cryptocurrency. It is also the major digital currency on which the blockchain technology is built. It has formed the yardstick with which other blockchain technologies are compared and assessed. In fact, Bitcoin is the source of inspiration for other digital currencies. It is thus important to understand the underlying principle behind the operation of the Bitcoin blockchain.

The History of Bitcoin Blockchain

In 2008, the concept of Bitcoin and blockchain were made public. It was initially presented as a whitepaper before it became open-source software a year later. The whitepaper was presented by an anonymous programmer, or a group of programmers, working under the pseudonym, Satoshi Nakamoto. Up until 2010, Satoshi worked with a couple of open-source developers on Bitcoin. Since 2010, however, this group, or individual, has transferred the control of Bitcoin to Bitcoin developers.

Regardless of the mystery surrounding the real identity of Nakamoto, he has created a credible and secure peer-to-peer payment system, where users can send and receive Bitcoin directly between two parties without the contribution of a third party. Since the Bitcoin blockchain carries out verification of each transaction, it ensures that the system is shielded from potential false transactions. Nakamoto realized that digital trust was a need. He thus decided to find a permanent solution to the problem. That is why he came up with blockchain. Blockchain has succeeded in providing satisfying answers to the legion of problems we have to contend with. One of the problems borders on how convenient it will be to trust digital information in view of the tendency of some people to be dishonest and provide the wrong information. These are problems that have been effectively answered by Nakamoto's blockchain technology.

The principle guiding blockchain technology has gradually made the technology the missing link that has finally made online transactions possible with the utmost trust and confidence. By recording all the transaction information in the blockchain, it is made permanent, so that alteration becomes impossible, and this has drastically reduced the vulnerability of the users to fraud.

Blockchain technology is a refurbishment of some other old transaction practices that have been in existence for decades. It combines these practices and makes a newer, practical application of them. For instance, cryptocurrency is the merging of payment and cryptography. In the past, payment through a valuable token was a norm. The same can be said about cryptography that represents the practice of using third-parties for securing communication, where the third-party ensures that the terms of agreement of the two parties during a transaction are strictly abided by. The merging of cryptocurrency and the reliable payment method is what is currently known as cryptocurrency. Thus, blockchains act as third-parties for the verification of the terms of the agreement reached by two individuals during a transaction.

Blockchains are also ledgers. For thousands of years, people have kept millions of financial accounts on ledgers. Nakamoto made a revolutionary innovation by merging all these practices and made it appealing to users across the globe. Nakamoto's original purpose was to design a system where sending Bitcoin cryptocurrency would be easy. In time, however, he realized that it can be put to a better use. That led to the alteration of Bitcoin's architecture, so it could be designed to easily record more data than token-related information. This led to the birth of the Bitcoin blockchain, the largest and oldest blockchain in the world. The Bitcoin blockchain contains thousands of nodes that are saddled with the responsibility of running the protocol that blockchain uses to create and secure the blockchain.

Bitcoin is here to stay. Developers are working around the clock to ensure that the Bitcoin blockchain is ever-changing to meet the needs of the users. As a result, developers are committed to making the system stronger and faster to ensure the long-lasting value of the blockchain.

The Battle Against Bitcoin

In spite of the numerous benefits of Bitcoin and the Bitcoin blockchain, it is not without some challenges, too. The first challenge centers on the question of whether Bitcoin's core should be left as it is, or if the functionality of the software should be enlarged. Although this is a seemingly simple decision, it has enormous repercussions. This is connected to the billions of dollars in assets, and the permanence of the information secured by Bitcoin software means that any code change should be critically debated and reviewed. The internal conflict is not the only issue that Bitcoin has to contend with. The decentralized nature of this digital currency has made it a formidable foe for traditional currencies. This does not sit well with regulators, and they have made it their primary target. Recent events in China and other countries is proof of the general disapproval that central authorities have for cryptocurrencies.

The popularity and wide acceptance of this coin also poses another problem. Many illicit business transactions can hide under the privacy offered by the coin. It can also be used as an avenue for money laundering, or transferring money from a controlled economy to one with more relaxed rules and regulations. As a result of a barrage of attacks on Bitcoin, its reputation has been tarnished in some ways, as many have criticized the cryptocurrency. Entrepreneurs who wanted to leverage Bitcoin technology had to rebrand it. This rebranding gave Bitcoin a facelift, and eventually led to the birth of blockchain. In time, people's fear of Bitcoin and other cryptocurrencies has been replaced with excitement and a deepened appreciation for digital currencies.

Some Bitcoin Misconceptions Debunked

Many have default reactions to any new innovation, especially one without a precedent, and that is difficult to understand: suspicion and condemnation. These reactions are usually borne out of ignorance and misconceptions. As a new innovation without precedence, Bitcoin comes with its own fair share of misconceptions, such as these below:

Bitcoin was Hacked

This is one of the biggest misconceptions about digital currency. The story goes that millions of dollars of Bitcoin were hacked. However, the truth is that no hacker or group of hackers has ever launched a successful attack on Bitcoin. The security behind Bitcoin is simply impenetrable. However, many central systems that are built on Bitcoin have fallen into the hands of hackers. Bitcoin exchanges and wallets have also met a similar fate due to their porous security. The Bitcoin community did not just sit back and watch hackers undermine its security, however. Instead, the community developed practical solutions to fortify their security and make the digital coins safe. These preventive measures include multiple signatures, paper wallets, wallet encryption, hardware wallets, offline wallets, and more.

Bitcoin is Used for Extortion

It is true that some daredevil hackers exploited the semi-anonymous feature of Bitcoin to use it in ransomware attacks. When hackers breach networks, the users are held hostage, pending the payment of the ransom. Recently, several hospitals, schools, and other public places have been subjects of such attacks. Unlike cash, however, Bitcoin leaves a trail in its blockchain that investigators can easily trace.

Bitcoin Has a Limit of 21 Million Coins

The story goes that there is a limit to the number of expected Bitcoin in circulation, and that the currency will collapse, after 21 million coins have been created and released. It is estimated that the last of the 21 million coins will be released in 2140. However, no one really knows what will happen between now and 2140.

Bitcoin is a Pyramid Scheme

This is another misconception. Many consider everything on the Internet to be a scam. Bitcoin and other cryptocurrencies are not spared from this attitude. The truth, however, is that Bitcoin is the opposite of a pyramid scheme. In fact, every miner that joins the network increases the difficulty of mining the digital currency. Also, the price of the currency is dictated by several factors, including demand, supply, as well as the perceived value of the currency.

Hackers May Take Over the Network

It is true that the Bitcoin network, like every other network, is susceptible to attacks. However, the resources required for hacking the Bitcoin network are so large that potential hackers would not be able to afford to do so. According to an online source, "an attacker would need the equivalent of all the energy production of Ireland" to pull this off. Most hackers would also be discouraged by the limited payoff of such an attack. A Bitcoin attacker would only be able to retrieve their own transaction and nothing else. They cannot just take other users' coins out of the blockchain. An example of a hack was carried out by Theodore Pierce. After he reportedly stole an estimated $40 to $40 million worth of Bitcoin, he still had to steal his girlfriend's parent's jewelry and laptops. This was because he had no access to the stolen funds.

Trade with Caution

Although there are countless misconceptions about Bitcoin and other cryptocurrencies, there are also some facts and figures that suggest treading with caution as well. It is important to understand the real players in the industry before investing hard-earned money in cryptocurrency. There are unscrupulous exchanges out there that will rip off investors. Consider the story of OneCoin scam, one of the most celebrated cryptocurrency crimes in history. That heist underscores the importance of taking all necessary security measures before dealing with Bitcoin, as scammers always find more innovative ways to scam. Some of these ways to scam investors in cryptocurrencies follow.

Fake Exchange Websites

For a cryptocurrency as popular as Bitcoin, there is no denying that some fake exchange websites spring up with the goal of robbing people of their cryptocurrencies. Over the years, a great many of these fake exchange websites have been created. Although cyberattacks are common on the Internet, Bitcoin and other currencies have also recently become the major targets of such attacks. This is due to the huge amount of money that is involved in a single attack. Moreover, many scammers are of the opinion that they can make money through identity theft by stealing the login information of users, or misleading users into sending Bitcoin to them. How to avoid being a victim?

Send Currency First

Sometimes one may come across sellers who promise to deliver goods, but only if the purchaser has first made the full payment. If this is a first transaction with the seller, it is advisable to proceed with the transaction with great caution because this scam has been successfully used by scammers for years to defraud people. After making such a cryptocurrency transfer, it will be the end of the conversation--the goods will never be delivered. Falling victim to this scam means the money is gone forever. It is practically impossible to get the money back because Bitcoin has a semi-anonymous nature that makes that impossible. The inability to initiate a charge back is another factor that works in favor of scammers.

The government could help if it put some measures in place to protect Bitcoin transactions, but that is not yet the case. Without a government's protection, users still face risks. Many scammers do not use direct scams; they try to gain trust instead. They will often impersonate someone a user knows, such as their boss, a family member, or a friend.

A user can avoid falling victim to a scam by trusting their instincts. If not comfortable with a conversation, cut it off, and move on to another seller. Do not invest anything more in a project than what one can afford to lose. Try to verify the identity of a buyer. If skeptical about the identity of a seller, find out as much as much about the seller as possible, or be prepared to let go of the transaction. If any doubt exists about a transaction or the other party, never be in a hurry to complete a transaction.

Get-Rich-Quick Schemes

The cryptocurrency world is already saturated with get-rich-quick schemes that have been created for scamming unwary victims. These employ many effective strategies to lure potential prey before robbing them of their coins. The good news is that such scammers can easily be identified, if one pays close attention. Most of the time, scammers promise something that is too good to be true. This often includes a promise of massive returns on investment. Scammers often use a recruitment process, and other techniques, for brainwashing potential victims. The recruitment process may involve asking that one register members of their family, or friends, as potential members of the scheme. They also promise there will be no loss on an investment. One must always resist the temptation to invest in such schemes. No matter how alluring a scheme is, take the time to do due diligence before investing in it. If the conditions surrounding the scheme are uncertain, stay out of it.

No Local Exchange

Another feature of a genuine digital currency is that it can be exchanged into a fiat, or local currency. Cryptocurrencies, such as Ethereum and Bitcoin, have this feature, and thus can be exchanged locally. A digital currency that cannot be exchanged locally does not deserve an investor's attention or money. Those types of crypto-coins are destined for failure and are usually scams. Be certain also to check whether the currency is traded internally. This is because a genuine digital currency cannot be traded internally, while it can be converted into a local currency through local exchanges, such as Bittrex, Poloniex, and others.

The Cryptocurrency Has No Background

Bitcoin and other legal cryptocurrencies have popular historical backgrounds that can be confirmed or are well-known by anyone who is interested in investing. Perform research to identify the background information of a coin in order to determine its legitimacy. It is safe to conclude that a cryptocurrency without a solid background is a scam. For instance, valuable information about the owner of the cryptocurrency and the company's address, as well as other relevant information should be readily available. Avoid any coin without this information.

It Lacks Fundamental Characteristics

Cryptocurrencies are defined by some common characteristics. Digital currencies that possess these fundamental characteristics are legitimate and will be a good investment. If a digital coin does not possess these characteristics, this is a red flag that it may a potential scam. Some of these characteristics are:

Controlled supply: Legal cryptocurrencies are not thrown into the economy without any control. Bitcoin has an estimated cap of 21 billion coins. Whenever the total Bitcoin in circulation reaches that figure, Bitcoin mining will automatically be stopped. This precautionary measure was put in place to prevent an uncontrolled release of the coins into circulation, as well as to prevent inflation.

Decentralization: Cryptocurrencies are not controlled by any central authority but are instead decentralized. This quality is one of the major factors behind the success of cryptocurrencies. Since the power to control digital currencies is not exclusively reserved for only some individuals, but by miners residing in different geographical locations across the globe, the coins cannot be misused like traditional currency. No artificial inflation, money-laundering, or financial mismanagement are possible.

Security: Cryptocurrencies are secure. The blockchain technology and other features of cryptocurrencies, such as decentralization, boost the security of the coins.

These are the fundamental characteristics that a real digital currency should possess. A digital currency that fails to have any of these qualities is far from being legitimate.

Chapter 13: Unraveling the Ethereum Blockchain

One of the most accessible blockchains is the Ethereum project. It is also one of the leading names in blockchain innovation. Its wide range of application makes it a potential contender for the best blockchain, a feat it can achieve in the future. The objective of this chapter is to explain the concept of Ethereum blockchain, and its numerous areas of application, with an overall view to better understanding of this cryptocurrency.

History of Ethereum

Ethereum is one of the earliest cryptocurrencies, which was created after the success of Bitcoin. In 2013, this powerful altcoin was first described in a whitepaper by Vitalik Buterin. Buterin previously had a reputation as an active programmer and writer in the Bitcoin community. He believed that governments and businesses could also utilize blockchain technology. As a contributor to Bitcoin, Buterin saw the huge potential of Bitcoin, outside of its ability to move value, without being attached to a centralized authority. He knew that Bitcoin could be put to better uses that would increase its value.

In those days, there was a fierce debate about the perceived overvaluation of the Bitcoin network from below-par transactions that were carried out by applications attaching themselves to Bitcoin. There was also a growing concern over the possibility of Bitcoin-based applications finding it challenging to scale in volume as a result of these parasitic applications.

Buterin and some others realized that the Bitcoin blockchain must be overhauled, if developers would be able to utilize Bitcoin blockchain to build decentralized applications. The alternative would be to build a completely new blockchain for these purposes. Since Bitcoin was already a household name, conducting a massive code overhaul of Bitcoin blockchain was not feasible. In 2014, Buterin and his team settled for the latter option and established the Ethereum Foundation. Their goal was to raise funds for building a new blockchain, one with a built-in programming language.

Between July and August 2014, the Ethereum Foundation raised some $18 million by selling its token, *ether*, as was the norm among cryptocurrency companies. Because the project was considered cutting-edge, developers and entrepreneurial talents from around the world flocked to the project, thereby making it a success. This is because many people realized that decentralization can help the world to find a permanent solution for eliminating corruption by authorities. The foundation used the fund for the project to hire a large, experienced development team for the project.

In July 2015, the first Ethereum network, known as Ethereum Frontier, was launched. The software was so restrictive that only developers who were technically savvy could use the software for building their own applications. A year later, Homestead was released, which is the current Ethereum software in circulation that is more user-friendly. Most anyone can use the template that is available on the platform for developing their application. The user interfaces are friendly and intuitive. It also has a large development community and is an improvement over the last network.

Their network for the future is Metropolis, which will offer a model where applications can be tested and developed. The applications will be easier to use, thereby giving them unprecedented market appeal to non-technical users.

Ethereum will be completed with the Serenity network. Serenity is the future of Ethereum, with its move from proof-of-work to proof-of-stake. This will be a switch from the model where miners compete with each other for the creation of the next block, to one where there will be a pseudo-random selection of nodes. The chances of choosing a node increases with a stake in the Ethereum network. The stake is a measure of the amount of cryptocurrency a node possesses. This change will lead to a gradual reduction in the cost of the energy used by proof-of-work. The cost-effectiveness of the stake will make it more appealing to users who wish to run some nodes in the Ethereum network. This will increase both security and decentralization.

The Power of Ethereum

Ethereum is considered to be one of the most complex blockchains in existence. It also comes completely packed with a functioning programming language that users can use to build any applications of their dreams. Whatever a programming language can do, the Ethereum protocol has the ability to do it. The Ethereum programming language is built inside a blockchain and offers more security, among other benefits. If a user can think of a programming project, Ethereum can handle it.

The amazing features of the Ethereum ecosystem have turned it into one of the best platforms for building strong decentralized applications. The friendly user- friendly interfaces and second-to-none documentation makes jobs easier. It also has security for small applications and fast development time. Ethereum-based applications have easy, smooth interactions with each other, without problems. These wonderful characteristics of the Ethereum system have made its protocol attractive to developers all over the world.

Its built-in programming language is the single most important feature of the Ethereum blockchain, making it more powerful than the more popular Bitcoin blockchain for application-building. Ethereum can also be used to create smart contracts. The Ethereum protocol makes the creation of new application extremely easy and possible because it offers the opportunity to take any process from government, business, or any other organization and build a digital representation of their processes with Ethereum.

Decentralized Applications

Decentralized applications are software programs that are designed to be controlled without any central authority. The creation of the Ethereum blockchain has led to the gradual rise in the number of decentralized applications around the world. More individuals and organizations are leveraging blockchain to create applications that work independently of any entity. These apps work on peer-to-peer principles to fully establish their decentralized nature. Ethereum is a leading supporter of decentralized application. It has a dedicated blockchain, with a Turning programming language, that allows professional developers to create decentralized applications on the Ethereum blockchain. Some companies and international organizations have taken full advantage of the opportunity offered by the Ethereum blockchain to develop decentralized applications for various uses.

Crowdfunding

One of the earliest users of Ethereum was WeiFund. The company leveraged the power of the Ethereum ecosystem to provide crowdfunding solutions, using its Web 3.0 enabled technology. The company promises to provide "world-class open-source modular and extensible" utilities that are readily accessible to everyone. In conformity to the principle, all the core aspects of the WeiFund platform are decentralized. Although WeiFund has an interface that is quite similar to some other crowdfunding platforms, such as GoFundMe and Kickstarter, all the funds raised on the platform will be kept safe in either ether, or digital currency. Unlike these conventional crowdfunding sites, the company takes advantage of smart contracts for the application. The implication is that all donations made via the platform can easily be converted into complex agreements.

Micro-Blogging

Micro-blogging is another application of decentralized applications. Eth-Tweet is a decentralized microblogging service designed for this purpose. This decentralized app runs on the Ethereum blockchain and provides some basic functionality that is reminiscent of Tweeter. The app allows tweets up to 160 characters in a message at once. As a decentralized system, no individual has any authority on whatever is published via the app. Any posted image cannot be altered or removed, except by the publisher only. In addition, donations can be made to the accounts in ether.

Developing Businesses

Helping develop businesses to survive is another application of decentralized applications. These projects have been taken to another level by 4G Capital. The company provides small businesses in Africa with funds to support their growth. To make these projects easy, a smart decentralized app has been created for use with smart contracts. Donors to the project will be able to use this app to fund businesses in Kenya, with the aid of a digital currency. The money that is lent to such businesses will be distributed among ones that are using the transactional system of 4G. The goal is to provide small business owners across Africa with the capital that will support their dream of becoming financially independent. The organization will also provide self-employed market traders, with unsecured debt funding for marketers, without collateral security for securing conventional loans.

The Power of Decentralized Autonomous Organizations

Wikipedia defines a Decentralized Autonomous Organization (DAO) as "an organization that is run through rules encoded as computer programs called smart contracts. A DAO's financial transaction record and program rules are maintained on a blockchain." DAOs are Ethereum applications that are built as an entity on Ethereum. They are created for fundraising and have been used by many companies and organizations for that purpose. A typical example of the DAO is The DAO. This is a venture capital fund that was launched in June 2016, with $150 million. The money was raised through crowdfunding by implementing Ethereum-based smart contracts. Apart from its use as a fund-raising application, DAOs can also be designed for nonprofit and civic purposes. Ethereum makes it easy for developers to create DAOs at their convenience as the digital currency has templates that developers can use for creating them.

How a DAO Works

DAOs follow a strict pattern that helps users to get the best out of them. An example of how DAOs work follows below based on a group of developers who designed a smart contract to be used for governing an organization:

- Investors contribute funds to the DAO and are rewarded with some tokens, which serve as proof of their ownership. The principle is similar to that of buying a stock in a company, but the difference is that investors in a DAO have control of their funds from the beginning.
- The DAO is activated and becomes operational, after the fund has been raised. This causes the members to propose a plan on how the fund is to be utilized.
- The members sit to vote on the proposal.
- The proposal is deemed to have passed or failed when the allocated time for the proposal has elapsed and the expected number of votes has been collected.
- A DAO is a service used by individuals who volunteer themselves as contractors.

The mode of operation of a DAO is at variance with conventional investments. In a conventional setting, a central party, or a board of directors, is responsible for the running of the investment. In contrast, investors in a DAO have absolute control over their assets. They are responsible for any decision about their investments. They vote on all decisions and potential investment opportunities. The flexibility and the entrusting of power with members make DAO more appealing to people than traditional investments. As a result, traditional investments feel threatened by DAOs.

Another difference between the two is the security provided by DAO for the assets that are built on it. While traditional investments are susceptible to fraud and financial mismanagement by those in control, DAO is fraud-proof because they are built on codes that are difficult to change at will. This has prevented hackers. Although there still exists a chance that hackers can still find their way around the code, the chances are so slim that it probably is not worth the effort.

An example illuminates the problems with attempts at hacking DAO: When The DAO was launched, it raised $150 million from over 11,000 members. However, they only had the money for a week because hackers worked on the DAO and drained The DAO of $50 million worth of cryptocurrency. The following week, however, the hack was reversed and the stolen funds were restored via the Ethereum blockchain's hard fork. Therefore, hackers have little incentive to hack DAO because the rewards are not worth the efforts they have to put into the hacking.

The attack mentioned above was not exactly a hack, although many people are of the opinion that it was an actual hacking of the DAO system. Ethereum is an imperfect system, and that has turned out to be its major weakness. The withdrawal of the funds necessitated restarting the system to correct such an action. Ethereum can accomplish this in just one way: to create a hard fork. This allows a fundamental change to the Ethereum protocol, so that previously valid transactions and blocks will be rendered invalid. The objective was that Ethereum could protect the stolen funds. This made it possible for The DAO to reverse the theft.

Nevertheless, hacking and scam attempts are a real, frequent occurrences in the digital currency space. A large percentage of these attacks are targeted at applications and centralized exchanges. The value attached to cryptocurrencies makes these a focus of attack for many hackers. Whenever one hears about hacking in the cryptocurrency world, it is usually not an entire system that was attacked by cybercriminals. It is more often only a website, or a wallet, that is hacked because hackers find it more convenient to hack a single wallet or website than a complete network.

The fact that cryptocurrencies are anonymous by nature complicates the situation. That is one of the reasons why crooks are attracted to cryptocurrencies. However, the cryptocurrency community is constantly putting more measures in place to increase the security of cryptocurrency and applications that are built on these digital currencies.

Discovering Ether

One cannot talk about Ethereum blockchain without mentioning *ether*. Ether is to Ethereum blockchain what Bitcoin is to Bitcoin blockchain. Ether is the digital currency of Ethereum. Without ether, Ethereum would be impossible. Ether motivates the network to seek self-security through proof-of-work mining. It is also needed for the execution of any code written within the Ethereum network. It is further used for the execution of contracts in Ethereum, and is thus referred to as *gas* in the process.

Some amount of ether is also needed for the execution of the built-in code in a smart contract. That is one of the reasons why the Ethereum token keeps appreciating in value. As long as Ethereum continues to be used for creating smart contracts and applications, ether will continue to hold a very high value. Over the years, ether has experienced an appreciable increase in value. This has made it a token with increased popularity and speculation. It has been listed on most of the cryptocurrency exchange websites and is now the financial exemplary for many new hedge funds. Although Ether had a slow start, it is now one of the leading cryptocurrencies in the world, with millions of investors.

How to Run Ethereum

Before one can use the Ethereum blockchain, the first step is to create a wallet. The wallet is where ether, the Ethereum token is stored. Once a wallet has been created, it can store ether. The following steps describe how to start using Ethereum:

1. Go to the official website of Ethereum, www.ethereum.org.

2. Click the download button at the bottom of the page. Download the Ethereum wallet. Note that this can be a time-consuming task. Make sure that the wallet is downloaded where it can easily be seen.

3. Open the downloaded wallet.

4. Click "Use Test Net." A prompt will ask to mine test ether. The difference between this test and the real ether mining is time. This is less time-consuming than real mining, although it still takes a reasonable amount of time.

5. Create a password. Ensure that the password is strong. The rule of thumb is to create a password that is long, and that contains alphanumeric and special characters.

6. Keep the password in a safe place because it will always be needed whenever performing any transactions with the wallet.

7. Check out the tutorials on the site. The start-up menu gives access to several tutorials.

8. Click "Develop."

9. Click "Start Mining."

Do not skip the "Start Mining" step because some of the later projects will require some ether. Upon completing the process, some test ether will be available for future projects on the Ethereum blockchain system.

How to Build a Decentralized Autonomous Organization

The future of business transactions will rely on DAO's. They will have an impact on how business transactions are conducted. They make it possible for individuals to create a company on the Internet that is governed by a set of rules that have been previously agreed on. These rules will be enforced via the blockchain network. Creating a DAO is not as difficult as many think. Note that a DAO cannot be created without setting up an Ethereum wallet. In addition, some ether must have been mined on the Ethereum test net before being able to proceed with the creation of a decentralized application.

To create a DAO, follow the steps below:

1. Go to Ethereum's official website: www.ethereum.org/dao.
2. Scroll down the page to find the code box. Copy the code.
3. Open the Ethereum wallet. This is where the DAO will be developed.

Test Congress and Net

After successfully opening a wallet, the next step is to set up the framework for creating the DAO by following these steps:

1. Open the Ethereum wallet and click "Develop."
2. Click on "Network."
3. Click on "Test Net."
4. After the Test Net page has fully opened, click on the "Contracts" tab.
5. Click on "Deploy Contract." Here, a set of test templates that the Ethereum team has created and set up for DAOs will be available.

6. Paste the copied code on the Solidity code box.

7. Choose "Congress" from the Contract picker.

When prompted to pick some variables, do so. Users can choose from these options:

Minimum quorum: This represents the fewest votes that are needed before a proposal can be executed.

Minute of debate: The shortest amount of time that must elapse before the execution of a proposal can be done. This is measured in minutes.

Margin of votes: This is for a majority. If the proposal gets more than 50% of the votes, including the margin, it is considered as passed. For a simple majority, leave the minute of debate at 0.

The next move is naming and setting up the governance for the DAO a user wishes to create. It is mandatory to set up a minimum for proposals and the merging of votes for a majority, which will determine the number of votes needed for a proposal, as well as the number of votes need for a proposal to pass. Do not forget to indicate the time frame to discuss new plans. When through with setting up the requirements for creating a new DAO, complete the following steps:

1. Name your DAO, as one would name a company.

2. Select 5 minutes for "Debate Times." This will determine the length of time that the new proposal will be available for conversation.

3. In the Margin of Votes for Majority section, set it to 0. This specifies the working of the democracy attached to contract work.

4. Confirm the DAO's price. The previous section gave steps on mining some ether in the test section for the wallet after initial set up. Use the mined ether to

proceed. If that section was skipped, one cannot proceed. In that case, go back to the previous section and mine some ether.

5. Using the mined ether, click "Deploy." This will prompt for the password. It may take the DAO a couple of minutes before it will deploy. When the new dashboard appears, scroll down to see that the DAO has been created.

6. A new icon will be generated that represents the newly-created DAO.

Click on it.

The Future of DAO

Decentralized organizations and smart contracts hold a lot of promises for the future. Both have a good rationale and democratic values that many find appealing. Currently, however, the full potentials have not yet been explored. DAO's may offer more possibilities than currently known, and that makes them more promising as well. As each contract is created, this may be the next step to either a massive failure, or a ground-breaking experience. One can achieve more success in the cryptocurrency world if considering Ethereum as the coin of the future. If the Ethereum network is approached carefully, its benefits far outweigh its drawbacks.

In contrast, if expecting perfection from the network and all its millions of participants, one is likely to be disappointed. While some of the users possess integrity and honor, there are also some unscrupulous bandits on the network as well. The hacking of smart contracts in 2016 was an eye-opener. That event underscored the importance of reviewing smart contracts regularly and thoroughly, while also paying attention to the security of such contracts. While some hackers may be working to bring the network down, other users and developers with integrity are working to ensure that everyone succeeds with their cryptocurrency.

Investing in a DAO

An important tip when dealing with decentralized applications and smart contracts is the need to be cautious before investing in such contracts and applications. This is especially true when dealing with contracts that are yet to be fully vetted or untested contracts. Do not forget that hackers are not after small contracts. Their primary targets are large contracts where they have a good chance of hitting it big once. The DAO hack described earlier is proof that hackers can hack contracts. Even well-thought-out contracts are not immune because hackers can explore flaws that may not be easily visible to others. Although the future of smart contracts and decentralized applications is promising, be certain to trade with credible and reputable parties only. This will drastically reduce susceptibility to cyberattacks.

One should also cultivate the habit of reviewing the best practices. This will keep a user abreast of new innovations, security tips, and other valuable practices that will reduce chances of becoming a victim of hacking. Also, create contracts in phases. Do this slowly so that there is sufficient time to manage the investments. And in the case of an accidental hacking, ensure that there have been some preventive measures in place to minimize loss. In the future, Ethereum blockchain, and everything attached to it, will mature. New solutions are expected to be put in place to make both the network and the wallets hack-proof.

How to Build Smart Contracts

Considering the threats by hackers, and other potential challenges, it is imperative to learn how to build smart contracts that are smarter than a standard contract. Programming a smart contract is more challenging than writing a standard contract because it requires being able to analyze and code a smart contract. In a smart contract, there is no need for a third-party. The implication is that if the execution of the contract is at variance with its expected result, then it is done. There is no third-party to correct the errors and make it work perfectly.

The complexity and distributed nature of blockchains have their drawbacks. One is the inability to make changes in the event of an unwanted outcome. It is important to note that smart contracts have the potential for flaws and failure. A user must build some safety valves into the contracts to be able to take the necessary steps to attend to any vulnerabilities or bugs whenever they come up.

One must also remember to include a switch in the contract. This will serve as an exit if things go wrong. One can then pause a contract, and thus prevent an unwanted outcome. To deploy a big contract, seek the assistance of the community to identify any vulnerabilities and fix them immediately. Offer bug-hunting rewards for the community to incentivize them to assist. To fortify a contract against attacks, keep the contract logic as simple as possible. Keep each section of the contract in a small module to make it simple. The more complex a contract is, the more likely that it will contain attack vectors and errors. When keeping a contract simple, it reduces the likelihood of dealing with bugs and makes it easy to isolate issues for correction whenever there is a need.

Finding Bugs in the System

The community already has some tools to find bugs in the system. Use these tools. Also, remember that a user's contract is their domain. That's where a user has absolute control over everything. There may be external calls from other contracts; be cautious if this occurs. Ignore these. Most of these are malicious calls that can overthrow a user's authority if given them permission for your contract.

Chapter 14: Understanding the Ripple Blockchain

Ripple is one of the biggest names in the cryptocurrency world. It is an amazing blockchain for trading and moving value globally. The Ripple protocol is known for its low cost, speed of operation, and high security. Its applications include trading and banking. Currently, Ripple blockchain is driven by a technology that makes the digital currency a leading blockchain in the commercial world. The technology has found a good use in the commercial industry.

The History of Ripple Blockchain

Although many people are of the opinion that Bitcoin is the leading cryptocurrency project, the fact is that the Ripple project is actually far older than its Bitcoin counterpart. The Ripple project was developed by Ryan Fugger, a Canadian developer, in 2004. He conceived the idea after working in Vancouver on a local exchange trading system. Fugger primarily wanted to create a functional monetary system that is decentralized, and that can be applied for the empowerment of communities and individuals, so that they can create personal money. He built the first version of the money system, which he named RipplePay.com. Over the years, however, the project has undergone several versions that have changed the original.

Developers, Arthur Britto, Jed McCaleb, and David Schwartz worked with OpenCoin to make some additions to Fugger's work. The contributions of these developers turned the Ripple project into a strong one, with the introduction of some features associated with blockchain, such as the digital currency system. This system allows members of a network to consensually publish transaction chains.

The pioneer CEO of Ripple, Chris Larsen, also contributed immensely to the popularity and wide-range of applications of this digital currency. The CEO founded companies, such as Prosper and E-Loan, to change the consumer market, with this radical approach. Larsen achieved much success because he enjoyed the assistance of these disruptive organizations. They helped him to achieve his dreams. He was Ripple's CEO from August 2012, to 2016.

Since Ripple came into view, it has achieved tremendous growth, so much so that it is currently a venture-backed start-up. Some of the biggest companies in the world are providing Ripple with needed support, such as Andreessen Horowitz, Google Ventures, and others. Ripple has capitalized on the huge support it enjoys from these companies to raise venture funding of over $93 million.

Politically, Ripple is very active. It is the leader of many companies and organizations, such as the Federal Reserve's Faster Payments Task Force Steering Committee. It is also the co-chairman of the W3C's Web Payments Working Group. To make its services available to people from all walks of life, it has offices in some of the major cities in the world. One can find Ripple offices in New York, Luxembourg, San Francisco, Sydney, and London. Ripple played a major role in the banking industry some years ago, having a disruptive impact on the industry. That eventually set the company up against authorities, especially, the Financial Crimes Enforcement Network (FinCEN).

In 2015, Ripple was fined $700,000 by FinCen for violating its Secrecy Act. The company had sold XRP to Roger Ver, who was a popular Bitcoin investor. Rather than file a report about the suspicious activities of Ver, due to its record of a felony conviction for using eBay to sell fireworks, Ripple kept mute.

That irked FinCEN, and Ripple was penalized for withholding valuable information.

Some banks, such as Oversea-Chinese Banking Corporation Limited and DBS Bank, withdrew their banking services to the Singapore branch of Ripple. The general belief was that the banks took this step because they believed that making assets available on blockchains exposed them to regulatory risks that outweighed the reward from such transactions.

Since this incidence, Ripple has decided to let go of those business interests and focus solely on regional and international banks. Ripple has gradually become a giant in the financial sector, as it provides financial settlement solutions for its global clients. The Ripple protocol works in a similar way as the Bitcoin protocol, and thus reduces the total cost of settlement that users are allowed to transact both directly and instantly. It is also built on an open-source and distributed Internet protocol. It uses a blockchain, and ripples are its official native currency.

Ripple has had a great impact on the financial industry, with its distributed financial technology. This technology makes it possible for users of the platform to make real-time international transactions across the Ripple network. Ripple has also made it possible for global markets to achieve their goals of rendering low-cost, fast, and global payment services to numerous customers.

Cross-border business transitions have never been better than what Ripple offers to its users. With Ripple, exchanging value and payments across borders is simple. Over the years, it has succeeded in creating an international network of market makers, financial institutions, and consumers. Hence, exchanging any value of choice to any part of the world, with the assistance of Ripple, is both possible and easy. The exchange can be made instantly and take place in any part of the world.

Another concept that Ripple is built on is the Internet of Value. The principle behind this concept is that any value, such as cars, money, commodities, and land can successfully be traded online, without the assistance of intermediaries to speed up the process.

The Ripple protocol will facilitate these processes and serve instead as an intermediary. Ripple is a trading platform as well as an exchange network, with a blockchain backend. Many institutions already use Ripple's distributed ledger to clear their transactions. Its distributed funds exchange also allows institutions to settle their obligations.

Interaction on the Ripple network can be accomplished in two major ways:

1. The users of the system for financial purposes can participate in the Ripple network by issuing, accepting, and trading assets to make these transactions faster.

2. Node operators also participate by keeping track of transactions, read consensus agreements about the validity of the transactions, and ordering agreements with other nodes that make up the network.

A participant in these processes must have some degree of trust for those issuing the assets in their possession. A node operator is also expected to have some degree of trust for other nodes, so that they work together and not collude to stop the confirmation of valid transactions. The Ripple network carries out exchange of its wide variety of values within its network through a trusted path. XRP, Ripple's cryptocurrency, is leveraged to facilitate exchanges between things of differing values, with no trusted path or a low trading volume.

Ripple has a basic infrastructure that can be used for optimizing payment processes and exchange of goods globally between the network, nodes, and the financial participants. Furthermore, Ripple has had a powerful influence on the banking industry. This is not accidental because Ripple has some core functions devoted to the banking industry in its protocol.

The Ripple protocol provides two important functions for this purpose:

1. It presents itself as a neutral transaction protocol. Therefore, Ripple can easily transfer the same type of value bilaterally. If it is a cross-currency transaction, it approaches its liquidity providers to source for funds. This can pose a challenge because many markets find liquidity to be an issue.

2. Ripple protocol sometimes connects payment networks and banks by acting as a common ledger between them. This allows both the payment networks and banks to clear transactions between them in just five seconds.

In these capacities, users have uninterrupted connectivity between each other. It is also easier to constantly monitor how transactions flow across its network. In addition, Ripple technology is favoured by banks because it helps them to eliminate the need for clearing houses and intermediaries. Instead, they can operate a system that is cheaper, faster, and has fewer risks attached. To take more advantage of this system, banks have also removed other intermediaries and paper from their transactions to make cross-border payments faster and easier.

Banks have also benefited immensely from this technology. Prior to the creation of Ripple protocol, foreign exchange operations were quite risky and expensive. The risks and the exorbitant costs of foreign exchange can now easily be avoided because banks have the opportunity to make direct transactions with other global banks, without added costs. In addition, Ripple has an open marketplace consisting of third-parties where they can easily source for liquidity.

The decision of banks to align themselves with Ripple has been rewarding. Some of the advantages of using Ripple for transactions are:

- It makes real-time payments possible.
- Comprehensive transactions can be traced without hitches.
- Reconciliation is nearly instantaneous.
- Almost all commodities, currencies, or tokens can easily be converted.
- It is the only open payment network. This means that the payment network can be used by anyone. A user can also make payments with the network in any currency in any part of the world, without worrying about logistics.
- Ripple is also a distributed currency exchange. With Ripple, anyone can make direct trade currencies, without any added margin or fees. With its Forex feature, cross-currency payments can be accomplished easily. This means payments can be made to anyone in whatever currency of their choice, while the recipient can also receive payment in his or her preferred currency.

Ripple offers several benefits that make it a leading name in the industry. With its impact on the financial sector, it promises to continue its rise to becoming one of the most powerful blockchains ever.

Differences between Ripple and other Blockchains

The Ripple blockchain is obviously making gains in the banking industry as a result of its numerous benefits and areas of application. In comparison to other blockchains, it has carved a good niche market for itself. There are a couple of notable differences between the Ripple blockchain and other blockchains, such as Bitcoin. Some of these differences include:

Structure: There is a significant difference between Bitcoin and Ripple, in terms of structure. Their modes of operation are also a bit different. Ripple employs one of the most-used exchange routes for structuring the transactions conducted on it as debts. It also uses its cryptocurrency for exchange between the wide varieties of values that people trade on the Ripple network.

Trust: Ripple is built on trust. Most other blockchains do not enjoy the same degree of trust that forms the foundation of Ripple. When a transaction is conducted by members of the Bitcoin blockchain, the network will ensure that none of the parties cheats the other party in the transaction. When it comes to balancing each block of transaction on the Bitcoin network, the network conducts regular checks to ensure that all the tokens used in the transaction have never been spent before.

Proof-of-work: This is another outstanding difference between Ripple and others. While the majority of other blockchains use proof-of-work, Ripple distances itself from it. The Ripple team has instead found a convenient way to completely eliminate the power requirement that must be met if other blockchains are to secure their blockchains. This has drastically reduced the amount of electricity that Ripple uses during its operation. Its speed of operation also exceeds that of traditional blockchains.

Nature of decentralization: Ripple and other blockchains do not execute a similar mode of operation. They work differently. One of the significant differences between these blockchains is the nature of decentralization of Ripple and others. Ripple adopts a very subtle decentralization. It is possible for a node to add other nodes of its choice to its validator list to peer into the transactions that the other nodes intend to confirm.

It acts as middleware: Ripple acts as the middleware between some institutions and financial products. To make use of the Ripple network, one must be licensed beforehand, such as a mobile money operator or money services provider. In contrast, the Bitcoin protocol is open for use to anyone. Although Bitcoin has changing regulations, it is not mandatory to be licensed before using it, while it is illegal to work on Ripple without being licensed. That is one of the reasons why Ripple focuses primarily on financial institutions.

Faster transaction confirmation: Ripple counts on its trusted nodes to provide it with probabilistic voting. Since this is consensus voting, the nodes can easily come to agreement whenever they want to confirm a transaction. Thus, while Bitcoin transactions usually take hours for confirmation, Ripple transactions are confirmed in just five seconds.

Number of units: Ripple has an estimated 100 billion XRP units. All the units were created at the beginning of the network. These units were distributed to Ripple owners and other investors. In contrast, Bitcoin token are theoretically limited to 21 billion tokens. Unlike Ripple, these tokens are not created once. Instead, they are created each time a new block is created. The nodes that are victorious during consensus are awarded these tokens. Over time, the supply of the tokens will increase.

Self-protection: Ripple has an internal self-protection built into it. It uses this built-in protection mechanism to prevent itself from denial-of-service and spam attacks. It does this by demanding minimum costs for each transaction on the blockchain. The transaction fee is usually 0.00001 XRP, which is referred to as ten drops. If the transaction volume exceeds the normal transaction volume, Ripple will automatically increase the required number of drops. Although Bitcoin has a similar mechanism in place, it does not impose a minimum transaction fee. Bitcoin miners may also deliberately ignore a transaction and not confirm it without including a fee.

No need for a "trust path": Trading Ripple can be done without a trust path. This is advantageous in transactions where both parties have no path. An XRP exchange is needed in the middle of the transaction to make any transaction between low-liquidity market and untrusted parties faster. In contrast, on Bitcoin parties can conduct their transactions even without the parties knowing or trusting one another. In this case, the trade cannot be made outside Bitcoin token. The extra feature incorporated into Ripple allows users of the blockchain to make exchanges of anything without problems.

It selects its nodes: Unlike Bitcoin that operates an open policy where participation in the Bitcoin network is open to all, the Ripple network is more centralized because it picks the nodes that will be used in securing their consensus system.

Unleashing the Power of Ripple

In recent years, Ripple has taken some steps to reduce its focus on consumers to fully concentrating on the banking industry. For instance, it has stopped updating Ripple Trade, which was its portal for consumer-related products, by no longer opening new consumer wallets on the platform. The company has also removed all the products that are primarily for consumers. This is because of the inability of Ripple to keep pace with the regulatory burdens associated with servicing consumers, as stipulated by the Financial Crimes Enforcement Network (FinCEN). FinCEN made its stance clear: any participant in the virtual currency industry must be registered under federal law as money services business.

By backing away from the customer aspect of its business, Ripple is able to devote more time and attention to large enterprise customers, such as banks. They are the only industry that can afford to accept the offers offered by Ripple, without any negative impact on their ROI. Individuals who want to can access Ripple via a third-party, such as GateHub, Ripple's preferred third-party.

Different operations can be performed in the GateHub wallet, such as sending money, trading silver and gold, Bitcoin, and XRP from the wallet on the Ripple network. From the wallet, one can also monitor the state of other currencies and be kept updated of their real-time worth in response to fluctuating cryptocurrency values.

Self-identification is a requirement to use the GateHub wallet. This can be time-consuming because setting up an account in this wallet store takes some time. Access to the network is only permitted after successfully creating an account.

To create an account on Ripple's wallet store, follow the steps below:

1. Visit www.gatehub.net.

2. Click "Sign Up."

3. Provide the necessary information. This will include password, email address, and other required pieces of information.

4. Click "Sign Up."

5. A recovery key is generated. Keep it safe.

6. A link will be sent to the given email address. Click the link to verify the email.

7. Verify identity.

Some pieces of information GateHub will ask for identity verification include:

- Name
- Phone number
- Photo
- Some supporting documents

After providing all the personal information, GateHub will complete its verification process and clear the user to being trading via the Ripple protocol. If one has a Bitcoin wallet, then funds can be sent to this newly-created account. To take the advantage of Ripple protocol for building anything, one must usually be a programmer or have access to one. To meet this requirement, count on the Ripple support team to provide help via their documentation and direct assistance.

Note that Ripple was created for cheaper and faster money transfer. One should understand that this is a heavily-regulated part of the economy. According to Ripple itself, the protocol is primarily designed to perform transaction tasks. It is left to a user's discretion whether to comply with regulations or not. For resources to use the Ripple network to build a custom project, follow this link: https://ripple.com/build/. This is the official Ripple build page.

Need for Caution

Similar to every other blockchain that depends on cryptocurrencies to be functional, Ripple has its own fair share of risks. This requires that one is always cautious when dealing with the cryptocurrency world. Although the cryptocurrency world in general presents many risks, some risks that are peculiar to Ripple are as follows:

Transaction manipulation: Due to its structure, the Ripple network is prone to buying assets and selling them in different markets, when a stakeholder wants to take full advantage of the differences in prices for a single asset simultaneously. This practice is called *arbitrage*. Many people are encouraged to engage in this practice because Ripple has multiple markets and a number of currencies. A determined programmer may take full advantage of that to manipulate transactions' orders.

There are two forms of arbitrage:

1. Advantageous arbitrage transaction placement: This is done before the closing of the ledger. It involves taking undue advantage of the differences in prices between some markets. Ledger closure occurs every five seconds. Unscrupulous traders employ the services of bots to fully exploit the market before the ledger closes. The small discrepancies between markets are usually capitalized on by these bots by striking a combination of deals that are identical or matching. They also engage in other malpractice, such as giving undue advantage to their transactions by pushing them into the best position in the ledger.

2. Large trade front running: The Ripple network is exposed to the front-running of huge trades by its structure, as well as the existing latency in its consensus. This is possible because the nodes in the network have the habit of broadcasting transactions to other nodes that have earned their trust. This occurs when bots are fully in action, monitoring transactions and looking for any opportunity to place themselves in front of big transactions. The bots do this in two ways:

a. Bots first buy up initial offers to make a large purchase fulfilled. A bot later sells the initial offers to the original owner.

b. The bots also manipulate the position of the transactions to make this happen by repositioning the transactions in the ledger. In the long run, the original owner of the initial offers will be given a trade that is lower in value than what he or she deserves.

Unethical trading: The original description of Ripple was as a platform for moving values across the world at a cheaper and faster rate than other existing networks. That is why Ripple needs clusters of markets to function. These markets share some trusted nodes that are used for transaction confirmation. At times, there can be some significant differences in prices of these groups. Some traders capitalize on these differences to encourage ethical trading.

Ripple is aware of the risks faced by its investors and is working to ensure that their users enjoy more protection than previously. For instance, it has an open offer to experienced programmers to help it seek out potential exploitation, vulnerabilities, and bugs from its protocol. The goal is to completely rid Ripple protocol of such potential threats and make the protocol overall less risk-prone.

Chapter 15: Understanding the Factom Blockchain

The cryptocurrency industry has tons of powerful, dynamic blockchains, and Factom blockchain is one of them. Factom blockchain is built and supported by Factom, Inc., a large corporation that is responsible for using the Factom protocol to build products and tools. Factom is a powerful tool, with the potential to turn blockchain technology into a formidable power. The Factom blockchain is unique from other blockchains. Its unique properties, however, make it the best blockchain for providing adequate security for systems and publishing data streams.

When it comes to securing things, the best way to ensure that is through the installation of Factom software on a system. To increase the interoperability of other blockchains and make Factom more secure, Factom blockchain also bridges and integrates other blockchain technology and blockchains.

The Purpose of Factom Blockchain

Each blockchain is designed for a particular purpose. For instance, the Bitcoin blockchain is designed for investors, while Ethereum blockchain is the power behind decentralized apps and smart contracts, as well as the driving force behind future transactions. Therefore, Factom also has a specific area of specialization. Factom is designed primarily as a publishing platform. Validating and publishing data is the core reason for the creation of this blockchain. All the other tools that are available on the Factom blockchain are designed with the goal of supporting the functionalities of the blockchain, making publishing of any type of data easy.

Factom is a strong platform with the ability to handle large transactions up to 10 kikibytes. This is because larger transactions can effectively be handled with multiple entries and special restructuring, and that is what Factom offers. The protocol can also publish the hash representing the data. Similar to Bitcoin protocol, the Factom protocol is also an open source that is available for the general public. The protocol offers individuals the opportunity to publish whatever they like, while enjoyong the protection and security of the Factom blockchain. This has allowed individuals and corporations to publish different content in a wide area of interests. To also ensure that spamming is curbed to a minimum, a small amount of money is charged per entry.

Factom also has its own cryptocurrency: *factoids*. This cryptocurrency is available for trading in way like the other more than 1,000 cryptocurrencies. It can also be used for purchasing entry credits on the Factom network. An entry has a fixed price. In contrast, factoid has a fluctuating price. A user can increase entry credits purchases whenever there is an increase in the value of factoid.

In the Factom system, users and tradable tokens are different entities and are also treated differently; for instance, consumers can get factoid at a fixed price, while others can take advantage of the free market for factoid. This separation was incorporated into Factom to make it appealing to governments and industries that are heavily regulated, so they can make the best use of Factom blockchain technology, without the challenges of tradable tokens.

At the outset of 2017, some 40,000 entries were recorded by the Factom network each day. Some of the entries included the daily prices of all altcoins and the Russel 3000 Index. These records can be used for historical purposes and as input for smart contracts. The industry has thus successfully solved the problem of accessing and storing data. It is now easier to replicate computer backups and archive them in great quantities. One of the biggest problems, however, is how to determine the most recently-revised document, especially if many organizations are involved.

There exists a way that many organizations can make certain that they use the same document as their partners. The simple solution is using a blockchain-based document management system. Since the system is built on the blockchain technology, it will be quite easy for an organization and its partners to be on the same page with regards to documents. Proof-of-work consensus is the adopted verification process adopted by Ethereum, Bitcoin, and other blockchains. Factom blockchain, in contrast, adopts a consensus algorithm that is based on the technique used by a blockchain to agree with a newly-entered data in the system. The consensus first examines the validity of the newly-entered data.

Such a strong system is needed by public blockchains due to the open source nature of such blockchains that makes it possible for anyone who wants to update the blockchain by adding data to it. The rules of these blockchains determine what criteria also determine the validity of a block and a chain that can be trusted. Proof-of-work is attractive, however, it sometimes requires huge amounts of electricity and investing in special computer hardware. Although proof-of-work provides security for blockchains, it is very expensive and consumes too much electricity. In this system, only the fastest computer wins. The addition of more gigahash to the network, after a successful operation, makes the competition even stiffer.

The degree of ease in validating a block is proportional to the amount of data contained within the block. In Bitcoin and other related systems that adopt the proof-of-work system, the validation of specific data in the system is impossible without the blockchain. The whole Bitcoin must be downloaded before the validity of any transaction in the Bitcoin blockchain can be proven by others. This is a time-consuming activity that can take days before completion.

Factom takes a different approach to transactions. Rather than focus on the validity of a data as does Bitcoin and the rest, it focuses on whether payment has been made for the entry. In this case, the validation of entries is done by the users of the Factom system.

To spare the users the stress of having to download the blockchain before validating an entry, Factom structures its data in subchains that individuals on the system can easily parse. This makes validation of data faster and easier. This structuring of Factom was done to make it useful for commercial applications and convenient for an industry to make its validation, without downloading a full blockchain with irrelevant data about some other industries. For instance, to make insurance verifications, there is no need to deal with unrelated data from the banking industry. This saves some time and resources as it also makes validation faster and easier.

Data corruption is another problem for which Factom has found a practical solution. To provide the right immunity for its network against the corruption of valuable data, the Factom blockchain automatically spreads itself out. It does this often, as it creates an anchor into both Ethereum and Bitcoin, with the following goals:

1. To prevent the server that is used for building the Factom blockchain from rewriting history accidentally without notice. Since the capacity of these servers does

not involve controlling Ethereum or Bitcoin, the history recorded on these two is permanently stored.

2. For the purpose of ensuring that people get the same version of the blockchain. Many giant organizations and corporations have the habit of frequently customizing their web pages to avoid this problem. When different companies receive different business transaction histories, it may trigger misunderstanding between the companies. The existence of a single Bitcoin blockchain makes it impossible to create different versions of history.

How to Build on Factom

Factom was created to serve as the foundation for other applications. The platform was built for its speed of operation, scale, and cost-effectiveness. Factom was also created to mimic the security that is the trademark of Bitcoin blockchain, and to make it permanent. Factom has some well-designed application programming interfaces that are designed to help development teams authenticate and manage documents. They can also use them to build special identities for both things and people. To take full advantage of the features of Factom, one needs a skilled and experienced developer to help. The API's should only be run for big organizations, as they are not currently designed to be used for small projects.

The public can take full advantage of two core offerings by Factom:

1. **Iris:** Factom designed this platform for developers to build identities. This is the principle behind the Department of Homeland Security's Internet of Things (IoT) identity project. It is an extension of the Apollo platform as a tool for record management.

2. Apollo: This is used as an authentication option, in addition to being used for publishing. Apollo makes it possible for users to refer to a huge volume of data fed into Factom. The data can be referred to historically. Apollo can be used for updating protocol or publishing a website's archive.

These API's can further be used for the original purpose, without running a cryptocurrency wallet or setting up a blockchain. This makes the process easier for the user and is the best for individuals who are unduly concerned about cryptocurrency's regulatory grey-zone.

Who can use Factom?

The question of who can use Factom can be answered with a simple statement: Factom is an open source platform, meaning that it is available to all. Anyone who is interested in taking advantage of the Factom platform can use it for building a safe, honest system with its blockchain technology in order to keep records safe. As discussed earlier, a nominal fee paid by the users prevents scammers and others from spamming the platform, so that honest users can reap the maximum benefits from its use.

Using Factom

Factom technology makes life easier for people. It can be used to secure personal information and make it available for those who really need access to it. For instance, it can secure medical records and make these available to a personal physician alone, without making it a public knowledge. One can also cast a vote from the comfort of their home, without making personal information public.

The Factom blockchain and data layer have a huge potential in areas of applications spanning both private and personal identity, such as financial and real estate records. With the Factom platform, users have a tool for building a more secure record-keeping system by taking advantage of its three types of proof:

1. **Proof of Process**: Any existing document will be linked to this updated document.

2. **Proof of Existence:** At any point in time, a document exists as a proof of existence.

3. **Proof of Audit**: When a document is updated, it can be checked to see if it has changed in accordance to some established rules.

Factom ICO

Factom is one of the blockchains that achieved success with its ICO. On March 31, 2015, Factom launched its ICO. Within 24 hours, potential investors bought more than a million tokens with Bitcoin. The Bitcoins were released in three batches, each batch making up 33% of the total. The first batch was released when Factom reached Milestone 1. Milestones 2 and 3 triggered the release of the second and third batches. 323 investors bought Factom ICO, thereby helping Factom to raise a whopping 2,278 Bitcoin, with a total worth of $1.1 million.

About Factoid

As aforementioned, factoid is the official cryptocurrency of Factom. Factom has a special token system that uses the factoid. The factoid can also be traded or purchased on some cryptocurrency exchanges, although its currency status is different from that of Bitcoin. If a factoid owner desires, he or she can convert factoid into entry credits. These are tokens that cannot be transferred and can be used by the owner for purchasing the power to publish whatever they want on the Factom network.

Some unique aspects about Factom transactions are that they are both permanent and irreversible. A user cannot undo a transaction once it is completed. And factoids are taken out of circulation after they have been completely burned. Factoids do not have a fixed price, following established cryptocurrencies. Its price is determined by utility and speculation in the cryptocurrency market. In contrast, entry credits are quite different and have a fixed price of $0.001. As a result, if a user wants to publish, they already have an idea of the price.

In order to raise funds to finance Factom development, the Factom team put some tokens up for sale when crowdfunding. The Factom network has yet to reach its 32 nodes full federation, in conformity with the condition outlined in the Factom whitepaper. The network will start rewarding all audits and federated nodes with new tokens when the network eventually reaches the 32 nodes.

The audit notes refer to the nodes that are saddled with the responsibility of checking the degree of honesty of nodes and that can replace a federated node whenever a federated note breaks the system's rule(s) or goes offline. A federated node is a node elected together with others by the network and given the responsibility of validating transactions and maintaining consensus. Value transfer occurs when new factoids are issued to the server, and when factoids are extinguished by users. Obviously, users are thus responsible for maintenance of the operation of the Factom servers.

How to Anchor an Application

Blockchain technology has changed the overview of consumer services as it made way for new services and products. Blockchains have proven to be the platform on which old technology can undergo reinvention, while new innovation can also find a place. Each blockchain comes with its own peculiar properties that are designed for specific applications. Factom has some unique properties as well. When it comes to information security, Factom is very good at it. The only limitations are the cost of publishing, which increases with the volume of the data to be published as well as the size of the individual entry.

When contemplating choosing the best platform for storing massive files, Factom is the undisputable leader. It can be used to store large files by leveraging the storage capability of a cloud solution, and then use the pointers inside Factom to find the location of those files when needed them in an application. The primary use of Factom is as a system for managing data, documents, and for building identities. It forms alliance with other blockchains and can be used for creating smart contracts.

How to Publish on Factom

Factom is a developers' software that is designed to provide assistance for other developers. If a developer wants to enter data into the network, or use his or her wallet, the developer must download special software and use his or her terminal. The developers behind Factom are working around the clock to ensure that the system is a strong one. They have also fully documented the system that will assist a user with the publishing process. To review Factom's open-source software and make a contribution, visit the GitHub repository to find the documentation to assist. It is expected that the Factom platform will soon offer a more user-friendly site for customers in the future.

The Role of FreeFactomizer

The Factom team is not the only stakeholder with the goal of helping users achieve the best uses of the Factom blockchain. In addition to the spirited efforts of the Factom team, some Factom fans are also contributing in their own ways to make the platform more accessible and easier to use. One of the fans built an app called FreeFactomizer. From the app, a user can explore the world of Factom to find out what functionality it possesses, even if not a developer. A user also does not need to know how to code or open a terminal before they can explore Factom with the assistance of this efficient app.

The app works by creating a hash of data, while uploading a file, or that is entered as a text into a text box. Factom then goes through the other documents submitted by other users and gathers their hashes. The collected hashes are then combined into a single entry within the Factom blockchain every ten minutes. The app is a demonstration of the proof of existence. Since this is a solo project sponsored by an individual, it comes with no warranty and may not be available forever. To check out this amazing app, follow these simple steps:

- Visit www.freefactomizer.com
- Upload the document to hash. Since the security of the service is not guaranteed, it is advisable to use a document that contains no sensitive information.
- For an estimate of the time it will take to add the file to Factom, click "Factomize the file Signature."

- After clicking it, wait while the file is being added to Factom. This will take about 10 minutes. The file will be combined with other data and documents while waiting. After completion of this process, FreeFactomizer will link back to Factom Explore through a link it provides.
- Factom Explore can be used to check the entry. Factom Explore is designed as a search tool that can be used for looking up entries in the Factom database.
- Another verification process to try is to upload the document again. If the entry is already confirmed, a message confirming that the signature is already registered will appear. This is an assurance that it has already been added to Factom.

Introduction into the Mortgage industry

Factom was the first company set up by this network for commercial purposes. It was established for managing blockchain documents. The goal was to make it a site for mortgage originators. Factom Harmony is used for mortgage documents and has a simple mode of operation. It first converts the imaging systems used in banks into a blockchain-based vault for storing documents. It also creates entries and manages them in real time, while the mortgage processing is ongoing. It then ensures that the data records within Factom are properly secured, so that metadata can transparently share this metadata between trusted parties. It makes reference to confidential data between these parties as well.

Factom Harmony, as a mortgage application, is far better than existing systems. Individuals who use this system have the confidence that they have identical records to the records they used for the loan, even many years later. As a result, mortgage buyers will now have the opportunity to carry out their transactions without the interference of intermediaries.

Factom hopes to take advantage of the benefits that arise from reduced costs from document assembly. Currently, banks and other lenders that provide mortgage loans spend a huge amount of time to make certain that records and audits are properly executed with the right data. This old system occasionally breaks down because multiple stakeholders are involved in the coordinating of all the processes, while using documents from different sources.

Secure Data on Factor Harmony with a Digital Vault

One of the most important uses of Factor Harmony is its ability to permanently store documents and data to a blockchain. It can also be effectively used for compliance and decision-making. This is in addition to its use for sharing data with any interested party. Data that are stored in the Factom system have a distinct version of history. Any missing data can also be clearly seen. Factom Harmony was also designed for handling lawsuits, audits, loan-trading, regulatory reviews, foreclosures, and securitization.

Up until 2008, the core technology was designed for maximum throughput, speed, document collection, and checklist management. As a result, records and data collection did not precede in a way that evidence of actions and decisions could be preserved permanently. Newer regulation demanded that businesses exercise more diligence in their record-documenting efforts as well as do their best to ensure accurate maintenance of any data they used for decision-making. This was due to a general lack of accountability, where there was always one excuse or the other whenever the documentation of any process was flawed. The inability to put in place a functional system that could preserve evidence of data and any related decision-making made it imperative that a system was designed to address this issue.

How Factom and Harmony Work Together

Both Factom and Harmony contribute in different ways to provide users a valuable experience. Factom's technology, on its own, is a combination of digital signatures, blockchain technology, and some cryptographic functions that were developed by the reputable US National Institute of Standards and Technology (NIST). NIST ensures that presentation of documents and data for future use is possible with the preservation of a cryptographic proof and some data points that users can use for preservation. The method used by NIST ensures the electronic creation of files that any authorized party can easily access and validate whenever they want.

Factom uses the SHA-256 cryptographic function for the generation of hashes for each data file and document that are stored on the Factom blockchain. It is the responsibility of the hash to create a cryptographic proof that a file is still valid without any alteration or change. The hash acts like the human fingerprint for some data that stands for the contents of a file. This eliminates the risk of accidental exposure of the content.

To further ensure the complete security of a set of data, Harmony generates some meta-data points and the hash for all the documents and files that are connected with a record. It also stores the generated meta-data points. Within this meta-data, data files and documents are linked together with the cryptographic tools. Both the file hashes and the meta-data are all recorded in the Factom blockchain.

Using Blockchain as Public Witness

Factom performs several functions, including acting as a public witness. It creates a number of public witnesses for any data it secures, although it does not have a huge blockchain, in comparison with Ethereum and Bitcoin. This is what serves as an incentive for nodes to become parts of the network. Factom finds a convenient way to ensure its security by anchoring any data that is placed in the blockchain in-between Ethereum and Bitcoin. It does this through hashing every ten minutes. Factom takes the data and hashes it until only one hash that has the capacity to represent the Factom blockchain is left.

Using dLoc for Verification

A new way of using blockchains to secure physical objects was created through the partnership of Factom with Smartrac. Smartrac is the world's leading name in RFID transponders manufacturing and supply. The company merged its experience with Factom to produce dLoc. This is a sticker that is designed for nearly everything. It is incorporated with a special utility that is specifically useful for breeder documents and other paper-based documents.

dLoc combines the power of software and hardware to serve as an end-to-end document management system. To secure an object, dLoc has an adhesive Smartrac that is a Near Field Communication transponder sticker. It has an embedded chip that can be place on any goods or documents to secure such documents or goods with the Factom blockchain.There is a simple principle behind this: with the NFC communication protocols, it is possible for two electronic devices to be connected to each other, if they are placed beside each other.

The combination of NFC's cloud-based software with the technology behind Factom has the result that is the creation of an immutable identity for whatever that is over time. The dLoc app can then be used by some people with high security clearance levels to access any physical documents and validate them. dLoc applications are not limited to document validation alone. Issuing agencies can also leverage the power of dLoc to take their business to the next level. They can use it to convert all their offline documents into digital documents. These can then be connected to all the digital systems for the purpose of bridging the existing gap between online and offline.

dLoc can also be used in a wide range of personal documents, such as land titles, birth certificates, medical and court records. Prior to the existence of dLoc, there was a huge integrity gap between the data in the digital and physical worlds. dLoc is the first document authentication system built on the Factom blockchain to offer a practical solution to this problem.

Over the years, dLoc has established itself as the best solution because of its being the first credible technique for using digital data to secure pieces of information on a paper-based document by leveraging the power of blockchain technology. The identity authentication offered by dLoc will have a great application for both the private and public sectors. These sectors are notorious for their wide use of paper documents. With the help of the dLoc authentication system, they can easily authenticate all these paper documents. However, it is not yet possible to use dLoc to completely eliminate fraud. As with any technology, criminals will find ways to bypass the authentication process and steal vital information. Circumventing dLoc technology, however, is quite costly, and this may discourage scammers. However, dloc helps discourage identity theft. A system has been created in dLoc with the objective of minimizing the possibility of having someone's identity or information stolen. The system will send alerts whenever an attempt is made on a user's identity.

Factom technology is gradually changing the way records are stored and protected. The current cases of hacking into conglomerates, such as Target, Sony, J.P. Morgan, and others is proof of the vulnerability of vital information to accidental exposure and theft. This has called for a more secure method of storing information.

This need for a secure method has necessitated a shift away from centralized databases that were the norm, to decentralized databases that are fueled by cryptocurrencies. For this reason, Factom has proven to be a reliable decentralized alternative to the vulnerability of centralized databases. By using Factom technology for record keeping, these can now be made secure. By analyzing and assessing all records, it is easy for Factom to identify potential security breaches that may lead to loss of data.

The success of Factom in ensuring the security of records is the beginning of a revolution that will have a positive effect on business practices. Factom blockchain technology, and its data layer, will also have various areas of application that will have a huge impact on our personal lives as well. Since its method of storage makes records more secure, financial records and identity thefts will be drastically reduced.

Chapter 16: DigiByte Blockchain

DigiByte is another blockchain that is ruling the gaming world. DigiByte is a multipurpose blockchain with a wide variety of applications, including document management and gaming. The DigiByte team is busy exploring many attributes of blockchains, such as speed, utility, and accessibility, realizing that the proper combination of these attributes will help everyone get the best results from blockchains.

DigiByte's strength comes from its structure. It is quite unlike other popular blockchains, such as Bitcoin, et al. For instance, while most blockchains have a single algorithm for operation, DigiByte is driven by five algorithms. Of course, this has its own advantage. In the blockchains run by a single algorithm, it is the survival of the fittest for the nodes. Only the fastest of these wins the tokens. The situation is quite different with DigiByte. Each of its algorithms allows for a different miner, and that has gradually made the blockchain more appealing to an increasing number of users. It has also let to the increased decentralization of the blockchain.

DigiByte protocol increases the security level of blockchain. Potential attackers will have a huge task before them to succeed in hacking the protocol. The increased decentralization makes it a matter of necessity that the hacker gains over 60% of the total hash rate of the network to have any significant impact on the network. To do so, the hacker would have to gain control of over 50% of four of the algorithms and a minimum of 93% control of the fifth algorithm. This makes the work of a potential hacker much more difficult. Therefore, chances of a breach decreases.

This is a plus when compared with Bitcoin blockchain, with its single algorithm. A hacker only needs to get 51% control of the Bitcoin algorithm to have access to the blockchain. Therefore,

DigiByte provides much more security than Bitcoin blockchain. If a hacker or a group of hackers can gain absolute control of over half of the miners in the Bitcoin blockchain, they automatically have control of the network, and that increases the possibility of manipulating Bitcoin. This is sufficient for them to wreak havoc on the network. If that happens, and the network is compromised, it will have a negative impact on the value of the token. All the data that secured in the network will also be compromised.

DigiByte Technology

DigiByte is a blockchain that is designed primarily for payments, gaming, and security. It also goes by the cryptocurrency name, DGB. DigiByte's headquarters is in Hong Kong.It is a cryptocurrency that was founded by Jared Tate. For a couple of years, Tate was a part of the Bitcoin community. He has a Computer Science and military background. In 2014, Tate's frustration with the Bitcoin core eventually led him to the launching of DigiByte.

His team of developers has created a lot of useful tools used by other projects. For instance, while Bitcoin only processes seven transactions per second, DigiByte processes a whopping 300 transactions per second. By 2021, the team also proposes to increase its transaction speed to match the enviable transaction speed of Visa.

The DigiByte network is highly distributed. At present, it is over 8,000 nodes that are spread across 82 countries. It can also be used for moving values between two parties without delay. In addition, it is cost-effective and affordable. Similar to Bitcoin, DigiByte blockchain can be used for securing small amounts of information. It can thus be used for securing documents, data, and contracts at an improved speed over that of Bitcoin.

The DigiByte team is also busy working to make the project appealing and fun. It does this by offering prizes for gamers via the platform. The team also makes sweet tweets about the gamers. Like most blockchains, it has a gitHub. DigiByte is an MIT-licensed open-source project.

DigiByte Gaming

The gaming division of DigiByte is a platform that utilizes cryptocurrency for promoting a new form of digital advertisement within the gaming world. The user-base is over 10,000 and keeps growing. To outperform its competitors, DigiByte gaming makes micropayments possible. This is a perfect technique for having a competitive advantage over others. Due to the borderless nature of its micropayments, companies can reach far more audiences than previously possible. In this manner, companies are at liberty to make small payments to people across the globe, regardless of the volume of the payment or the size of any prize they want to deliver for any gamer. DigiByte has a bright future both in and outside the gaming world. In the future, DigiByte marketing is expected to spread around the globe, even beyond the gaming industry.

Mining with DigiByte

As aforementioned, DigiByte has five algorithms. It uses these algorithms for transaction processing. Each of the algorithms has 20% of all the blocks in the network under its control. This is the secret behind both the blockchain's diversity and uniqueness. The DigiByte team saw an opportunity to gain more users, if it allowed a couple of mining types on the platform. In technologies such as Bitcoin, with only one algorithm, only the latest and fastest technology will gain an upper hand. For this reason, the nodes are always in a constant struggle to be the fastest and to use the best technology. In contrast, since DigiByte technology allows an array of nodes to compete and win tokens, the system allows much more participation and diversity. This gives it an edge over its competitors.

The five DigiByte's algorithms are discussed below:

1. Scrypt (https://dgb-scrypt.theblocksfactory.com/https://dgb-scrypt.theblocksfactory.com): To run this algorithm for DigiByte, use either GPU or ASIC mining equipment.
2. SHA-256 (https://dgb-sha.theblocksfactory.com/https://dgb-sha.theblocksfactory.com/): The ASIC mining equipment is needed to run the SHA-256 algorithm for DigiByte.
3. Qubit (https://dgb-qubit.theblocksfactory.com/https://dgb-qubit.theblocksfactory.com/): This is a GPU algorithm for mining DigiByte.
4. Groestl (https://dgb-groestl.theblocksfactory.com/https://dgb-groestl.theblocksfactory.com/):%20): This is another GPU algorithm for mining DigiByte.
5. Skein (https://dgb-skein.theblocksfactory.com/https://dgb-skein.theblocksfactory.com/): Mine DigiByte by this GPU algorithm, too.

Many are encouraged by the multiple algorithms run by DigiByte. It makes it easier for potential miners to have access to the blockchain, without undergoing a rigorous competition, such as when mining with mono-algorithm blockchains. The barrier is lower and access is easier.

This has also resulted in better decentralization as well. It is now possible for cryptocurrency miners to alter the purpose of outdated Bitcoin mining equipment, so that they can use it. In essence, if a user still possessed old Bitcoin mining equipment, they can also use it to mine some DGB. However, before embarking on DGB mining, check the costs to find out whether mining DGB will be worthwhile, to gain value for investment.

To mine on DigiByte follow the steps below:

1. Visit www.coinwarz.com/calculators. On the site, there is a calculator for estimating payback time when considering mining different cryptocurrencies. The calculator will show the cost and profitability of mining.
2. Enter 3 in the Pools Fees field. This is an estimate of what it will cost to join in the mining. The figure is usually between 0.5% and 3%.
3. Enter 500 in the Hardward Costs field. Specialized mining equipment does not have a specific cost, but rather varies. The average cost of good mining equipment is $500. Enter this amount.
4. Enter 470,000 in the Hash Rate field. The figure represents the estimated speed of a mining machine. It is an estimate of how many hashes it can hash at kilohashes per second, or 1,000 hash computations/second. The ease of mining a cryptocurrency depends on the hash rate for mining it. Cryptocurrencies with high hash rate will be more difficult to mine than cryptocurrencies with a lower hash rate.
5. Click "Calculate." The calculator processes the information and provides a general idea about the cost of mining the cryptocurrency and how profitable that mining will be.

Leveraging the Power of DigiByte's DiguSign

DiguSign is another valuable tool from the DigiByte team. The tool was created to serve as a reliable and more efficient alternative to e-signature and cloud storage services. The tool combines the basic functionality of cloud storage and e-signature, as well as supplements them with the verifiability and permanence that is the trademark of blockchain technology.

With the assistance of DigiSigu, a user can digitally append their signature on documents, while using the DigiByte blockchain to secure them. It is the belief of the developers that the areas of application of this tool will spread across different fields, including the healthcare industry, law, and financial services. These areas are where it is imperative that contracts should have a well-defined version history and a pre-determined time line when documents were provided, as well as the recipient of the document.

Upload each document to DiguSign individually, or connect a DiguSign account with other cloud services, such as Dropbox, Google Docs, and OneDrive. A user can create as many as three free contracts and documents that are based on blockchain by taking advantage of the free testing version provided by DiguSign for its service. Although DiguSign is a relatively new innovation, one can notarize a document, as well as store and ascertain the credibility of digital documents.

To publish a document's SHA256 hash, DiguSigh embeds the hash directly into its blockchain transaction. The DigiByte blockchain is then used to secure the transaction.

To set up a DiguSign account, follow the steps below:

1. Visit www.digusign.com.

2. Sign up for the account.

3. For verification, upload the document.

4. There is an option to create a contract template or a document. Choose "document creation."

5. Some fields will need to be configured as well as signatures, too.

6. Supply emails of those who will also be signing the document.

7. Several options are available after the emails. Choose "Secure Final Version."

8. When all the signatories have appended their signatures, clicking the "Secure Final Version" option will send the final document to the DigiByte blockchain.

This creates a fingerprint for your document that can be used whenever needed.

Earning DigiBytes While Gaming

DigiByte appreciates the affinity for both blockchain and digital tokens. Many gamers will play games where tokens are given as rewards. DigiByte capitalizes on this knowledge by using cryptocurrency tokens to serve as an incentive for gamers. Some of the games that can be played to win DigiByte tokens include League of Legends, Counter Strike, and World of Warcraft. The ability to mine is not the only factor here because some large gaming companies are behind the awards.

This is a symbiotic relationship for the gaming companies and DigiByte, where DigiByte gets sponsorship from these companies; in turn, the gaming companies are given the opportunity to retain their existing customers. The allure of earning cryptocurrency moves even more gamers to take part in the games. This helps the gaming companies increase their customer base.The greatest benefactors from these relationships, however, are the gamers. Some gamers who win DigiByte tokens will eventually have an opportunity to earn cryptocurrency they may decide to store for future appreciation. They may also decide to spend the digital currency.

As a gamer, the website devoted to gaming by DigiByte is the platform where a gamer has a good chance of earning cryptocurrency, while also pursuing their gaming passion. Each day, DigiByte offers players a couple of Quests they can use to earn XP. They can convert their XP into DigiByte, according to a predetermined daily rate. Playing any of the games on DigiByte's gaming website increases the chances of earning this coin.

To convert these earnings to Bitcoin or any other cryptocurrency, visit cryptocurrency exchanges, such as blockchain.info or Poloniex. It is fairly easy to earn DigiByte as a reward for gaming time. And one does not have to invest in mining. There is no requirement to write a line of code to earn it. One only need to play any of the games from the comfort of their home, and thus can join the club of cryptocurrency earners.

To earn DigiByte coin through gaming,follow the steps below:

1. Visit www.digibytegaming.com.
2. Create an account. Use social media login for faster setting up.
3. Verify account by clicking on the link sent to email.
4. Visit www.battle.net. Create a personal profile to link to the account on DigiByte. The profile will be used to link DigiByte to World of Warcraft.

5. Connect to the game, or if needed first, set up the game on computer.
6. Go back to www.digibytegaming.com.
7. Select World of Warcraft.
8. Connect it to battle.net account.
9. Click on World of Warcraft app to open it.
10. Start playing the game and earning DigiByte.

Chapter 17: Hyperledger

Hyperledger is defined as: "a community of software developers and technology enthusiasts who are building industry standards for blockchain frameworks and platforms." These are the people with the responsibility of guiding the blockchain industry, enhancing the usefulness of blockchains, and making them acceptable in the commercial world. Business enterprise teams view Hyperledger as their deployment platform.

The company was formed in 2015 by the Linux Foundation and was tasked with the responsibility of developing an open-source and enterprise-grade ledger framework. The objective was to direct the attention of the blockchain industry and use it to build applications that are industry-specific, as well as strong, applications, hardware systems, and platforms that are designed to be of assistance to the business community.

Linux realized that most of the blockchain technology builders lacked goals and direction. Most of the stakeholders were busy with copying existing technologies, rather than focusing their attention new inventions that would be of help to the blockchain community. Learning from the mistakes of its competitors, Linux and was convinced that it needed an open source strategy, if it was to reach its full potential, something that was missing with other blockchain technology companies.

Linux's different approach to blockchain technology did not come as a surprise, considering the track records of Brian Behlendorf, its Executive Director. Behlendorf has years of experience that was garnered from his days at Apache Foundation, and as the CTO of the World Economic Forum. As such, he had the experience to steer Linux Foundation in the right direction. His experience has had a positive impact on Hyperledger, leading to its wide acceptance by users.

The track record of Behlendorf and his vision of the company have convinced some A-list companies to buy into the foundation. Some companies that have expressed their desire to work hand-in-hand with Linux Foundation are J.P. Morgan, Cisco, Intel, Accenture, Fujitsu Limited, Wells Fargo, and a host of others. A number of high-ranking blockchain organizations have also joined the company. Other investors in this company include R3. This is a company known for its contribution to the banking industry. It has offered Linux Foundation a working architectural framework that will have a positive impact on its financial transactions.

Linux has also received assistance from the Factom Foundation and Digital Asset. While the former offers Linux Foundation its developer resources and other related resources, the latter has given the foundation a couple of enterprise-grade codes for their project. These are not the only companies that provide software resources for Linux Foundation. IBM has also provided the same. Many reputable software organizations have also contributed software resources, such as code, to the project.

Hyperledger is an ever-growing organization, with an increasing number of projects as well. As of this writing, the company has over 100 companies under its control, in addition to a huge volume of projects in progress. The company has designed a lot of applications that are used in a many areas of the economy. Some of their applications are Iroha, Explorer, and Sawtooth. While both Sawtooth and Iroha are blockchain platforms, Explorer is a web application that serves a lot of different purposes. Furthermore, although Bitcoin and other blockchains existed before the Hyperledger project, it has proven to be a formidable foe for those blockchains because it has an impressive list of applications:

Manufacturing Supply Chain

Hyperledger is currently exploring opportunities in supply chain management, using a blockchain with the potential for turning the supply chain into a useful scheme. Under this scheme, all the components parts that are used for the creation of a product can be more easily managed. If running a supply chain, one can capitalize on this to quickly respond to demands from customers. The technology can also be used to track the origin of all the components of a product. This knowledge can be used to determine the authenticity of each of the parts used for a product. In the case of product recall, the faulty part can be easily identified. It can also be used as a preventive measure to verify the authenticity of all the parts before putting them to use.

When the scheme, known as Fabric, is fully completed, it will make it possible for everyone using a supply chain to track all the parts that are produced either by them, or that are used for making a specific product. The ability to determine the best parts for making a product will provide consumers with the best products.

Business Contracts

To make its presence felt in the business community, Hyperledger has defined some practical ways that private and public contracts can be established. It defines private contracts as contracts with a minimum of two parties, where each party usually has confidential information about the contract. Public contracts, in contrast, are contracts that can be viewed by anyone at any time. Someone who desires to view these contracts can do so via Hyperledger search. For instance, one can use a public contract for bidding to make a public offer, or to offer a product for sale.

Direct Communication

The future offers more possibilities for Fabric users. It can also be used by companies for making offers or public announcements. A company may call a meeting of its shareholders for fundraising or any other purpose. This can easily be done with the assistance of Fabric. By using the same principle as the Decentralized Autonomous Organization implemented by Ethereum, Factom shareholders can easily make decisions based on their investments and execute their decisions without delay. This is because Fabric makes processing the decisions of such shareholders in real time possible. As a result, it becomes easier for shareholders to vote or meet without problem.

Assets and Securities

Blockchains can also be easily used for assets and securities. This is possible due to the elimination of third-parties via the automation of the functions performed by the third-parties. The introduction of Fabric into assets and securities makes it possible for asset owners to have direct access to their assets. In the process, intermediaries will be completely bypassed and eliminated.

Asset Interoperability

Fabric will share this quality with Ripple in the future. In the future, companies may find a way of exchanging assets that are low-liquidity with others by matching people with similar concerns. The process will be very simple. Rather than play the role of an intermediary between two parties, both buyers and sellers will be connected together, so that they can find the best match from the available asset classes. The goal is to develop Hyperledger to the stage where it can trade derivatives.

Chain Core Technology

The Chain Core protocol is another powerful blockchain technology that defines how assets can be transferred, issued, and controlled on any blockchain network. The platform helps individuals and organizations to move financial assets. The protocol also makes it possible for a group of organizations, or a single entity, to operate a network in order to ensure that different types of assets are supported. The platform is specifically built for financial services and has some admirable features that make handling these services easy. With the Chain Core platform, it is now easy for institutions to launch a blockchain and operate the same internally. They can also connect to a list of other networks that are working ceaselessly to transform the movement of assets around the world.

Chain Protocol was designed to define the transfer, control, and issuance of assets on a blockchain network. It is a permissions and open-source protocol that was built by the blockchain startup, Chain, in collaboration with some telecom and financial firms. Chain's list of partners includes major A-list firms, such as Street, Capital One, First Data, Nasdaq, Fidelity, Citi, Orange, Visa, Mitsubishi UFJ, and Fiserv.

Some of Chain Core's features include:

Native digital assets: Chain Core is a new platform that can effectively be used for securities, currencies, and other instruments that are designed for financial services. Regardless of what is needed for financial transactions or businesses, Chain Core can provide the right tools for it. Its native digital assets also provide all users with a unique medium for securities, currencies, and other financial instruments.

Full-stack security: Account security is further ensured with the implementation of a full-stack security measure that involves stable cryptographic primitives, HSM integration, and an open source stack that is equally auditable. The protocol also ensures instant payment to the users.

Multi-signature accounts: Whether representing a business, conducting business as an individual or representing an institution, a secure account is available that reduces chances of security breach by ensuring that there are many signatories to the account. These multi-signature accounts can help users have access to secured account management for businesses, individuals, and institutions. This is an effective way to guarantee that no one can singlehandedly defraud the owner(s) of the account.

Permission network access: A user can participate in, access, or operate a network according to their role in a financial setting.

An immutable ledger: Chain Core offers a platform where a record of transactions remains valid and cannot be altered or forged under any condition.

Transaction privacy: The privacy of transactions is guaranteed. Apart from parties involved in any business transaction, no one can have access to these transactions without authorization.

Smart contracts: With this protocol, a complex agreement can be made without bringing in counterpart risks via automatic enforcement of agreement. This functions in a similar way to how the Ethereum protocol drives its smart contracts.

Instant settlement: Within this protocol, transactions can be confirmed immediately. This is possible because of its Federated consensus mechanism.

Reference data: The transaction structure includes compliance data, assets definitions, and arbitrary annotations. The inclusion of these makes it convenient for a user to reference data without any challenges.

Scalable and available: Chain Core is available to millions of current and potential users. The protocol has the potential to scale to tons of servers across data centers. This is a preventive measure put in place to minimize the impact of any component failure on the protocol and its users. The overall system will still remain strong as other servers take over from the failed one. Therefore, there is an assurance of uninterrupted services, without any concerns of a complete system failure.

Fast: Users demand a system that can has speed and efficiency. They have no patience for slow systems. Chain Core is engineered to meet the high performance that is expected of a system built for financial transactions. It only takes some milliseconds to create a transaction, sign, and validate it.

Connectable and extendible: The developers of Chain Core insightfully designed it to make it connectable and extendible, considering the potential for growth of the financial services sector that may have a corresponding increase in demand for a protocol that will simplify the job of stakeholders in the financial sector. The protocol comes with well-documented SDK's, data format that is easy to digest, and a couple of API's to make extending its functions easier.

The Chain Core protocol is also designed for developers. It is a platform where experienced developers can put their skills to use by developing platform-based applications. To make the protocol useable for developers, these unique features are incorporated:

Intelligent queries: Its APIs can be used to conduct intelligent queries on transactions. These queries may be on asset ID's, account aliases, or arbitrary reference data.

Developer dashboard: Dashboards are powerful interfaces are some of the powerful tools of developers. This protocol has an interface that makes exploring blockchain data and building applications easy for developers.

Multi-language support: Chain Core has tons of SDK's that are available for developers in a few programming languages, such as Ruby, Java, and Node.Js. Thus, developers can "speak" to the protocol for their use.

With the array of features incorporated into the Chain Core Protocol, it is not surprising that it is gradually becoming a popular protocol among users. One can gain a comprehensive understanding of this protocol and its potential future benefits in the Chain Core whitepaper.

Elements Blockchain Platform

This is an open-source protocol specifically designed for extending Bitcoin's functionality. It affords developers a platform to explore Bitcoin, and to extend its areas of application and functionality. Elements is one of the best blockchain platforms that will help realize the potentials of Bitcoin.

Some key features of Elements protocol include:

Confidential Transactions: Transactions can be kept confidential and made available for viewing by authorized personnel only.

Confidential Assets: Multiple assets can be controlled without having knowledge of the amounts and identifiers, and can also be audited.

Deterministic Pegs: This feature allows the construction of cross-chain transactions, with some elements of decentralization attached to it. Tokens can also be moved from one blockchain to another using this feature.

Segregated Witness: This is a protocol developed to protect people from transaction malleability, and thus boost a block's capacity. The structure contains data that is required for checking the validity of a transaction, although it is not needed for determining the effects of a transaction. Otherwise known as SegWit, this is an invention supported by the Bitcoin community due to the huge fundamental changes that it brings to the Bitcoin platform. It removes unwanted data out of a transaction in order to increase the throughput of the transaction by reducing its size. SegWit offers other benefits that are part of the reason for its growing popularity.

Additional opcodes: The inclusion of opcodes in the protocol is a welcome development. Some previously eliminated opcodes, such as substrings, string concatenation, integer shifts, and other bitwise operations, have been added to the protocol. Others include a DETERMINISTICRANDOM operation that can be used for producing random numbers, within a given range, by using a seed. There's also the CHECKSIGFROMSTACK operation too. This is another operation that verifies whether a signature corresponds with a message on the stack instead of verifying it on the spending transaction.

Signed Blocks: The signed blocks allows blocks to be signed cryptographically. The implication is that creator of a block has the liberty to verify the identities of the created blocks in the future.

The Periodic Table: The Elements protocol is composed of open-source bundles. They can be combined with each other for the construction of new and novel applications via the Bitcoin blockchain.

Sidechains: There are also sidechains features which are extensions to blockchains that are already in existence. Their incorporation into these existing blockchains will lead to the enhancement of the functionality and privacy of such blockchains by adding some extra features, such as confidential transactions and smart contracts.

Relative Lock Time: Timing a transaction is possible with this feature. It allows the user to specify when a block can be updated with the input. The time is determined by the elapsed time since the output spent by the input was also included in one of the blocks on the blockchain.

The Elements protocol and its wide range of applications thus makes it a good complement to the Bitcoin blockchain.

HydraChain

Hydrachain is another blockchain technology that has a bright future. This platform extends the Ethereum platform and adds the needed support, so that it can be used to create Permissioned Distributed Ledgers. The HydraChain platform can primarily be applied in the consortium chain or private chain setups. This protocol is also designed with unique features that combine to make it appealing:

Compatibility with the Ethereum Protocol

HydraChain enjoys 100% compatibility with the Ethereum Protocol via its contract levels and on its API. Many tools chains that were previously used for the development and deployment of DApps and Smart Contracts can be reused again.

Instant finality

The validators negotiate new blocks. Before the system adds a block to the chain, it will require a quorum by whoever signs the block. This prevents the existence of forks or any revert. New blocks can only be created if there are pending transactions.

Native contracts

Like most of the protocols discussed here, HydraChain gives developers the right infrastructure they can use for developing smart contracts through the Python programming language. The language makes debugging easier and development times are reduced compared to other languages. By bypassing the Ethereum Virtual Machine, it becomes relatively fast to execute a native contract. Native Contracts also offers maximum support to the ABI, in addition to being interoperable with the contracts that are EVM-based. Although these contracts are written in a different language, they can exist on the same chain without issues.

Open Source

The software behind this technology is open source. It is also available with the MIT license. This ensures that it can be accessed and used by anyone.

Customizability

Most of the aspects of this system can be customized to meet particular needs. For instance, a user can adjust some values, such as gas limits, transaction fees, block time, genesis allocation, and more.

Microsoft Azure and Blockchain Technology: The Beneficial Alliance

Microsoft Azure is another innovation that has made a splash in the technology world in recent years. It is interesting that there is a correlation between blockchain technology and Microsoft Azure. This has led to exciting innovations in the Azure platform, with the potential to have positive impact on the efficiency of businesses, and to create new business opportunities. While blockchain technology has proven to be a potent tool for changing business models and opening new markets for businesses, Microsoft Azure is also contributing its share to make the technology acessible for traditional business. The connection between Microsoft Azure and the blockchain technology is possible due to certain tools:

Bletchley: The Fabric for Modular Blockchain

The Project Bletchley is a product of Microsoft and serves as its answer to its vision for a modular and open blockchain platform. It is powered by another powerful platform, Azure. The project focuses on some new innovations and elements that are believed to be in the architecture of the enterprise of blockchain. The Project Bletchley is known for its ability to provide business enterprise customers with building blocks. This is specifically a members-only system of permission networks, where the use is restricted to members of the permissioned networks for the execution of contracts.

Bletchley's blockchain fabric platform does not function independently of other platforms or technology. Instead, it depends on Microsoft's cloud computing platform, Azure, to function. Azure serves as the cloud platform for building and delivering distributed applications. According to its official website, "Microsoft Azure's availability in 24 regions across the globe, hybrid cloud capabilities, extensive compliance certification portfolio, and enterprise-grade security enable blockchain adoption, especially in highly regulated industries like financial services, healthcare and government."

Some of the areas of application for Project Bletchley are:

Private keys management: The project enhances the use of private keys. It is a technique that blockchain investors can use to safely keep their private keys safe.

Digital identity: As discussed earlier, creating a digital identity is a necessity. With this project, a user can easily create an identity that will be digital in nature.

Data security: The security of data is guaranteed and cannot be breached.

Customer privacy: Privacy is guaranteed as Bletchley allows anonymous transactions.

Azure is blockchain's provider of cloud layer services in Project Bletchley. It serves as the platform for building and delivering applications. The project is proposed to be available in dozens of regions across the globe. Azure has some traditional products, such as compliance certification portfolio, hybrid cloud capabilities, and security that is different from other blockchains. To make it easy for its clients to quickly adapt to blockchain technology, Microsoft decided to form an alliance with Azure, especially in some areas as financial services, healthcare, and government.

Azure works in cooperation with a couple of blockchain protocols to achieve the goal of its alliance with Microsoft cloud. These are part of the Hyperledger project discussed above. They are also included in the Unspent Transaction Output (UTXO) protocols. The implication is that the platform does not use a cryptocurrency, and this may make it more appealing to customers. Customers may also be able to enjoy good integration with Ethereum and other sophisticated protocols that naturally do not use a cryptocurrency for securing their network.

Project Bletchley and Cryptlets

There are two fundamental ideas behind Project Bletchley:

1. Blockchain middleware: This is specifically for identity management, cloud storage, machine learning, and analytics. It also provides intelligence and data services and operations management. With the assistance of these technologies, there is immutable and secure operation from blockchain. It can also deliver business reporting and intelligence, as demanded by business regulations and leaders. This middleware is designed to work with existing Azure services, such as Key Vault, Active Directory, and other blockchain technologies, in order to deliver the best platform, as well as provide a set of solutions.

Marley Gray, the director of business development and strategy for Microsoft explains the usefulness of the blockchain middleware: "The blockchain middleware is designed to help users take advantage of the increased security of blockchain and its immutable record of transactions, while at the same time delivering business intelligence in the form of reports required by regulators and others."

2. Cryptlets: This ensures that communication and interoperability between the project and Microsoft Azure is executed smoothly.

Much is expected from blockchain as the vehicle that will revolutionize business trade value online. It is unfortunate that some enterprise organizations do not see blockchains's value as investors do. Instead, they consider it to be a tool that will disrupt their industry in the future.

The challenge still facing the most ardent believer in Project Bletchley is building new ecosystems and applications on the distributed ledger technologies at our disposal. For instance, blockchains cannot succeed without having an effective way to secure the execution of off-chain code, as well as to receive external data variables securely. The good news is the soon-to-be-released *enclaves*. These enclaves are security advances that will be incorporated in silicon chips. They will provide blockchain users a new security measure in the architecture of CUP. The introduction of enclaves will make it possible for code execution to be performed in an isolated and secure container, thereby enabling the results of such computations to be accurate and tamper proof.

To help enterprises achieve their goal of reinventing business processes collaboratively, Bletchley promises to come up with a Blockchain Application Fabric for that purpose. It is in this Cryptlet Fabric that we find Cryptlets. They provide some of the most important functionality, such as privacy, integration, management, secure execution, and more. As such, Cryptlets have become the tools that developers can build to meet their functionality requirements, to enable them have a foundation they can use for building applications that are based on distributed ledgers.

The Cryplet Fabric provides blockchain applications with a proven, secure third-tier. Since blockchains are distributed, it is expected that Cryptlet Fabric will be used as an application, or a service in Google, AWS, and other cloud platforms. Developers will have abundant opportunities to focus on some of the limitations of blockchain platforms such as scale, performance, and security during the development of Fabric.

Cryptlets can be used as a service in libraries that can be found in the cloud. They can also be created in a wide variety of environments, as well as hosted in these environments. SmartContract modelers and developers will work hand-in-hand to publish the Cryptlets, so that these can be included in development and application designs. This project will not only be handled by Microsoft. It will be accomplished in conjunction with some third-parties who will offer Cryptlet libraries to showcase the functionality of Cryptlets.

For instance, to use Cryptlets, the opportunity exists to go through Cryptlet libraries, whenever a Cryptlet is needed to alert to trigger a SmartContract, if it meets a specific condition. The possibility also exists to demand extra functionality from Cryplets, such as providing market prices whenever it is triggered.

After a user finds the best Cryptlet for their use, they can use this Cryptlet for subscribing to a notification service, so that it can alert when set and with the data type that is desired for the notification. To be assured of the authenticity, security, and reliability of the data and service, the Cryptlet infrastructure will verify them.

Other Cryptlets that can be developed include those that can integrate logic or data, such as validating a customer's data without revealing the data to the blockchain itself. A user can choose the language to write the Cryptlet and use the

Bletclhley SDK to deploy it to Azure Stack, Azure, or localhost. As both consortium and public blockchains gradually take over the globe, Azure can conveniently deliver data that is open and secure execution, too.

Although Cryptlets and blockchain oracles share some similarities, Cryplets outperforms blockchain oracles in terms of trust and security in a scalable ecosystem. The Cryplet Fabric provides top-notch software, with the latest advances in hardware, in other to provide consortiums and developers the tools needed to provide solutions that can be used to drive distributed computing onto other frontiers.

Cryptlets have also been used in some other areas as well. These can also be used in UTXO systems and smart contracts. This has been very helpful when there is a need for an additional information or functionality. They have also been helpful in bridging the gap between in the execution of programs, when there is a need for more secure information. With Cryptlets, a trading platform or customer relationship management can easily establish a connection with cloud storage to ensure its security.

The Bletchey's middleware does not work alone. Instead, it works together with Azure services and Cryptlets as well as some other blockchain technologies to provide a complete solution that will ensure a blockchain integration works smoothly. Bletchley's marketplace is the selling point for Cryptlets that are built by experienced developers. These Cryptlets also understand a wide range of functionality sets that are crucial to creating applications that are based on distributed ledgers and address those functionalities.

Some customers are in need of some essential functionality, such as integration, secure execution, and privacy, and the market is ready to meet their needs. Other needs that the market will meet include interoperability, management, and other data services.

Types of Cryptlets

Cryptlets are divided into two types:

Utility: These Cryptlets come equipped with timestamping, encryption, external data access, and full authentication. These are known as UtilityCryptlets. They make transactions both strong and trusted.

Contract: Contract Cryptlets are user-oriented. They can be deployed as bots or autonomous agents that will deliver. These work outside the blockchain to provide the execution logic that is normally provided by smart contracts.

Contract Cryptlets and smart contracts are connected. They are usually created upon the publishing of a smart contract. There are two factors behind the success of Cryptlet: 1) This is a system that runs together in alignment with a virtual machine, and 2) They also outperform smart contracts that are built inside blockchains due to their demand for less cryptocurrency for execution. Cryptlets are the favorite of users who do not use cryptocurrency blockchains. In this case, smart contracts and chaincode are both signed by parties that know each other. Another important tool here is CryptoDelegates. This tool makes it possible for Contract Cryptlets and Utility to function effectively. They serve as the link between a smart contract and the Cryptlets. That makes transactions both authentic and secure.

A CryptoDelegate works within the Virtual Machine on which SmartContract functions. This tool extends the authentic and secure envelope for all the transactions that are conducted off the blackchain by calling a Cryptlet from a SmartContract that extends both the authenticity and security of such transactions. A Cryplet that is called from a CryptoDelegate is deserving of trust because it is signed with a validated and trusted digital signature when the CryptoDelegate was under design or being written. Each call via the CryptoDelegate will check the validity of signatures at runtime as well as record those signatures together with the corresponding transaction.

Cryptlets can be accessed through a tested host that is equally trusted and has the ability to expose the source of the Cryplet with a trusted hash as a property. When a host is attested, its source will not be revealed but can still be trusted by both parties in a transaction. This host will be shared via https, a secure channel that will have certificate validation via the execution environment. It is thus possible to use an enclave for running Cryptlets for data, secure execution, signing, and encryption. Furthermore, Cryptlets leverage the power of enclaves to ensure advanced functionality, whenever there is a need for encryption, process isolation, and advanced threshold signing. Either the software, or hardware, will provide enclaving.

Writing Cryptlet is made easy for developers by offering them a wide range of programming languages to choose from. They can equally write it on any platform of their choice. Some platforms, such as C#, node.js, F#, and Java, have modules for code compiler verification, so that optional type, determinism, verification checks, and security can be provided. This is to ensure that there are no compatibility issues with SmartContract, whenever it is required.

To provide a Cryptlet Fabric cloud for developers that can be used for an array of distributed ledger platforms, Cryptlets take advantage of Runtime Integration with CryptoDelegate, Aspects in Programming Languages, Azure Service Fabric, and Secure computing. Cryptlets can be tested in AzureStack,

213

Azure, or LocalHost, depending on the user's choice of platform. LocalHost is ideal for developing and testing the Cryptlets where there is no network access

Building in Azure Ecosystem

Azure is a cloud computing and digital ecosystem that connects cloud partners with enterprises, without the contribution of a third party. It also helps in the connection of enterprises to SaaS. This has a positive impact on enterprises because they can make reliable data transfers, without worrying about security.

The Microsoft Azure ranks second as the biggest infrastructure service (Iaas) in the world. To store some data, or use cloud computing, Microsoft Azure is a convenient platform for doing so. The security of the data is guaranteed. Azure has another service that complements its efforts. This service, ExpressRoute, serves as the intermediary between Azure and consumers. This is to ensure that communication between the two is as smooth as possible. This also serves as a protection against security and performance issues that have, over the years, become a source of concern on the Internet.

In 2015, when Microsoft made the decision to use the Hyperledger and Ethereum blockchain systems for expanding its Azure ecosystem, the first of the long list of offerings by Azure blockchain was built on the Ethereum blockchain. Ethereum is a good system for building applications as demonstrated by its use in different areas of smart contracts and decentralized applications. It was Microsoft's goal to use both Hyperdledger and blockchain technology for building more offerings. Microsoft also works towards the growth of the Azure marketplace, while moving to the Azure, a portal designed for customers.

Microsoft Azure has an incorporated Stack program, Azure Quickstart Templates. They use the Azure Resource Manager to use the different Azure resources, to improve overall working efficiency. This manager provides a platform for customers to get their work done as a group by sharing resources. Therefore, they have all the tools to do their jobs in a coordinated manner. The Azure Quickstart Templates have wide areas of applications, which include staging, production, and testing. Through its resource manager, a user has access to many features that include auditing, tagging, and guaranteed security. As a result, one can easily manage resources after they have been carefully deployed.

Project Bletchley, from Microsoft, serves as the blockchain architecture that works in alliance with other enterprise technologies in the same line of business. This offers Azure the needed marketplace and blockchain backend. The project was an attempt by Microsoft to ensure that both distributed ledger networks and blockchain are available to a wider audience, without compromising the safety and effectiveness of both tools. Their goal was to use these tools to help the users find a personal solution to their problems, as well as to address major business challenges that had been plaguing them for years.

Azure vs. Chain Core

Chain Core blockchain technology, and its potential to work together with other blockchains in the future, will have a positive impact on global economy. Azure and Chain Core both work together to achieve this goal. Chain uses the Azure platform for releasing its Chain Core Developer. This is an open-source version of Chain's distributed ledger platform. A user can take advantage of this free version to issue assets and make transfers via an authorized blockchain network.

Developers can start a blockchain network by leveraging its test net. They can also have access to documentation and technical tutorials via the test net. If desired, they can create personal networks on the network as well. The network offers developers opportunities to take full advantage of the Chain Core for the improvement of the global community.

Installing Chain's Distributed Ledger

The Chain Core Developer Edition is fully-loaded with a Java SKD, some code samples, and a guide for intended users. It also has installers and dashboard interfaces for Mac, Linux, and Windows. All this makes the installation process easy. To install, follow the steps below:

1. https://chain.com/docs/core/get-started/install
2. Select your operating system from the provided list.
3. Click "Download" after selection.
4. Open the downloaded program and run the installer.

When through with the installation, a SKD will give the developer and user the tools needed to create blockchain assets and applications.

Creating a Private Network

Azure provides a platform where a private blockchain network of Ethereum consortium can easily be created following the steps below:

1. Sign up for an Azure account or login. (A free trial is available.)

2. Visit https:goo.gl/Ixu5of
3. Click "Deploy to Azure."
4. Complete the form.
5. Click "Purchase."

Using Azure's Financial Services

The Chain developer platform comes fully-loaded with a Microsoft-operated network, the Initiative for Cryptocurrencies (3CI) and Contracts, and Chain. Chain launched this platform as a blockchain technology solution that users can use for issuing and transferring assets on blockchain networks that are credible and authentic. Some financial companies and Chain collaborated to create this platform. As a result, the Chain Core platform can be used for developing different financial applications.

The goal is to launch innovative products on the platform. Since it can be used in different sectors of the economy, it can be used for producing products for banking, capital markets, insurance, and payments. Chain additionally has a partnership agreement with Visa, so that it can produce a simple and secure way to process and deliver business-to-business payments anywhere in the world.

How to Use Blockchain Tools on Azure

Azure's use is not limited to the handful of services mentioned above. It has some other tools and practical applications. To make the platform easy to use for this purpose, Microsoft partnered with ConsenSys to build a new project, known as Solidity. With Solidity, a user can easily build any decentralized application of choice on Ethereum. Ethereum Blockchain, as a Service (EBaaS), enables both clients and enterprise developers a platform for creating a cloud-based blockchain environment. Azure offers two tools for deploying Ethereum blockchain on the platform:

Ether.Camp: This is a developer environment in Azure.

BlockApps: There are two of these: 1) the private and semiprivate environment for Etheruem blockchain, and 2) BlockApps for deploying into Ethereum's public environment. These tools facilitate the development of smart contract-based applications.

This is possible because the Ethereum platform on which it is built is an open system that is equally flexible. This allows its customization to meet the diverse needs of different customers.

Chapter 18: Blockchain Technology and Financial Services

While many organizations were reluctant to adopt blockchain technology, financial institutions, governments, and banks were the first. Today, this trio constitutes the fastest-growing users of blockchain technology. Global financial services are the most powerful industry in the world. Trillions of dollars of transactions are conducted each day to meet the growing needs of billions of people.

New technology has not yet been fully integrated into the financial industry. For instance, Internet banking was only introduced a few decades ago and has continued to be one of the most accepted innovations. However, the banking industry has not fully taken advantage of these innovations. Many still use paper checks for banking transactions, and these transactions are still often run on computers that were designed and manufactured decades ago.

Another problem is peculiar to multinational companies. Some of these have different accounts across the globe to facilitate transactions between two or more countries. Whenever there is an urgent need to transfer money from one subsidiary to another, the money may be transferred immediately; however, it will still take a couple of days for confirmation. This is a big challenge for these institutions. While they cannot get the funds for immediate use, in contrast the intermediaries take their cut immediately. It is ironic that transactions can still be held for days, with all the advancements in technology. Obviously, customers would prefer a swift transaction instead.

There are also endless fees on small transactions. Transferring a couple of dollars from one part of the world, to another, may be challenging, considering the different charges, exchange rates, flat fees, and other insidious hidden costs. In the long run, banks are not really interested in the needs of their everyday customers but in the super-rich, for whom they can charge fees more conveniently. What banks often consider as a minimum fee may be far beyond the ability of some customers.

The financial industry itself contributes to these problems. And financial regulators and monetary policymakers may not be receiving full or actual information from the financial industry. This may lead to problems that have a huge impact, such as the 2008 financial crisis that rocked the world.

The financial crisis was as a result of some human problems, such as lack of transparency, excess leverage, criminal activities and fraud, and other preventable errors that eventually prevented the stakeholders from preventing such a crisis. Many did not have, or ignored, the information that could have prevented the world from having to deal with a financial mess that had a huge impact on the global economy. It is still true today that the financial sector continues to run on principles and technology that were devised centuries ago.

Some notable financial experts, for instance, are now questioning the rationale behind the existence of points of sale, when the proliferation of smart phones indicates that POS's are no longer the best option. Today, there exist better ways to make money transfers both easier and faster. Erik Voorhees exclaimed that: "It is faster to mail an anvil to China than it is to send money through the banking system. That's Crazy! Money is already digital, it's not like they're shipping pallets of cash when you do a wire!" Obviously, there are better ways to handle financial transactions than the current practices. Nothing justifies waiting days or weeks before a wire transfer can be confirmed.

Banks are culprits in this case. They have too much power and liberty to control the sector as much as they want. They have the social and political license and huge scale to take as much as possible from their customers, regardless of the country of operation. There are also the powerful intermediaries, who build on that to create a monopolistic economy that favors them. Although they benefit greatly from this, it comes with a price: the system runs at a slow speed and is also quite expensive to run.

Since financial institutions deal primarily with money, basically just moving it from one place to another, new tools are currently built into the blockchain technology to meet the needs of these organizations. The goal is to change the world with a new method for carrying out financial activities.

It is not surprising, then, that Financial Technology, otherwise known as Fintech has taken over.

Future Banking Trends

The banking industry was the first to recognize both the threat and potential that blockchain technology possesses to transform the industry. The banking sector, of course, is one of the most highly-regulated industries and requires a huge amount of money to set up and operate. Many potential investors are put off by the huge capital needed to set up a bank. This has served as a protective shield for the industry against invasion by unqualified investors. However, it has turned out to be a burden, too.

Digital money, however, makes it so there is no need to handle hard currency. It is also an efficient, fast means of moving money, without the tradition risks attached to traditional practices. Banks found this to be both appealing and threatening. Many financial institutions were awed by the possibility of running a decentralized system beyond the control of governments and other regulatory bodies that have served as central authorities for years.

The relationship between these authorities and blockchain technology, however, was also problematic. It was initially a war between them as governments tried to no avail to kill off blockchain, with anti-blockchain regulations. Their stance against blockchain, however, was temporary. Without much success, they have embraced blockchain, as it continues to become an accepted technology in many parts of the world.

In an attempt to end interest in blockchain, the U. S. Securities and Exchange Commission (SEC) rolled out a list of potential risks hidden in investing in virtual currency. The warning was borne out of the perceived possibility of potential investors being brainwashed and lured into investing in digital currencies by promising them high returns on investment. The SEC was of the opinion that the promise of such a financial reward may override some potential investors' ability to make a rational decision. The SEC also believes that digital currency ranks among the top 10 threats that investors should be on the lookout for.

However, the SEC has now realized the potentials hidden in digital currencies and is ready to invest in cryptocurrencies by partnering with investors and companies as cryptocurrency continues to thrive, despite such opposition against it.

A couple of years after some financial institutions opposed cryptocurrency, some countries rolled out plans on how to become major investors in digital currencies by creating their own currencies. Countries such as China and the U.K. took practical steps towards achieving this. Their positive outlook towards digital currency was borne out of the realization that these currencies offer more rewards than challenges, as was previously erroneously believed. Take Bitcoin, for instance: Over the years, this digital coin has singlehandedly defied all odds to continue to maintain its position as the leading digital currency. The most important thing about it is how it did this in the face of negative regulations, while still serving investors.

Hackers have tried their best but have failed on numerous occasions to bring Bitcoin down. The ability of Bitcoin and other digital currencies to withstand and successfully overcome such challenges have made them appealing to investors, and helped to increase interest in cryptocurrency in recent years.

In addition, the strong, secure platform offered by innovations in blockchain technology has the potential to handle several billions of transactions, with the goal of supporting global economies and making these stronger than ever before. Therefore, it is not surprising that cryptocurrency has continued to rise.

The permanence and unalterable nature of transactions recorded in blockchains make it an appealing digital ledger. If a country decides to adopt blockchain and keep a record of all in it under the control of a central bank, that will be a plus for the economy. This is because there will be a complete record of transactions that can always be referenced, even if they are not viewable to the general public.

The security level offered by blockchain is another factor that contributes to their ease of use in the banking sector, especially in government. For instance, a government can rest assured of the security offered by blockchain, as well as a reduced risk of fraud. Thus, they will have the ultimate control over taxation and other monetary policies. They can also easily trace any digital transaction conducted by organizations and individuals.

The future of the banking industry looks bright as blockchain technology becomes the platform for conducting transactions. Consumers are spared the stress of banking, as they can make payments to their business partners and others through their phones. There is still a challenge, though. Some regulations, such as anti-money laundering and Know Your Customer regulations, stipulate that it is mandatory for banks to know their customers and be aware that they are not involved in any financial fraud, such as money laundering or any act of terrorism. This problem is common among banks that are already issuing cryptocurrencies. These banks may find it difficult to meet the requirements set by AML and KYC. Some countries are already using blockchain ideas to drive their banking industry.

Another problem is the ability of the blockchain to handle a huge volume of transactions in some cases. Some nations have a huge economy that may be far beyond the ability of the blockchain to handle. This is peculiar to the world's biggest economies such as the U.K., U.S., Germany, France, and others. Some of these countries process billions of transactions each day. It is doubtful that blockchain, a new technology, is yet strong enough to handle such a huge volume of transactions. This raises an important question: What happens if a huge economy, such as those mentioned above, uses blockchain and it gets hacked? This is perhaps better imagined than experienced.

The banking industry and other stakeholders are doing their best to address this issue promptly, so that they can maximize the benefits of the blockchain. Many financial organizations, such as the World Bank, International Monetary Fund, the Bank for International Settlements, and national central banks have held meetings to address this issue to find a way to take full advantage of the blockchain technology, despite the challenges it poses to them.

The financial industry has realized that the most effective practice for sending money internationally, without wasting time and resources, is the adoption of blockchain technology as the ultimate protocol. This will make an interbank settlement and bank transfers easier. It is true that banks cannot be completely eliminated. Consumers still rely on traditional banks. Nevertheless, there will also be an affinity for banking through blockchain. The acceptance of other payment options, such as Cash, PayPal, Payoneer, and others is proof of the readiness to accept other options, aside from the traditional banking system.

Now that blockchain has a formidable security that makes the risk of being hacked less likely, and developers will continue to boost the security of blockchain in the future, there are fewer worries involved in using the technology. Remember, that 51% of the nodes working on a particular network must reach an agreement for a takeover of a network before they can actually take over the network. This would be difficult to achieve and thus reduces the chances of a blockchain being compromised, thereby assuring depositors of the security of their money. The widespread application of blockchain technology may, however, raise some serious issues in the future. Two of the most important issues that may arise are digital privacy and data sovereignty. However, the adoption of cryptocurrency by all will go a long way in the prevention of fraud.

The availability of an audit trail for all transactions carried over the Internet by a debit or credit card means different things to different people. Financial institutions consider the existence of the audit trail beneficial because it ensures transparency of documentation and can help to easily determine the movements of assets from one region to another. In this manner, individuals can trade assets, without the need to question the legitimacy of such trading, and it also allows parties in transactions to comply with the terms and conditions attached to the transaction.

There is still a huge challenge that blockchains must overcome if they hope to have any significant impact in the future. There's the "right to be forgotten" law, which empowers customers to prevent organizations from keeping their data for eternity on the Internet. This will be quite challenging for blockchains because they are created to keep information stored in them permanently.

The nature of blockchain to have information permanently stored on them may also have dire consequences for companies and governments. If competitors are using the same blockchain, it makes it possible for a competitor to have an idea about the investment plans of a company. Corporations and government may have access to the historical records of all transactions that are recorded on a blockchain. As aforementioned, this is quite risky and may constitute a national security risk, if such information is accidentally made available for public consumption.

Another concerning issue is how to ensure that a fund is not transferred to another country to sponsor terrorism. This is an important issue both for organizations and individuals that are using Bitcoin and Ethereum. These permissionless digital currencies make it possible for someone to do this without oversight. This is due to the anonymous nature of such digital currencies, in addition to their being available for anyone to use them. This creates room for anyone to move funds at any time, and for whatever purpose the individual wants.

These are some of the challenges that experts are working on solving in order to allow both individuals and organization to take full advantage of blockchain technology, with all of its amazing benefits.

Chapter 19: Blockchain and Global Financial Products

Blockchain offers many financial products for the future, such as several investment products, services, and an array of securities. In addition, individuals can now find it more convenient to calculate risks as more transparency is brought into the issue of collateral, one of the many benefits of the new markets that will come along with blockchain. As discussed earlier, a significant problem is that the majority of the world's poor do not have access to titles for their homes and land. Many of them also do not have registered businesses, and this makes it easier for them to lose their assets or source of livelihood to the government at any time.

According to a famous economist, Hernando de Soto, while campaigning for dead capital, he was of the opinion that the world's poor could have access to over $9 trillion worth of assets, if they could only get titles for their homes and land, as well have their businesses registered. He was of the opinion that if countries can make this dead capital available and turn it into real property, they will be able to sell these assets in the global market. In fact, even more countries will have the need to make their dead capital available for others in the future. For instance, owners of undeveloped lands and properties that cannot be financed can decide to put up such properties for sale in the international market. This will be a welcome development because such assets will catch the attention of potential buyers, as they are drawn to such properties by the transparency offered by blockchain technology that makes it possible for asset managers to verify the status of these assets.

When blockchains are fully integrated into managing real estate assets, real estate managers will be able to use the information provided by blockchain technology to remove assets that are underperforming, as well as to focus on the best assets. The real estate industry will never be the same if managers can take advantage of this technology to improve the industry and offer their clients nothing but the best.

Investors can also take full advantage of blockchain technology to invest in assets, without resorting to the use of intermediaries that take a percentage of whatever investment conducted through them. From the comfort of home or office, one can search for assets that meet certain criteria, find them, and make payment via the blockchain technology, without the need to contact a bank for a loan or verify the ability to pay for the asset. Instead, everything will be done on blockchain.

This means more individuals can choose to invest in the real estate market, without the fear of being taken for granted by intermediaries. Decentralized autonomous applications have already been providing a platform for savvy investors. It is predicted that more investors and managers will be confident enough to invest even more for investment opportunities that are based in DAO.

Investing can be both time-consuming and challenging. Proper due diligence must be done before a potential investor decides to part with his or her hard-earned money. In most cases, it may take a buyer several months before making up his or her mind up whether to proceed with the investment or not. This challenge is overcome by the use of DAOs.

The bureaucracy and other paperwork that are usually involved in investing will be eliminated with these decentralized applications. These will make this possible by creating a voting system that is fully-based on blockchain, so that investors can receive shares that correspond to their investments. Thus, the risks associated with conventional investment in properties will efficiently be eradicated, and a space will be created for a blockchain-driven economy, where investing in assets will be less challenging.

Payment without Borders

The advent of the Technology era turned the world into a "global village." We now live in a world where national boundaries have been eliminated through modern innovations, such as the Internet and technology. Companies now capitalize on these innovations and operate without borders. They have extended their services beyond their geographical location and can offer these in any part of the world. This has also made instant payment possible as many organizations now do not have to wait for days or weeks before their payment will be confirmed by their partners. However, this does not always go smoothly, or without some drawbacks.

The greatest risk one faces is losing their funds to hackers after being paid in cryptocurrency. The ability of the hackers to operate anonymously makes it impossible to catch them and to retrieve the stolen funds. In addition, since cryptocurrencies are decentralized, there is no one to register your complaint to, no customer service, and no dispute resolution center. Therefore it is possible to lose all of the funds, if a victim of hacking.

The current structure of blockchain, however, makes it the personal responsibility of each consumer to put some security measures in place for prevention against hacking. This is in sharp contrast to the opportunity offered by modern technology that offers customers the freedom from any need to protect themselves from a potential loss. This is the responsibility of governments and big companies. They are responsible for offering insurance and protection against any loss. Governments have taken responsibility for the security of the lives and properties of their subjects for centuries. The assurance that governments are in control of the security has been a great relief for many people over the years.

Despite these changes, some companies still make payments with cryptocurrency. Some big companies are fighting for the opportunity to use Bitcoin as their payment option due to their foresight and the assurance that blockchain technology holds the key to the future and will determine how the world's economy is run in the foreseeable future. Some pay their clients and employees in digital currency in order to encourage acceptance if of the use of digital currency. This is proof that the technology is gradually gaining people's trust.

Faster and Better Trade

Blockchain also has another appealing quality: it encourages faster trading. The banking sector has been hit by some challenges in recent years, and that has obviously had a negative impact on their speed of operation. Moreover, there has been a sharp decline in global trade finance recently, and many companies are still in need of capital for running their businesses. Most of these companies are yet to recover from the economic meltdown that hit the global economy in 2008, while some have partially recovered but still lack the capital to keep their business at the level it was before the economic crisis hit them.

These challenges can be met by micro-investments and DAOs. These can provide such companies and businesses with what they need, as well as offer them better, more profitable returns than they can currently get from the market. In addition to providing them with more profitable returns, they also have more attractive offers, such as better security identity, transaction transparency, and convenient global tracking that increase the accountability of goods. These are some of the outstanding benefits that investors will derive when blockchain technology becomes the foundation on which transactions are built on. This is a huge opportunity for small-scale investors. This has led credence to the belief that blockchain technology offers a promising future, especially in the financial sector.

The days of the traditional finance are numbered. There will soon be a gradual shift to the use of blockchain technology to drive the financial sector. The future should remove the numerous challenges that consumers have to contend with during current business transactions, especially in the banking sector where monopoly is the order of the day. That obviously comes with a lot of challenges as well. It will definitely usher in a period of immense opportunity, however, for consumers who welcome the new development.

The global financial services sector is currently in a big mess. It is an old-fashioned industry that was built on obsolete technology some centuries ago. Its attachment to the old technology is one of the main reasons why it is ineffectual and irrelevant in this digital age. The system is also centralized and can be turned into a puppet by the powers that be, can be exposed to a data breach, often does not provide the basic tools needed by the consumers, and has so many other shortcomings that are responsible for its inability to meet up with people's demands. No wonder that a lot of people are rooting for a complete overhaul of the system. They yearn for a lasting solution to the perennial challenges that the industry has been struggling with over the years.

The introduction of blockchain technology into the industry will immensely improve customers' experience of the financial industry. It will also signal the end of the status quo that does not encourage innovation, competition, and a passion for excellence. Incompetence will be replaced with efficiency.

Blockchain promises to offer these benefits and much more as entrepreneurs and innovators work hand-in-hand to find an effective way to maximize the opportunities offered by blockchain technology.

Blockchain has repeatedly been seen as a panacea for all the financial issues that the current technology cannot handle. Its long list of potential future benefits, covering all the sectors of the global economy, has justified the confidence people have placed in the technology. Many experts are of the opinion that blockchain technology will outperform the existing technology. It is also the expectation that blockchain will help eliminate the monopoly of many financial institutions due to the many reasons that follow:

Cost

It is more cost-effective to run financial services on blockchain. If banks harness all their potential, they have a better chance of reducing their back-office expenses, according to Santander. If banks decide to do so, they will conveniently improve their services and offer their customers better services, access to markets, financial services, and capital. This will be a welcome idea to aspiring entrepreneurs and start-ups. Rather than depend on banks and greedy intermediaries for financial assistance, anyone living in any part of the world can have access to the huge resources available for use through the blockchain technology. They only need a smartphone and Internet connection to tap into these opportunities. That makes it a lot cheaper than other technology that has been used in the past.

Attestation

One of the greatest challenges that have been plaguing humankind forever is lack of trust. That has been a formidable obstacle and has led to the abortion of many transactions, leading to many lost business opportunities. However, blockchain technology is poised to eliminate this trust issue and give people a platform where individuals, with little or no knowledge about each other, can do business together, without being overly concerned about trust.

The era of making identity verification the exclusive rights of financial intermediaries is over. Blockchain can handle that even better than these intermediaries ever could. It is designed with the capability to verify the capacity and identity of potential business partners by going through the blockchain network to check the transaction history of both parties. There are other economic and social indicators where they can gain valuable and reliable information from, too. The availability of these numerous tools at the disposal of the technology is responsible for the avalanche of benefits it offers the users.

Speed of Execution

Speed of execution is another important benefit offered by blockchain technology. It can be quite disheartening if remittances take a few days before they settle. The same can be said about stock trades and other investments, not to mention the lengthy process for most bank loans. In most cases, these usually take about 23 days before they are available for use, and that is after meeting stringent conditions.

Some commercial institutions, such as Bankers' Automated Clearing System, Clearing House Automated Payment System, Electronic Fund Transfer, SWIFT, and Automated Clearing House (ACH), handle huge volumes of payment orders daily. This translates to trillions of dollars annually. In terms of speed of execution, these organizations can boast of an impressive execution time, as they confirm such transactions within a few days. However, their amazing delivery speeds are still nothing compared to the awesome speed of execution that blockchain offers. The Bitcoin blockchain takes only 10 minutes to confirm transactions. There are also even faster blockchain networks that get transactions confirmed faster than one can imagine, at the speed of light. This is what the conventional banking system cannot promise or currently guarantee. The CEO of Ripple Labs, Chris Larsen, told the truth when he said:

In the corresponding banking world, where you have a sender in one network and a receiver in another, you have to go through multiple ledgers, multiple intermediaries, multiple hops. Things can literally fail in the middle. There are all kinds of capital requirements for that. This is good news for users who conduct a series of transactions each day. The allure of getting instant confirmation of a transaction can be irresistible. Imagine not having to wait for days or weeks for a transaction to be confirmed, while a bank benefits from the float. No capital trapped in transit. No selfish intermediary to deal with. Blockchain assures a smooth transaction that is devoid of all the issues that are the trademarks of the traditional method of banking.

Value Innovation

Although the Bitcoin blockchain was specifically designed for making Bitcoin transfers from one Bitcoin wallet account to another, it was also designed to create room for developers to put their creative skills to use as an open source. This has led to the creation of altcoins, or alternative coins, by some experienced developers and investors. The altcoins have wide areas of applications beyond what Bitcoin can conveniently handle. Some other investors had a different idea. They are interested in leveraging the sheer size of Bitcoin, as well as its liquidity, for the creation of sidechains that are "colored" to serve as a representation of any physical or digital liability, or asset.

Sidechains are a form of blockchain with their own peculiar functions and features. These new coins are quite different from the Bitcoin blockchain but are built by taking advantage of Bitcoin's hardware infrastructure and established network. They used these features as their building foundation and made some changes to make them distinct. As a guarantee that they will perform beyond expectation, they may come in different forms: a barrel of oil, a stock, a car, a currency, and others.

Many financial institutions are not waiting until blockchain becomes a household name before taking advantage of blockchain technology for exchanging, recording, and trading their assets and liabilities. If they wish, they can equally replace centralized markets and traditional exchanges with the blockchain technology, so that value can take on a better definition of how it is traded.

Risk Management

Another important benefit is risk management. Among the long list of benefits offered by blockchain technology is that it will assist many people to manage their risks without problem. There are different risks that blockchain can help manage. For instance, there is the risk that some irregularities in a payment process may lead to a trade bouncing back. This is called *settlement risk*. Another is counterparty risk. This is the risk of a counterparty defaulting for whatever reason before having settled the trade. Finally, there is *systemic risk*. This risk is the most important of them all. It covers all other risks that may stem from counterparty, with the exception of counterparty risk itself. The systemic risk can be completely eliminated with a single step: instant settlement. There is no worry of counterparty risk if a transaction is immediately confirmed.

It is not unusual to see unscrupulous managers take advantage of the long delay in the confirmation of transactions to carry out financial misappropriation. This risk will also be completely eliminated. Blockchain makes it easy for an accountant to go through a company's transaction history and see the previous transactions as well as the current ones. Transactions that are conducted on blockchain are also irreversible. Therefore, the manager can easily spot any irregularities in such transactions and prevent the potential mismanagement of funds and other resources. That action can help eliminate another form of risk: *agency risk.*

Open Source

Making changes in financial services technology is not as easy as one may think. The difficulty stems from the fact that each change or improvement made to the sector must be compatible with previous efforts to make it effective. Blockchain technology can handle this backward compatibility as an open source technology. Thus, it can be used for iterating, innovating, and improving the sector by making appropriate use of the consensus that is available in the blockchain network.

Some of the huge benefits that may arise from such adaptation include attestation, high speed, lower costs, reduced risks, and innovation of value. What is more, it also offers adaptability that makes it possible for users to transform investment banking, retail banking, securities industry, insurance, accounting and audit, and others.

Potential Changes to Financial Services

There is no doubt that the financial services sector will undergo a transformation that will have a positive impact. There are some areas of the financial services that are expected to experience significant changes as a result of the introduction of the blockchain technology into the sector. Some of these changes are outlined below.

Authenticating Value and Identity

For decades, intermediaries have played a significant role in identity verification during a financial transaction. They are also the go-to medium for establishing trust during such transactions. Without the roles played by intermediaries, applying for financial services, such as loans and bank accounts, may be challenging. A customer may be ignorant of the procedures needed to have access to financial assistance, what options are available, the basic requirements, and the best agents that will meet their needs. These are some of the many roles played by intermediaries to assist people whenever they need any financial services. As mentioned earlier, the introduction of blockchain technology into the sector will change this. This is due to the impact of the blockchain solving trust issues in transactions. Peers can take full advantage of the technology to establish a strong, verifiable and secure identity.

Storing Value

Financial institutions have been the storehouse of value for different institutions, individuals, and governments for centuries. While institutions settle for Treasury bills and Money Market funds, where they can gain small returns on their investments, individuals often settle for a bank account or a safety deposit box in a bank for storing value. However, it is really not advisable for individuals to depend on banks for storing their value, and neither should banks be the only providers of checking and savings accounts.

Moving Value

One of the many responsibilities of financial services is moving money from one place to another, as they move billions of dollars round the world each day. From minor transactions, such as making a purchase on Google Play, to making purchases to the tune of billions of dollars, financial services work to ensure a smooth transfer, without delay. However, blockchain will gradually become the only means of moving currencies, stocks, bonds, and other valuable assets around the globe. The services offered by blockchain will also come with some increased benefits, such as reduced friction, improved speed, encourage economic growth, and reduced costs.

Investing and Funding

Every individual has access to wealth creation through investing in assets or companies. They may get their returns as interests, dividends, or some other means. The financial sector has proven invaluable with their responsibility of matching potential investors with business owners or entrepreneurs to facilitate tier investing. Intermediaries, such as venture capitalists, investment bankers, lawyers, and a host of others, have been deeply involved in raising money for individuals who are passionate about investing in such assets or companies. Blockchain will take over all of these functions of the intermediaries by automating all the functions performed by the intermediaries and make peer-to-per financing easy and attractive. Other benefits include introducing transparency, efficiency, and security, from paying coupons, to recording dividends.

Lending Value

Financial institutions have been at the forefront of providing financial assistance to people for years. They do this via mortgages, issuance of credit cards, municipal bonds, corporate bonds, government bonds, and more. This is meant to assist individuals to meet their financial burdens and has helped some to cope successfully with their financial responsibilities. To cater for the growing number of people who need these services, many companies have been established that provide credit scores, credit checks, and credit ratings services. Sometimes, these companies complicate issues for an average customer. This has necessitated the need for the individuals to have a more efficient user-friendly platform that will ease the burden for users. On blockchain, each individual can trade or engage in any transaction without relying on an intermediary, such as these service providers. The result of such a direct transaction is transparency and speed. Consumers can have access to loans and other financial assistance directly. Entrepreneurs around the world will benefit greatly from this policy when it becomes fully implemented.

Risk Management and Insuring Value

Risk management is a large area that includes insurance. The goal is to provide a protective platform for companies and individuals against unexpected catastrophe or loss. Many people have found insurance, as a risk management technique, very effective in handling unpredictable crises. However, due to some lack of oversight, more than $600 trillion is still outstanding in over-the counter derivatives. This is one of the major insurance issues that blockchain will address. It will ensure that risk management becomes more transparent by taking advantage of its decentralized attribute that focuses on derivatives. By using information about an insurer, blockchain can easily determine whether the insurer is reliable, or not.

Exchanging Value

Globally, trillions of dollars of financial assets are exchanged each day. This is done through different buying and selling different products and services as well as investments and storing values. One of the greatest factors in support of blockchain is the reduced processing time of such transactions from a couple of days, to only seconds or minutes. This guaranteed speed of operation will also lead to improved efficiency. Thus, both underbanked and unbanked individuals will soon have access to wealth creation by leveraging the benefits of blockchain technology.

Accounting Value

Accounting is one of the richest industries in the US. It is a multibillion-dollar industry that has touched the lives of investors and other stakeholders in the financial services industry. Modern finance is more fast-paced and complex than it used to be. This has created a huge problem: its requirements are far beyond what traditional accounting practices can conveniently handle. The whole system needs a complete overhaul to meet up with the modern financial services. The introduction of a new accounting method backed by powerful blockchain technology will make a difference. The distributed ledger will also bring transparency to the financial services and make auditing as transparent as possible with real-time auditing. As such, financial transactions can easily be reviewed by stakeholders, which is a great improvement over the current practices.

Google Translate for Business

Accounting is considered to be the language of finance, meant only for experts in the field. There would not have been any need for accounting if all the transactions in the world were entered in the large public ledgers that blockchain can offer. Today's accounting managers are expected to maintain an order of books. However, management of high-profile organizations and companies have shown that management sometimes sacrifices their integrity, when pursuing a goal that will have either a short-time or long-term impact on the organization. Other problems that have continued to be a huge challenge for the sector include false reporting and corruption.

In addition, the sector has been unable to prevent human error. This has led to series of accounting mistakes across the world. Sometimes, what started as a simple mistake spiralled out of control and became a huge financial mistake, as the small mistake found its way into financial statements and calculations. This is not an isolated case. One out of three companies has had its employees enter incorrect data into their system.

When the Sarbanes-Oxley rules were established, the goal was to use such rules to curb accounting fraud. Over the years, events have proven the ineffectiveness of such rules to reduce the frequency of accounting problems. Some factors behind this failure include increased multifaceted transactions, the existence of more complex companies, and the unprecedented speed at which modern commerce is done. These factors and others have provided potential frauds a platform to securely hide their wrongdoing. There is also the inefficiency of the traditional accounting methods to meet the new business models. For instance, consider micro-transactions: One cannot have perfect micro-transactions with the current audit software that has 2 decimal places as the default.

Accounting has proven to be an invaluable practice in the business world. There is nothing wrong with accounting, but there is a lot that is wrong with the practice. Most of the modern accounting methods are badly implemented, and as such have a negative impact on the profession. Stakeholders in the accounting sector have been unable to create an efficient accounting method that will bring out the best.

The World Wide Ledger

Accounting is done with two entries – a debit and credit entry. This is the reason for the name, double-entry transaction. This is the conventional practice ever since accounting was introduced into the business world. The World Wide Ledger will come in handy here. This can be added as a third entry that will give a company's auditors, shareholders, and regulators instant access to the content of an entry book.

Many large companies carry out a tremendous number of transactions daily. This may include purchasing raw materials, selling products, or paying their employees. There may also be accounts for liabilities and assets on the balance sheet as well. The introduction of the World Wide Ledger will be useful, as it will be used for recording transactions and making the transactions available on a blockchain by publishing a receipt with the time of the transactions to the blockchain. This will give a company a financial report that is fully searchable, auditable, and verifiable.

This will make it easy for a company to prepare an up-to-date spreadsheet that is accurate, complete, and immutable. To restrict unqualified personnel from having access, executives can restrict access to the ledges to only managers and other key stakeholders who have been granted permission. Moreover, introducing the World Wide Ledger into the accounting sector has some significant implications: It may force banks to comply with regulators, and also gradually reduce the risks in accounting.

Barclay's Simon Taylor saw the potential implications of such a ledger when he noted that such a ledger will bring about transparency in transactions and financial records: Transparency "means that a regulator would have access to the same base layer of data. That would mean less work, less cost, and we could be held to account in real time. That's really powerful."

Some of the greatest beneficiaries of this new technology are regulators. Currently, privately-controlled and opaque financial accounting systems and ledgers are the only tools available for bank examiners to do their jobs. This will change completely when a shared ledger, such as the World Wide Ledger, is introduced. This public ledger will give bank examiners and auditors what they need to conduct automated examinations that will help them go deep into a spreadsheet, examine its authenticity, and how the financial strength of the corporation. This innovation may also have a permanent impact on the accounting industry, as it makes it possible to automate valuable processes of accounting and audit.

This will make it increasingly difficult for fraud to occur. The updating of records at regular intervals makes it impossible for someone to change the records later, thus ensuring that any record that is recorded in the blockchain can be completely trusted due to its invulnerability to alteration. The potential of blockchain to bring some accountability to the accounting industry is summarized by Austin Hill when he argues that: "A public ledger that is constantly audited and verified means you don't have to trust the books of your partner; there is integrity in the statements or the transaction logs, because the network itself is verifying it...If the ledger says it is true, then it's true." This technique is comparable to a continuous audit of the ledger that is done, not manually, but cryptographically.

Eric Piscini of Deloitte, one of the top four accounting firms in the world, understands this implication. He believes that the banking sector may be standing on the precipice of extinction, if blockchain is completely implemented, and that it may drive many banks out of business, because the banking business is all about risk management. If blockchain eliminates risks, what becomes of the sector?

Piscini also acknowledges that the audit business is in for a comprehensive disruption of its business model: "Today we spend a lot of time auditing companies, and we charge fees accordingly. Tomorrow, if that process is completely streamlined because there is a time stamp in the blockchain, that changes the way we audit companies."

Some accounting firms are already preparing themselves for the challenges ahead. They are aware of the potentials in blockchain and do not want to be pushed out of business by this innovation. Some of these firms have welcomed blockchain technology openly. Companies record their transactions into a blockchain, so they can easily audit the parties because the transactions have been successfully recorded. The introduction of blockchain as the third entry will make a huge difference. An automatic entry on the blockchain gives access to anybody to determine the accuracy of an accounting book, whether it is balanced or not.

Accounting records are some of the most guarded secrets of accounting companies. Most companies will not like the idea of having their transparent accounting record become public property. They also will not feel at home with regulators or auditors having access to their records. However, some experts are of the opinion that transparency will do more good than harm for those companies. According to these experts, when a company embraces a spirit of transparency, the financial department can easily be streamlined, the cost of carrying out an audit will be lowered, and this will also give the market comprehensive knowledge of the value of the company.

This will also make it possible for the company to enjoy a significant increase in price per share over some other companies, where transparency is taboo and investors have to wait a few months before seeing financial information about the company. For instance, Bornini, an expert in the field asks: "Who is going to invest in a company that shows you what's going on quarterly, compared to one that shows you what's going on all the time?"

Although the concept of triple-entry is strange, the probability that it will become a crucial point in accounting in the future cannot be ruled out. Some stakeholders are currently raising issues about the ability of blockchain to have perfect control of accounting. This school of thought believes that the services of competent auditors, however, will still be needed to handle some aspects of accounting. In any case, the input of blockchain technology may go a long way in reducing the stress of ensuring an accurate account by the auditors.

The introduction of triple-entry accounting will also bring about an unprecedented level of responsiveness and transparency. This can be achieved through verifiable transaction records, real-time record keeping, instant audit, and other related practices. This will empower blockchain to solve most of the problems that are peculiar to accounting.

In other words, rather than have a whole group of auditors handle auditing, especially for big auditing firms, only a single auditor is needed to correct some areas that blockchain cannot currently work on. Triple-entry accounting will not be the only blockchain innovations that will be introduced into corporate governance.

Managers in the accounting sector will benefit immensely from the increased transparency that blockchain offers. If those managers can do everything within their capacity to uphold transparency and embrace trust as a symbol of corporate leadership, that will open many opportunities to them. Although corporations often have the responsibility of publishing their dealings to the public, they also have the right to guard their secrets. The same applies to their staff and employees' privacy. There is a difference between privacy and transparency, however. Regardless of how strong the desire is for a corporation to protect the privacy of its staff and stakeholders that should not be an excuse for a lack of transparency.

Blockchain and Credit Scores

In the event of financial emergencies, one may need to apply for a loan or a credit card. When doing so, the bank will ask for a credit score. The score is usually used to determine eligibility for the loan and the ability for repayment. A credit score is the result of previous financial history. Without a good credit score, the chances of getting a loan are slim. Most retail creditors will not consider an application for a credit card without a good credit score. However, the process for calculating these scores is flawed.

While the credit score takes into account an applicant's credit history, some other important personal attributes are ignored, sometimes to the detriment of the application. For example, some individuals use their debit card for shopping and other purposes, a practice which does not contribute to building a credit score. Also, a young person's poor credit rating should not have a bearing on his or her credit risk in adulthood. There are numerous flaws that need to be addressed when calculating credit scores. These are factors that blockchain can handle. The series of factors covered by blockchain will make it a better platform for managing risks and issuing credit cards.

The most important attribute of a person is his or her reputation. It is one of the major factors that are always considered when the issue of trust comes up. Whether in the field of business, or in regular day-to-day activities, one cannot rule out the importance of reputation when trust is under discussion. Someone with a questionable reputation should not be trusted for any business discussion or transaction. However, this attribute is usually ignored, when financial intermediaries want to determine whether someone can be trusted or not.

For instance, consider the examples of two business owners who both need the financial assistance of a bank to grow their businesses. In most cases, the small business owner may not be given the right attention due to a biased opinion of his or her documentation and credit score. In contrast, a big businessman with a flawless credit history will naturally be shown favor.

The banking sector, however, is not concerned about other factors outside a credit score when an individual is seeking financial assistance. If a credit score is less than good, the chances of getting a loan are slim. This has cut some individuals off from enjoying the benefits of a loan, especially those who are in dire need of a loan to get their financial responsibilities under control. Many can be cut off from enjoying such services because they fail to meet some stringent conditions set by the creditors. People living in the developing countries feel the full impact of such practices.

A case study is the New York ID Cards issue that occurred in December 2015. Despite the fact that the card gained much acceptance by some over 67,000 people and the approval of the bank's federal regulators, many top banks still rejected it as a valid document for opening a bank account. That's an indication of a flaw in the system and is, in fact, the current fate of many people around the world.

The structure of blockchain makes it possible to solve this problem. It can provide individuals in need of financial assistance a better alternative to the traditional banking system by empowering them. They can easily create unique identities, with attractive attributes and immaculate transaction histories, for the participants. This will give people from all walks of life access to loans and credit.

This is not the only area where the blockchain technology will prove useful. It can establish trust between parties in a transaction, whenever that is absolutely necessary. Its structure ensures that the borrower will get the loan and make full repayment with interest. In that case, both parties are empowered with their own data and have strengthened privacy. Thus, they can create unique identities by leveraging their social capital and previous economic history on the particular blockchain. What the future holds for people in this sector is well-defined by Patrick Deegan, Financial Services expert. He foresees a future when individuals will "deploy and manage their own identity, and form trusted connections with other peers, and nodes."

This is because the blockchain keeps a complete record of all transactions in the blockchain ledger. That makes every transaction count, and it can help boost someone's reputation, as well as increase their creditworthiness. Individuals can also create a wide array of personas for use. They determine which personality is ideal for a particular person or institution and interact with the other party based on the appropriate personality.

Some organizations have experimented with this idea and have found it to be effective. Companies can extend credit to someone based on his or her reputation alone. When implementing this, a potential applicant for credit has a wide avenue of opportunities to build a good reputation. There can even be recommendations by friends and family on social media in order to boost your reputation.

When dealing with organizations that subscribe to this idea, one can build a profile and submit their credit score, in addition to other attributes, without the fear of having confidential information become public knowledge. Such platforms offer a unique opportunity to work on your credit score if it is low. On this platform, one can start building their reputation by first taking a reputation loan. This is a special loan that is offered to borrowers to assess their ability to repay their loans or not. The major requirement for qualification for this loan is a verified identity to check is an applicant is of age to take a loan.

The ability to make full payment within the agreed deadline will boost a user's reputation and credit score. There is a difference between reputation systems and others. Credit scores will no longer be the only factor that determines an applicant's creditworthiness. A couple of other factors will be considered as well, including the ability and wiliness to make full repayment of a loan.

Companies will also be able make improvements to their credit ratings. The criteria for rating someone will be other factors, such as vocational competence, shared values, trustworthiness, and so on. Therefore, the chance of having the right reputation to meet the demands of lending institutions increases drastically.

Role of Blockchain IPO

In 2015, an unexpected event demonstrated the far-reaching effect of blockchain IPO on the global market, when the global community woke up to devastating news: the Chinese stock marketed had suffered a severe crash. The crash was so big that experts were already forecasting another economic meltdown.

The Chinese stock market crash affected the global economy, including traditional IPOs and Silicon Valley. While everyone was discussing the potential impact of the crash on the economy, a company decided to make a daring move: Augur embarked on a crowdfunding campaign amid the crash that was eventually considered one of the most successful in history. Within the first week, over 3,500 investors from across the globe helped the company to raise some $4 million. This was done exclusively by these investors, without the input of an intermediary, such as investment banks, lawyers, and regulators. Stock exchange and mandatory filings were also excluded from the fundraising.

One of the major responsibilities of the financial services is matching entrepreneurs with investors. Financial services have played the middlemen, connecting these parties and offering platforms for meeting. For decades, raising equity capital has been done through the same process. This includes through secondary offerings, initial public offerings, private placements, and private investments in public equities. The process has not undergone appreciable changes for almost 90 years. However, changes from blockchain IPO are on the horizon.

The existence of new crowdfunding platforms has offered small companies the opportunity to find an alternative way to raise capital for their businesses through the Internet. Nevertheless, the contribution of intermediaries is still needed by entrepreneurs and investors. In addition to the intermediaries, the sector still needs a reliable payment platform that will ease moving money from one person to another.

The blockchain IPO is a deviation from this process. It looks at the flaws in the existing system and works on them. It has made it possible for companies to raise funds via blockchain by issuing cryptocurrencies or tokens to interested investors. The tokens can come in the form of bonds, equity, or anything of value. In addition to Augur, Ethereum has also changed fundraising methods. A few years ago, Ethereum was able to raise enough funds to sponsor a new blockchain by crowdselling its token, ether. Since the fundraising, Ethereum has grown to become the biggest digital currency, after Bitcoin. Its public blockchain is also regarded as the fastest-growing in the world. This would not have been possible without its IPO.

It is hoped that blockchain IPO's will continue to gain momentum in the future. If they live up to their expectations, they will take over some of the key roles of investment bankers, brokers, securities lawyers, and other professional stakeholders in the global financial system. This will change the face of investment for good. If blockchain IPO's can be integrated into exchange platforms, such as Coinbase, circle, Smartwallet and other new start-ups, this will eventually lead to the much-expected distributed virtual exchange. In that event, there will be a gradual shift from the conventional exchange to a virtual exchange.

Some exchange companies are gradually making necessary changes to take advantage of blockchain to up their games, without being pushed out of business by the emergence of blockchain-based exchanges. For instance, NASDAQ is gradually embracing blockchain technology in order to make it a part of its private market. The same can be said of NYSE. This company has also invested in Coinbase, one of the leading cryptocurrency exchanges. NASDAQ is investing in blockchain with a well-defined goal as expressed by its CEO, Bob Greifeld, that blockchain will "streamline financial record keeping while making it cheaper and more accurate." These are not the only companies making this gradual shift.

Blockchain technology will, in fact, take over the financial services sector in the near future. The impact will be felt in capital markets, retail banking, and accounting. Banks and other financial institutions will also feel the huge impact of blockchain technology, as it moves to have a complete control of the industry, thereby removing conventional and ineffective practices and replacing them with enduring, more efficient practices.

Conventional practices have some unappealing characteristics that make change inevitable, such as the speed of execution, changes are not usually welcome, and powerful intermediaries. The new order will bring big changes in the sector, such as transparency, security, more privacy, peer-to-peer solution, and innovation.

The financial landscape will experience transformation for some time to come that will turn it away from the exclusive property of intermediaries, to a platform where every stakeholder has an equal chance of achieving financial prosperity.

Chapter 20: Blockchain and Job Opportunities

It goes without saying that the economic conditions in some developing countries are appalling. For instance, in many of these countries a large percentage of the population depends on sustenance farming and other menial jobs for a living. Unemployment rates are high, with few jobs for young workers, and the living conditions continue to deteriorate. The harsh economic conditions in those countries also make it difficult even for skilled workers to access to all the tools they need to excel in their chosen career.

It can also be extremely difficult to access loans. Many banks require collateral before a loan application can be considered, and this has kept many individuals from receiving loans due to their inability to meet this requirement. Those who are fortunate enough to secure a loan are often burdened with high interest rate, making it so it can be difficult to run a business successfully, as the interest rate eats into the capital.

Blockchain technology, however, is a great tool for creating employment opportunities, for the more than over two billion people with limited access to job opportunities in most parts of the world, especially in the developing world. Even the developed world has yet to recover from the economic crash of 2008. This has gradually led to a decline in the standards of living even in advanced countries. Some families are witnessing the worst economic hardships ever due to the high costs of living, without a corresponding increase in income.

In 2014, at the annual meeting of the World Economic Forum it was revealed that it is riskier to grow inequality than combat the effects of war, global warming, disease, and other serious challenges. Blockchain, however, has the technology to create numerous job opportunities for individuals in different parts of the world. Although this may sound impossible to some, the fact is that the technology is up to the task.

One of its first applications is to lower the barriers to financial assistance that has been the bane of many countries. The easy access to capital will help a lot of prospective entrepreneurs put their skills to use. Artisans and other skilled workers will have access to capital to pursue their dreams and break free from the shackles of unemployment and poverty, thereby improving the economic conditions in some developing countries. In the coming years, it is expected that the blockchain industry will open up numerous opportunities for individuals. What follows are only some of the careers that blockchain will change:

Project Manager

There is an increasing interest in blockchain technology across the world. It has had a real impact in the business industry, as more companies are integrating blockchain technology to optimize their businesses. For these changes, each company must find effective ways to communicate with a blockchain company that will install the machinery to meet their business needs. Of course, the best results can be obtained by hiring someone who is knowledgeable in the field. A blockchain project manager has the responsibility of converting a client's needs to what a developer will easily understand by using the appropriate technical language. He or she is also an intermediary who will convert the developer's language to what the business owner will understand. A project manager will have the responsibility of brokering the deal between the parties, and both will plan the project and supervise its execution. A project manager also handles the following responsibilities:

- The cost estimates of a project
- The budget to finance the project
- Partnering with a blockchain company to integrated the technology into the business.

Security

One may wonder why security is mentioned among job opportunities in the blockchain industry, considering the already high security measures attached to the technology. There is more to the security than many know. While it is true that security measures incorporated into the technology make it unlikely that blockchain can be tampered with, one cannot completely rule out the possibility of fraud, although such a fraud will automatically be captured and recorded in the blockchain, which helps make easy detection possible. Detecting the fraud and ascertaining the degree of damage done, however, will require the services of skilled professionals in identity protection and encryption.

Developers

Developers have better chances than anyone else to get a job in the blockchain industry because all sectors of the economy will have a need for the introduction of blockchain technology, from financial institutions, to insurance companies, and government agencies, to tech companies--the list is endless. These companies have a need for the technology for driving their businesses forward, and to improve how they serve their users and clients. They can also optimize their businesses with the technology. Thus there is a need for the services of competent developers, to create the platforms on which the companies will accomplish their business goals with blockchain technology. As blockchain companies receive more inquiries from companies that need their services for incorporating the technology, there will also be an increase in the number of developers needed.

Web Designers

The boom in the demand for the blockchain technology will also open up more jobs for website designers. There are still a huge number of blockchain-related businesses and start-ups that are interested in raising funds through the sales of tokens. These businesses will need websites to inform potential investors, their clients, and the platform users of their intention to make token sales. They also need to inform clients of the company's mission, team members, their goals, and other related information that their target audience will find useful. Web designers are needed to handle many of these tasks. They must be available to create and update the websites with the relevant information that potential investors will find valuable.

Law

The increasing number of businesses that depend on blockchain technology will also lead to an increased demand for lawyers and other law professionals. They will be needed to handle the legal aspects to avoid any potential legal problems. In 2018, at a conference on the topic of "Working in the Blockchain Ecosystems in 2018," the attorneys in attendance revealed that there has been an increase in the number of potential clients who make inquiries about the governance and the structuring of ICOs. These aspiring blockchain investors need professional advice from law professionals before committing themselves to the business. This is an assurance that attorneys will also find good job opportunities there.

The world should be ready for an explosion of job opportunities in the blockchain technology industry. However, there may be legitimate concerns about the eligibility for offers in the industry. Some may not have much experience in the field, and thus are not qualified to apply. However, the truth is that jobs in this area require little knowledge of blockchain technology. Blockchain technology has only been around for less than 10 years, so most employers will not expect extensive experience in this area. As a web designer, however, your chances of getting a job are very high. Employment opportunities will abound in the blockchain industry in 2018 and beyond, and now is the right time to gain the right knowledge that can lead to employment in the industry.

Customer Support Agent

The increased number of job opportunities created by the blockchain technology will make it a necessity for companies and organizations that want to take advantage of the technology to have a customer support department to attend to the complaints and inquiries of their customers or clients. Due to the new nature of the technology, many customers or clients may want know more about the technology, or want to inquire about how the technology can benefit them. Of course, more human agents will be hired to handle the complaints or inquires.

Customer support will also assist in the sales department by selling the company's services, or a range of products, to their clients or customers. Even if the agent is not directly involved in selling the product or service, he or she may be have the responsibility of providing information about the product or service to potential customers or clients. This may involve encouraging the clients to consider the benefits of blockchain technology to take advantage of them.

Systems Architect

With a degree in Computer Science and other certifications in relevant fields, the cryptocurrency world offers a golden opportunity to work as a systems architect for companies that are interested in boosting their businesses with blockchain technology. As a system architect, the job specification requires keeping the company running with input, as well as installing both the software and hardware the company needs to use the technology, and the responsibility of maintaining the systems in the company. To meet the needs of the company and clients, technical support will also be necessary. Thus there will also be a need to provide system backup management services, troubleshooting and diagnosis, and other services that will ensure the smooth running of the company.

Smart Contract Developer

Smart contracts are some of the most important parts of blockchain technology because almost all of the uses of the technology are rooted in smart contracts. Smart contracts have uses in politics, education, entrepreneurship, and numerous other sectors, so they are obviously a pivotal component of blockchain technology. In view of the rising number of smart contracts and the need to develop more of these to meet increasing needs, smart contract developers will be in high demand.

Blockchain Bootcamp Instructor

Some coders are trying to learn how to get fully involved in the cryptocurrency world. This requires qualified instructors to train them. One can build an interactive website for the bootcamp, host workshops to build awareness, and support the desire for coders, and others to increase their knowledge of the technology.

Overcoming the Banking Challenge

As previously discussed, the banking sector is another important sector of the global economy where blockchain technology is expected to have a huge future impact. In developing countries, there still exist many challenges in the banking sector. The banking sector depends on customers and volume of transactions to thrive. Banks cannot function without the customers because their patronage automatically determines how much the bank will succeed. It is worth noting that banks are only interested in customers whose money can add to the overall growth of the bank. In essence, they have little or no interest in one's money if it has little economic value to offer to them. That is why they go out of their way to win rich customers, while those at the bottom of the financial pyramid are considered inconsequential.

The challenges that individuals who are not financially stable have to contend with when dealing with banks starts from the moment they want to open a bank account. While the developed countries have a simple process for opening a bank account, it is a quite different process for those in developing countries--one must make a physical visit to the bank and fill out an application for consideration. That is just the beginning of a long process that may take days or weeks, depending on the bank, their requirements, and a client's ability to meet these requirements without delay. Some of the requirements can include government-issued ID cards, which may sometimes be another battle to obtain one. In some countries, one can only obtain government-issued IDs on special occasions.

While it is easier to open a bank account in developed countries, a potential client still has to meet some basic requirements, some of which include anti-money laundering and Know Your Customer regulations, as well as anti-terrorism financing rules. They are simply not interested in the client; they are interested in their credentials.

According to the World Bank, "Three quarters of the world's poor don't have a bank account, not only because of poverty, but the cost, travel distance, and amount of paper work involved in opening an account." Imagine the huge implications of these unnecessary restrictions. One of the grave consequences is the unconventional saving techniques adopted by such individuals. Someone without a bank account in the developing countries may resort to some risky measures that may have dire consequences, such as using alternatives like piggy banks or keeping money under the mattress. Such practices make it difficult, if not impossible, for an individual to build up reserves, and as such they also cannot have access to insurance, credit, or other financial services.

All this clearly shows that the financial services sector is missing out on a good opportunity to provide much-needed, affordable, and safe financial services to billions of the unbanked. Many use alternatives to banks, such as credit associations or savings clubs. Each week, each member of such associations contributes according to their financial limits a stipulated amount of money that is then handed over to a predetermined member to take care of his or her financial needs.

The process will be repeated the following week, and the deposits are given to another member, until all the members of the club gain the needed financial assistance. This is a common practice in sub-Saharan Africa. In this part of the continent, the informal saving techniques are used by some

48% of the population. The figure is higher in Nigeria, where almost 70% of the adults use this saving method, popularly known in the local parlance as *cha, ajo, esusu,* or *adashi.*

The need for good financial services for women, and others, who exist below the poverty line, is highlighted by Melinda Gates, Co-Chair of the Gates Foundation: "Financial tools for savings, insurance, payments, and credit are all a vital need for poor people, especially women, and can help families and whole communities lift themselves out of poverty."

With blockchain technology, one can bypass the aforementioned requirements by leveraging a different financial identity that is promoted by the technology. This new identity is independent of paper credentials but focuses on a personal identity, or reputation, instead. The new method thus provides an easier way to open a bank account than the conventional method, with all of its requirements.

Rather than go through vigorous traditional ID tests, one only needs to create a personal digital ID and maintain a sterling reputation that can be verified at any time for any type of transaction they want to engage in. With the assistance of blockchain, this can easily be achieved. The technology also makes a digital ID trustworthy to pave the way for unlimited access to financial assistance and services from banks and reputable financial institutions.

This will overturn the current inability to use a personal reputation to secure financial services without the verification of some paper ID's that have little or no value to a borrower's ability to make repayment after taking a loan. There are billions of people with no access to documents that can be used for verification, and these changes can positively impact their lives. This new method introduced by blockchain can easily create a permanent, standardized digital identity for use in any part of the world. What is more, there will also be the freedom of releasing only a fraction of an identity during a transaction. This means parties and not compelled by any law to reveal their full identity during a transaction.

By taking advantage of micro-lending agencies, individuals with restricted access to bank loans can have access to lenders on a platform that can allow them to track the repayment of micro-loans to determine the credibility of a lender and his or her ability to get bigger loans in the future. By repeatedly taking small loans and making timely repayment, a borrower can increase his or her credibility. When that is combined with a global payment platform, an individual has everything he or she needs to succeed in a business due to the availability of easy financial services.

Even in economies where women are grossly discriminated against, especially in the banking sector, blockchain technology will offer everyone a fair and unbiased platform and access to financial services. In an online article titled "Helping the World's One Billion Unbanked Women," it reported that a "One billion women – more than 40% of the women around the world – still don't have access to financial services, despite women's growing share of global consumer spending." It is a serious challenge for women to find a convenient and safe place to obtain credit, save their money, obtain insurance, receive their pension, and gain access to other financial services. Such discrimination works against the economy of a country, thus sinking the country deeper into economic hardship.

Blockchain technology is a better alternative to the banking system. When borrowers have credible reputations, it can lead to more global entrepreneurship that has access to financial assistance. Financial institutions and other counterparties will not have issues with granting access to value. This will ultimately widen the scope of opportunities through the distribution of opportunity on a global level. Blockchain will make it possible for everyone to create a verifiable, unique identity that is specifically based on the reputation of such an individual. Thus, individuals of all backgrounds will be provided with an unprecedented, profound equality.

Blockchain stakeholders and experts anticipate that the future will witness the enfranchisement of the underbanked and unbanked. This will occur with an increase in the number of micro-lending services that encourage investors to create different portfolios, covering a wide range of portfolios of microloans for interested parties. The repayment of the loans, as well as their use, can easily be traced via blockchain. This will make it easier for individuals both to get loans as well as to make repayment as agreed. Billions of entrepreneurs will have more opportunities to raise capital for building their businesses.

Chapter 21: The Roadmap to Financial Freedom with Blockchain

The inability of individuals to have a credible financial identity has continued to prevent them from achieving financial opportunities. However, now that blockchain technology has embarked on the journey of taking over the financial landscape, these worries should disappear. Blockchain has created a platform for individuals from all walks of life to carefully design a working formula that will gradually assist them towards achieving financial prosperity. This is incredible, as it offers billions of people the opportunity to create their personal wealth, without depending on the government or other entities to provide that.

The Tools

It is helpful that the tools needed for participating in an economy are readily available for all. All one needs are internet access and a mobile phone, which will open up access to other tools and resources.

Personal Identity

Personal identity is a part of an individual's reputation. A reputable identity can be built in a number of social networks for different transactions. The availability of a good payment system and a reliable means of storing your values and conducting any transactions with potential business partners from across the globe has the potential to open up new opportunities. Eliminating the hindrances that have prevented access to financial resources will pave the way for many to launch their own businesses or work towards building their existing businesses towards success.

Entrepreneurs play a crucial role in the development of an economy. Experts consider them as the engines that drive the economic growth of many economies. Without their creativity and business innovations, the marketplace would suffer. Blockchain allows more entrepreneurs to meet the basic requirements for kick-starting their career. It offers individuals and small companies the features of big companies, so that they can leverage, launch, and maintain their businesses.

The existence of smart contracts and blockchain-based ledgers has led to a gradual reduction of the barriers that people have to overcome when contemplating starting a business. They have also been effective in expediting incorporation in developing countries. This is a big relief, considering the time and resources that are naturally needed to get a company incorporated in those parts of the world.

Blockchains are designed for streamlining, automating, and improving the three components that are crucial to business building: fund raising, formation, and sales.

The complete trust in blockchain as the gateway to business incorporation will lead to a significant drop in formation costs. It will also be an effective record-maintaining procedure that can always be used as a guide, especially in some areas without the rule of law as a guide. It also breaks the burden of financing a business. The free access to debt capital and equity makes it relatively easier for such individuals to raise the needed capital for launching their business.

One of the general problems that such investors have is exchange rates. The inconsistency of exchange rates is a major challenge that has prevented many people from floating a company. The same applies to conversion rates. These twin problems have continued to serve as a deterrent to potential businessmen for decades in the developing world. Using Bitcoin for business transactions, however, can easily overcome these rates, since the digital currency is not subjected to them. Therefore, buyers are no longer under the obligation of having a local currency, credit card, or a bank account before they can make purchases.

By leveraging the security and the immutability offered by the blockchain ledger, entrepreneurs can conduct several activities without problems. It affords them the opportunity to register their title of assets, business, and manage their payables, inventory, and receivables. Blockchain technology has all that they need to perform these easily. Some of the tools include blockchain-based applications, triple-entry accounting software, and the elimination of third-parties, such as tax lawyers, auditors, vendors, and others, who indirectly reduce the success rate of small businesses.

An entrepreneur can take advantage of smart contracts to automate some integral parts of his or her operations. Payroll, purchase orders, financial audits, interests on loans, and other operations can be easily automated to reduce the burden of handling all these aspects of their business manually, and thus save both costs and time.

Three business models may be of great help to these entrepreneurs:

1. **Sharing resources**: The distributed economy offers some benefits, which include the liberty to share resources. One can loan out some of their physical or non-physical resources, such as wheelbarrows, office, spare beds, and other valuable assets to the members of a network, who are in need of such assets but consider it cost-effective to get them as a loan rather than buy them new. One can also share some other resources, such as Netflix subscriptions, Wi-Fi, and others.

This can all be done through smart contracts and micropayments. The only requirement for getting such assets as a loan will be the reputation scores of the interested members. Individuals will be able to use blockchain as a tool for creating value and freely earning income.

2. Monetizing personal data: In addition to resources, one can also monetize personal data. Current systems do not recognize efforts and reputation. They are only interested in documents. There is more to an individual than what is reflected in his or her paper documents. Blockchain offers the possibility of monetizing such valuable data.

In the future, one will be able to contract and license their personal data in ways that will create a new opportunities for new sources of income. The current system makes us lose valuable data that can be successfully monetized. We freely give out personal information about ourselves in exchange for some services but end up losing our integrity and privacy. This will be reversed with the introduction of the term, *prosumers*, by blockchain technology. This term refers to the transformation of people from consumers to professional consumers, a term that reflects the new position of consumers as "product and brand advocate."

This simply means that people will no longer be satisfied with the status quo of being viewed as consumers only. They will have a say in what they consume and become the voices of the products and services they consume. Therefore, they will have a huge impact on the success or failure of products, companies, and brands by taking advantage of the social web and the power of technology via the blockchain technology. This will remove absolute power and control of brands from the producers and hand that over to the consumers, putting them in control.

For example, large companies and organizations currently depend on consumer information to make progress in their businesses. That is the rationale behind taking surveys, conducting polls, and doing everything possible to get necessary data from consumers. Why not contract the data to something valuable, rather than making it available for them free of charge?

3. **Distributed investment and ownership:** For centuries, wealth has become concentrated in the hands of a few, while the majority of humanity has battled poverty. That is the reason why a larger portion of the population remains poor, especially in developing world.

The good news is that we are gradually moving away from that trend, with a system that will ensure that more people can increase their financial status with distributed technology. This technology will offer individuals free access to financial markets and create amazing investment opportunities, to liberate people from perpetual financial slavery. There is an endless list of business opportunities to choose from. There are conventional business investments as well as other blockchain-based businesses, such as blockchain IPOs, microlending schemes, and many more.

All these can reduce the challenges of a cash crunch and open an avenue for raising capital for bigger businesses. There is also blockchain crowdfunding. It has become the go-to method for raising capital and has proven to be so effective that the method was used for raising some $2.7 billion, in 2012, alone. Since then, more entrepreneurs have leveraged crowdfunding for raising capital, especially cryptocurrency entrepreneurs. As more become accustomed to blockchain and crowdfunding, it will become the primary source of raising capital across the globe.

Blockchain IPO's offer more than just a platform for raising money. These can also be used to lower the costs of anyone who issues them. They can allow aspiring investors to participate and benefit from the IPO's.

Remittances as a Case Study

It is customary for foreigners living in developed countries to assist their poorer relatives in the developing world financially. A high percentage of these foreigners do that every payday. This has been the norm for a long time, but it is a costly and time-consuming practice that can easily be improved for the benefits of both the givers and the receivers.

A typical money transfer from a developed, to a developing country can be challenging for both parties. Sending money through intermediaries, such as Moneygram, can be stressful. The sender has to likely find a ride to the location where he or she can make the transfer. Sometimes, the journey to and fro may take hours, depending on the distance between where he or she lives and the point where the transfer can be made.
The distance is just one of the numerous challenges that the sender has to contend with. Others include the charges on the remittance. Some intermediaries charge as much as 10% of the total money to be remitted as a transfer fee. When that is added to the time spend in transit for making the transfer, the sender would have lost about $50 for making a transfer in the region of $150 and $200.

Getting the money is also not an easy task for the recipient as well. For instance, getting to the bank to withdraw the money will also take time and money. This is in addition to the local charges on the money by the appropriate body. The recipient may also have to wait for days or a week before the money will be available for withdrawal, after providing evidence that he or she is the real recipient of the money. In other words, both the recipient and the sender go through a lot of stress to transfer and receive money and pay a huge percentage of the money as fees.

This has been the experience of people living in diaspora, with their dependants at home. It is not a singular case but a common trend among such people. Billions of dollars are sent from different parts of the developed world, to the developing world, through this method and the story is the same. Those who benefit the most in these transactions are the intermediaries. Annually, they collect $38 billion in fees on remittances sent from one part of the world to another.

Remittances are one of the most important contributors to the GDP for some developing countries. This gives them the potential for having a positive impact on the standard of living of the most vulnerable people in the world. Some countries, such as the Philippines, Haiti, and others, receive tens of billions of dollars annually from remittances.

A study conducted by the International Monetary Fund explains that the remittance money is spent on the basic necessities of life, such as medicine, food, shelter, and clothing. In essence, the remittances are used to reduce the financial hardship of the recipients and increase their standard of living. Without remittances, the economic conditions of most of the world's poorest nations would be much worse because the remittances are estimated to be about four times the amount of aid from foreign countries. Nevertheless, the huge fees charged for these remittances still need to be addressed.

With the increasing number of smartphones in the world, one would expect such remittances to be made via these devices, and that would spare the senders the stress of traveling from one location to another just to make a deposit. However, many are still using old technology. Blockchain can address this issue by eliminating third-parties in order to simplify the process and establish a payment method that prevents people from having to wait in line for hours on end or travelling long distances just to make a simple international transfer.

Many companies and organizations are thus gradually becoming aware of the potentials of blockchain and leveraging Bitcoin technology and protocol to slash the cost of remittances. The collective goal of these companies and organizations is to take the huge fees charged for remittances away from the wealthy third-parties and keeping it where this money is most needed, with the world's poorest people.

Intermediaries have monopolized these businesses for years and have reaped extravagant amounts of money from them. They have transformed them into large industries and have turned themselves into multimillionaires. However, many of these intermediaries are beginning to realize that Bitcoin technology will soon replace them. Bitcoin protocol will wrestle the financial power from the wealthy and empower the over two billion people living in abject poverty.

Challenges of Blockchain-based Money Transfer

The prospect of giving power to the people is attractive. It is reassuring that the poor people can dare to dream of a future where they will have better economic prospects. However, before this goal can be realized there are still some challenges blockchain technology has to contend with. First, a high number of the senders send payments in cash, and not Bitcoin. The recipients, too, live in economies that are cash-based. Second, a large percentage of individuals have little or no knowledge of blockchain and may find it challenging to use.

This raises the question of how they will use the new technology, when many have little knowledge of it. This means that they will have to gradually make the shift from a cash-based economy, to a blockchain-driven one. Until payments are made in digital currencies and one can conduct transactions with them anywhere in the world, hard currency is still a necessity. This current trend may continue until a company comes up with a way to challenge the monopoly of Western Union and develops a system that makes Bitcoin and other digital currencies readily available to people that can be used for transactions. In addition, that company will need to simplify the process of getting hard currency in exchange for digital currencies.

For example, consider that a company I will call, e-Payment, has a mission of turning the millions of smartphones in the world into a handy teller that can effectively be used for dispensing cash. However, a user must be a member of the blockchain network to have access to this service. In this scenario, the sender will be Jonas, and the recipient, Aisha. Rather than take a long bus ride to the nearest Western Union office where Jonas can transfer the money to Aisha, imagine if both of them can carry out their transfer and receipt on their mobile devices. Aisha and Jonas, then, only have to download the e-Payment app on their devices to make the transaction possible.

Jonas can initiate a transfer to Aisha with just a click of a button. The money is transferred to Aisha in her local currency. Aisha may decide to withdraw the money in local currency or make online purchases with the local currency, especially on sites that accept e-Payment as a payment platform. Since Aisha may want to make some local transactions and purchases, such as buy food, go shopping, or pay rent, she obviously needs the local currency. The new system makes it easy and convenient for her to get cash if she wants it. Since this is a global payment system, there are possibly other people in her neighborhood who use the same payment method. Therefore, she can contact any one of them and exchange her digital currency for the local currency. When Aisha checks the e-Payment app, she realizes that there are dozens of users in her neighborhood. She believes that some of them may need digital currency in exchange for the local currency that she needs to handle some of her finances.

She messages the users in her neighborhood to see who is interested in the exchange and their exchange rate. They all respond and give her different exchange bids. By taking into consideration some factors, such as proximity to the seller, the exchange rate, and others, she decides to settle for someone who appears to have the perfect exchange. Without wasting time, she transfers her digital currency in exchange for cash, and each person goes his or her separate way. The entire process from initiating the transfer by Jonas, who lives thousands of miles away, to the time the exchange is completed takes place within a couple of minutes without making a long trip to an exchange. This simple process can take place soon in the future.

When comparing the speed of operation of the conventional money transfer services with this technology that will soon take the world by storm, one can see a clear distinction between the two. For instance, a simple transfer from one person to another via the Western Union will pass through about 8 intermediaries. These include local banks, individual agents, Western Union, and others. Each of these agents charges a fee for its role in the transaction. With the e-Payment system, only three parties are involved; the sender, the platform, and the recipient. The system thus reduces the charges on the transaction, as well as the time spent sending and receiving remittances. This is obviously a new development that many will welcome.

For the e-Payment system to fully meet the needs of the people, it must address some salient issues, such as the availability of other users that one can easily make the exchange with. This requires that the company exists in different countries across the globe and wins the patronage of as many people as possible. If the nearest user is some 50 or more miles away, the distance may defeat the original purpose of the system. It is hoped that this problem will be promptly addressed.

Trust is the second issue that needs to be addressed for the system to succeed. If there is no trust between the users of the app, that may lead to a big challenge that may overrule the whole the system. However, the trust issue is not what many would assume. Many companies have addressed this concern with astounding success over the years. Therefore, it is hoped that people will readily trust each other if they see a valid reason to do so. The key to this system is the smartphone. It can also play the role of an ATM, as it has successfully been used for a variety of services since its release. If users can order an Uber ride via their phone, book flights, and other services, in the future with blockchain, many other services, such as the transfer of money from developed, to developing countries, will be more readily available. With the increasing number money transfers around the world, the future will witness a transformation that will be beneficial to more economies than ever before.

Chapter 22: Blockchain and Humanitarian Aid

The huge benefits of blockchain also cover humanitarian aid. It can have a major mpact on how foreign aid is both delivered and utilized. For years, many countries have granted developing countries foreign aid that runs in the billions of dollars. However, the impact of such foreign aid has not yet been felt by the many of those who need it. This is because the use of those funds is often not transparent. Several studies have pointed to corruption as the problem that leads to the disappearance of such aid in a heartless misappropriation of funds.

Even before the funds are delivered to a needy nation, some unscrupulous intermediaries have been accused of helping themselves to the aid, removing a sizable part of the funds before sending the rest, to where some other corrupt government officials also take a cut before the needy even have access to the remaining aid, which in most cases is far below the original aid. Such selfish acts have thus reduced the impact of aid on the people who are supposed to be the recipients of the aid.

While this is a common trend that is common to government-funded aid, NGOs are not excluded from the problem, too. Many NGOs have turned out to be a farce, and are just an avenue for greedy individuals to get foreign aid that they later divert into personal use. For instance, the Red Cross came under heavy criticism after it was discovered that this internationally recognized NGO did not fulfill its initial vows to bring aid to the Haiti 2010 earthquake victims, but rather squandered the foreign aid received instead of alleviating the suffering of the surviving victims of the natural disaster.

Prior to the collection of this aid, the Red Cross promised to build 130,000 new homes for the victims but failed to so, despite collecting enough funds to cover its promises. Using the country's land title registry as an excuse, the Red Cross ended up only building 6, instead of the promised 130,000 homes. Their excuse was that most lands do not have clear owners, thereby making it difficult to know who owns what. On that pretext, the organization woefully failed to discharge its responsibilities and fulfill its promise.

Blockchain technology could have successfully prevented such neglect from happening. The issue of the confusion over the ownership of lands could have been prevented if the technology has been used to ascertain the ownership of pieces of land. Clear titles would have also then been provided to make the ownership of each piece of land clear. This would have prevented the Red Cross from using this excuse for shirking its responsibilities, and instead ensuring that aid got to the appropriate recipients.

This and other related cases have demonstrated the inefficiency of organizations when it comes to handling funds, especially as intermediaries. This is another area where blockchain can come in and correct the system. Blockchain can enforce honesty and a sense of responsibility when dealing with aid and crisis management. It can provide information from the Internet to find a wide area of application in providing know-how, connections, and the right data that are needed for both volunteer organizations and victims of circumstances, such as the Haiti hurricane victims and other victims of natural disasters. To ensure the appropriate delivery of such aid, without it being diverted by intermediaries, blockchain will first get rid of the intermediaries, who are the main culprits behind the misappropriation of such funds.

Blockchain is an immutable ledger. This attribute enforces integrity, so that aid groups, institutions, governments, and individuals who are involved in charities can do so with integrity and commitment. Failure to do so would result in their actions being seen by all the members of the blockchain network. The fear of being held accountable will override a desire to misappropriate funds.

Imagine how much can be achieved if other organizations, such as UNICEF, WHO, and others use blockchain technology for raising funds. If UNICEF can get money directly to the children who are in dire need of financial and health assistance, and WHO does the same, these bodies will bypass corrupt government agents and other intermediaries.

Such a smart move will open the door for individuals who are in need to sign up for some assistance through a distributed ledger, such as the blockchain and others, that is managed by nodes from different parts of the world. Whenever a grant or aid is delivered, it can be time-stamped for easy monitoring by the nodes. The move will result in the reduction of the tendency for the intermediaries to inflate their spending. In some cases, the complete elimination of such a dubious act is guaranteed. As a result, the aid will be judiciously used to meet the needs of the target audience without anyone converting the funds for personal use.

It is to the credit of UNICEF that it has decided to plan for the future by embracing cryptocurrencies. The international body is currently exploring these digital currencies, so as to maximize these benefits. In 2015, UNICEF launched a digital currency, Unicoin. This is a digital currency that can be mined by children to give them access to digital currency and its benefits. To qualify for this, a child only needs to submit an inspirational drawing to Unicoin. A successful child earns some coins that will be converted into a pencil or notepad as a reward for his or her efforts. In this case, the process takes place strictly between the child and the program, without a need for intermediaries.

As more organizations understand blockchain and are ready to take advantage of its features, we can expect to see many more direct transactions, as well as see people benefit directly from a program that is designed to meet their needs, or to help them cope with a disaster, such as was experienced by Haitians in 2010.

This can also be taken a step further, if the organizations mentioned above can create a program where children can also create personal accounts that will enable them to have direct access to these donations and benefits, without the input of a third-party. When corrupt officials and other greedy people do not have access to such accounts, they will thus be prevented from converting such funds for other uses. The opportunities offered by such a direct program are endless. Blockchain has the capability to make that happen.

In some cases, the input of intermediaries cannot be completely ignored. They can be a necessity when dealing with natural disaster relief and other related activities because the peer-to-peer system will be inefficient in this situation. Nevertheless, the introduction of blockchain will enforce integrity, transparency, and the judicious use of funds. Stakeholders will now be able to e-track the movement of aid from its origin, to its final destination via blockchain technology. This will ensure that the aid gets to the primary target, those that are in dire need of the aid. For instance, if one contributes to polio eradication in a developing country, water purification elsewhere, or towards natural disaster relief, they can easily monitor how their contribution is used and can ascertain whether it is used for the primary objective, or diverted to the funding of a civil unrest or some other personal projects elsewhere.

In the event of missing funds, the organization can be held responsible, since the whole community will be aware of the missing aid. Incorporating smart contracts into the project will also ensure that such organizations are automatically held accountable and responsible for their actions or inactions. Smart contracts will work hand-in-hand together with the blockchain to ensure 100% accountability. For instance, if the fund meant for the relief in Haiti was first released to an escrow, with the instruction for the fund to be released whenever a milestone is reached, the Red Cross would not have gotten access to the funds and reneged on their promise to build 130,000 houses. If the aid was supposed to be released at the completion of a building, they would have got access to the fund for just 6 houses, and not 130,000 houses. That would have drastically reduced the misappropriation of the funds experienced during such an unfortunate disaster. Accountability and transparency would have been enforced, and that would have benefited the victims of the disaster more.

Incorporating blockchain into the system will also bring some challenges. If the beneficiaries of such aid should directly communicate with the program, it simply means that everyone should have a good knowledge of blockchain technology. That is a big challenge that must be addressed and overcome.

Network failure is another challenge. During a disaster, there may be life-threatening challenges, such as an earthquake, hurricane, cyclone, and so on, and these may cause power and network failures. Mobile phone users would then not have access to the blockchain-based program that was set up to bring relief to them, if these services were not available during a crisis. Despite the best efforts of concerned organizations and individuals to prevent corrupt government officials and others from taking advantage of an aid program to enrich themselves, some will still find their way around the program to divert money meant for a relief program. These are just some of the challenges that still must be overcome. Regardless of these challenges, blockchain will still drastically reduce how unscrupulous individuals can misappropriate funds for their personal use.

Chapter 23: E-government: Estonia as a Case Study

Blockchain can also extend its reach to the concept of e-government, in order to make governance readily accessible and to demand transparency from leaders. It can also aimed at making voting and other government-related activities simple, so that the citizens of a country can participate in government from the comfort of their homes.

For example, Estonia is a small country with fewer than 1.5 million people. Regardless of its small population, the country is setting the pace in e-government. In 1991, Estonia had a unique opportunity to define a new form of governance upon gaining independence from Russia. Estonia took that opportunity and designed a unique way to run its government. Estonia's system of governance is now the model for many countries in the world. For instance, when Japan wanted to craft a system that will support e-government, the country did not approach the United States or the U.K. for assistance, but instead conferred with Estonia because the country has set the pace in digital government.

The Estonia government has taken full advantage of interconnectivity, decentralization, and cybersecurity to design a system that allows for more infrastructure to be incorporated into government as the need arises in the future. Currently, the citizens have access to online services and information that make it possible for them to contribute to how the country is run. With their digital identities, they can update their government records and/or conduct businesses.

e-identity

The Estonian government's achievement would not have been possible without digital identity. It is the driving force behind the country's e-government. The government made an effort to ensure that citizens have digital identity. The effort was rewarded by the impressive number of the citizens who now have a digital identity. As of 2012, 9 out of every 10 Estonians had an electronic identify card they can use for transactions, to travel the European Union, and to access government services.

The ID card itself is a database of information. It contains personal information about the cardholder, a PIN that can be used at any time, and two certificates that perform different functions. One of the certificates can be used for providing a digital signature, while the second certificate is designed for authenticating the identity of the cardholder. The citizens use this card for different purposes, such as voting, editing their tax form digitally, having free access to banking services, requesting social security services, and having unrestricted access to public transportation. This has eliminated the need for a bank card because they can perform all banking operations with the card. The card can also be used for checking e-Prescriptions, digital signatures, for proof of authentication when conducting banking activities, national health insurance, and other related activities. The ID card is thus every Estonian's gateway to a wide variety of e-services.

The result has been impressive, and it is proof that e-government can be achievable for all. Just a year after launching the program, 95% of the taxable citizens paid their taxes online, while a higher percentage (98%) conducted online banking. These are not the only sectors where the citizens have utilized their multipurpose ID cards. They have also used it in the education sector as well. Both students and parents in the country have used the e-School for tracking their grades and assignments in order to help them prepare in advance for their academic work. They have also used the card to establish a good relationship with their teachers. This has resulted in improvement in their overall academic performance.

e-Health

The Estonian government did the same in the health sector. It has citizens' health information that has been gathered from different sources to make it credible. Each Estonian can easily access his or her personal health record because the records are not kept in a single database. Each citizen also has absolute control over the degree of his or her health record that is available for the public consumption. Therefore, they can even control the amount of information that is available for their doctors.

The introduction of e-solutions is a revolution in the healthcare system for the country. After visiting a doctor once an online e-Health record will be opened, and this can easily be tracked by authorized personnel only. To ensure the security of the record and to give free access to authorized individuals, it is built on the KSI blockchain technology. This also ensures the reduction of internal threats to such information, while simultaneously ensuring data integrity. The e-Health record can also be used to retrieve data from a wide range of providers, and to present them in a format that doctors will find useful. They can use the tool to gain access to a patient's records, and read the results of tests and X-rays from a remote location.

The whole process is blockchain-based, in order to ensure that the integrity of any record retrieved from the system has not been compromised. This gives medical personnel access to reliable information that can provide the best medical assistance to their patients. For instance, a doctor is at liberty to utilize a patient's ID code for reading some valuable information about a patient, especially during emergency situations.

Some of the information they can have access to in real-time includes recent treatments, blood type, on-going medication, allergies, and related information that will assist the doctor to make the right life-saving medical decisions. In addition to being helpful to the doctors, the system is also useful to the nation because it helps the health ministry to make the best decisions, track epidemics, measure health trends, and ensure the judicious spending of the health budget. The ministry can make these vital decisions by working on the data compiled by the system for national statistics.

e-Voting

During elections, Estonians do not form long queues to exercise their civic rights. The majority of those who qualify to vote do so with their e-Voting cards during national elections. With their mobile-ID or ID card, their location from home is not a barrier during elections because they can log-in anywhere in the world and exercise their voting rights. To preserve the anonymity of the voters, their identities are removed from the ballot prior to sending the information to the National Electoral Commission.

While the e-voting practiced in some areas seem to share some similarities with this voting system, theirs is an elegant and hassle-free voting system, when compared to the time demand attached to other e-voting. Their voting method is also simple and comes with impressive security measures that make it the perfect voting method. What is more, it is highly-efficient and consumes less. It also eliminates the use of problematic and costly machinery that has continued to be the bane of many countries for decades. The results of recent elections have shown the effectiveness of their system during elections. Research shows that 11,000 working days were saved during the last elections that took place in Estonia. In this matter, many countries are doing their best to become the next Estonia.

During the European Parliament elections held in 2014, one third of Estonian voters participated in the elections from 98 countries spread across different continents. That's the power of their paperless-voting system. This figure is expected to rise significantly in the coming elections.

As discussed in the previous chapter, land registry issues formed the basis for the Red Cross to abandon their responsibility during the Haiti earthquake in 2010. That would not have been an issue if the earthquake had occurred in Estonia. The country has a credible electronic land registry system, and that has had a huge impact on the real estate industry in the country. It only takes a little more than a week to finalize the transfer of ownership of a piece of land from a seller, to the buyer. Previously, it would have taken a minimum of three weeks and required a lot of paperwork.

e-Residency

E-residency is another beautiful program that has assisted Estonian citizens, irrespective of their geographical location, to have the country's transnational digital identity. They can also get authentication that gives them access to secure services, to verify, encrypt, and sign documents, not manually, but digitally. Regardless of a place of residence in the world, one can register your company only in less than 30 minutes online. Over the years, the move by the Estonian government to practice e-government has contributed significantly to the development of the small country and has made it a model for other countries to follow. The convenient and safe digital system practiced in Estonia has brought about an unprecedented level of accountability and transparency that can hardly be found anywhere in the world. They have also successfully used the system to save some 800 years of work time every year, while also providing entrepreneurs the right environment that is conducive to starting a business and watch it grow.

e-Business

Estonia leads the list of countries where setting up a business is made easy. Most of the country's e-services are targeted towards making setting up a business and running it effectively to be convenient for the citizens. The country's solution of electronic tax claims, digital signatures, and an e-Business Register has removed unnecessary obstacles and has created an environment that is conducive to running a business as an entrepreneur. In the near future, Estonia hopes to roll out Industry 4.0, another digital revolution that will support the business world. The fact remains that when the environment for setting up a business is fertile and conducive, the chances of such businesses succeeding increase. That is the reason behind the country's impressive reputation as "one of the countries with most start-ups launched per capita than anywhere else in Europe."

Behind all this is cybersecurity. Without a solid cybersecurity system in place, their database would have been breached, and that would have had a negative impact on their efforts to digitalize the country. The country saw the need for an effective cybersecurity built on trust and seized the opportunity to create a strong security system. In Estonia, the technology behind their e-government is built, not on human trust, but is designed in a way that all the information on the government networks can embark on auto verification. This has made it compulsory that the government is as transparent as possible because there is no room that can be exploited and used for deceiving the citizens.

In terms of cybersecurity, Estonia adopted the keyless signature infrastructure (KSI) system. This system makes the verification of any electronic activity possible on a blockchain, even in the absence of cryptographic keys, system administrators, or a government official. This has led to accountability and transparency because the system makes it possible for the stakeholders to monitor the activities on the system. If someone accesses the system, all the information about when the visit was made, what information is accessed, what the person actually did on the system is made available to the public. Thus, everyone is encouraged to comply strictly with the rules governing the system. One can personally verify the integrity of their file and everyone else can do the same.

The system is both efficient and cost-effective. There is no need to sign documents repeatedly or be saddled with the responsibility of protecting keys. The KSI ensures that everything is well-protected. Nothing can be changed in the information protected with KSI. If other countries around the world can follow Estonia's example, we can hash valuable information, such as death certificates, health cards, birth certificates, land titles, business registration, school transcripts, and more from the multiple databases where they are stored into a single blockchain, and have access to integrated services without the assistance of a central processing body.

By implementing this, individuals will be guaranteed maximum protection of their information. As each individual has his or her personal identity information that is not under the absolute control of the government, they can live their lives independent of the government in some areas of life. When discussing the numerous benefits of such a personalized identification, the founder of the Institute for Blockchain Studies, Melanie Swan comments:

The blockchain—with its structure that accommodates secure identities, multiple contracts, and asset management—makes it ideal for situations such as marriage because it means a couple can tie their wedding contract to a shared savings account, and to a childcare contract, land deed, and any other relevant documents for a secure future together. The potentials of blockchain are yet to be fully explored.

As a further example, on Sunday, August 5, 2014, a couple made a world record as they held the first blockchain wedding. The couple signed the dotted lines, while a Bitcoin conference was ongoing at the Disney World, Orlando, Florida. The entire wedding was conducted without the involvement of any religious organization or government. Instead, the marriage was recorded through the Bitcoin blockchain. According to the source, the couple decided to take this step due to their strong believe that the blockchain technology will be here forever. The couple's wedding message reads: "For better or worse, till death do us part, because the blockchain is forever."

When the wedding was over, the couple showed the QR code that was linked to the "transaction," the storehouse for the data associated with their wedding. One of the attendees, a blockchain advocate, expressed the desire of many blockchain enthusiasts in his speech: "In the future, we'll have real, enforceable contracts between loving partners encoded in blockchain."

Chapter 24: Blockchain and Freedom of Speech

The prosperity of a society is determined by many factors, including the freedom of speech and privacy. This implies that the citizens of a society should be free to exercise their freedom of speech without fear of intimidation. They must also be able to enjoy the freedom of anonymous, private communications with their friends and family. Many have been denied these basic rights through online censorship, hacking of information, and data fracking. These factors have created fears that have reduced freedom of expression. These are the major reasons why many have resorted to the use of encryption technologies, such as the use of VPN and other technologies that offer them some degree of anonymity when communicating over the Internet.

Those using these technologies have mastered the art of disguise and can scramble their messages to prevent them from getting to unauthorized personnel. However, encryption technologies are not considered a legal means of communication in many countries. Moreover, they are scarce and cannot be used by those who really need them for identity protection during communications. In some countries, such as China and Russia, access to these technologies is restricted without permission from the government, regardless of whether a corporation or an individual. Without authorization, it is considered illegal to use them. Some countries give permission to use them but through a "backdoor." This requires using a security code or other security measures to bypass the established authentication process and gaining access to a computer while avoiding detection. In most cases, users are ignorant of the existence of these backdoors, and thus are denied the opportunity to use them.

Anonymous and encrypted communications sometimes work in violation of the law and frustrate the efforts of the counter-terrorism agencies and law enforcement due to their ability to make surveillance extremely complicated. This is a source of concern among developed countries, where these technologies are readily available. To address these concerns, some countries have adopted the unconventional methods of censoring websites, even when they are not authorized to do so by a court of law. Russia has taken the lead in this. The country has succeeded in silencing indivisuals and limiting their freedom of speech and expression. The Putin government has also succeeded in banning many print media houses. The goal is to reduce their freedom of expression.

Russia is not the only country that is guilty of stifling freedom of speech. China is another country that has suddenly developed a passion for cutting off individual's freedom of expression. In recent years, the Chinese government has succeeded in blocking almost 90% of individual's access to Google services and has imprisoned many who dared to express their displeasure at the government on social media.

All this was taken a step further in 2015. After the collapse of the Chinese stock market, over a hundred people were arrested for allegedly leveraging the power of social media for spreading harmful rumours that could cause panic and cause disorder in the society and the stock market itself. Governments such as Russia and China are taking advantage of the ease at which people can be victimized and oppressed with technology. However, these trends cannot continue forever. It is hoped that blockchain technology will also provide answers to these problems, just as it has addressed numerous others in the past. For instance, governments will no longer find it convenient to silence opposition, if blockchain is used as a replacement for the present technology. There are a couple of reasons why they will not find blockchain easy to manipulate.

First, the public key infrastructure that will be used by the individuals for encrypting and concealing their identities will be difficult for government agencies to breach. Without easy access to individual's information and communication, governments will find it challenging to oppress anyone or to deny them the freedom of speech that is their basic fundamental right. Second, consider another potential solution to these problems: distributed peer-to-peer micro-blogging. This principle involves working on a platform that is decentralized, so that no one has the means of shutting it down. By using end-to-end encryption for safeguarding communications, communication is well-protected because a potential attacker will have no way of gaining access to create an attack.

One such microblogging platform is Twister, a Twitter clone that works on blockchain technology principle. This fully P2P microblogging platform offers benefits that have increased its appeal since it was created in 2013:

Free speech: Because the platform is completely decentralized, it cannot be censored. Posts are securely kept on the platform, and no one has the authority to remove them. Blocking is also impossible. There is unlimited access to free speech, without the fear of being penalized for expressing a fundamental human right.

No IP recording: While using the Internet, many believe that they are an anonymous user of the Internet. In reality, though, that is far from the truth. They are not anonymous users of the Internet because their IP is recorded and can be used to track a user after their location has been confirmed. This is one of the challenges of anonymity that Twister has addressed. On Twister, an identity is unknown because the IP has been blocked and no one can have access to it. This is the true definition of an anonymous user.

No spying: On Twister, one can also send direct messages. The platform is fully-protected by trusted end-to-end encryption. Both metadata and the content are well-protected. Thus, communicating is anonymous.

The creator of Twister leveraged the powers of BitTorrent protocols and Bitcoin to deploy an end-to-end cryptography that makes it impossible for government to spy on communications. This prevents users from the prying eyes of the government officials that are always on the lookout for people who speak against the government.

In addition, the government will also find it challenging to use the withdrawal of funds to blackmail journalists or journalism. If a government decides to do so, a reputable media house can always seek financial assistance from members of a blockchain network. Investors who appreciate such honest journalism may provide the funding for the media house, especially if they are sympathetic to their cause and against the government's abuse. Since investors can hide under the anonymity offered by the blockchain technology, they will not have to worry about being identified with the opposition. This is an incentive to provide funds for such reputable media houses.

In an attempt to stamp out opposition, some governments are fond of destroying pieces of information that can be used against them. Sometimes, this has proven to be very effective for many governments. The introduction of blockchain technology will eliminate these practices because the decentralization and high security measures attached to the blockchain technology make it a formidable technology beyond the control of the government. Whatever information is already recorded on the blockchain has been permanently embedded and can neither be altered nor destroyed. Such information can thus be used for holding institutions and governments accountable for their actions.

For example, crowdfunding is an effective fund-raising strategy that has been used for raising billions of dollars. Imagine if that fund-raising method were also used for financing media houses, and thus such media houses were no longer on the payroll of the government. This will offer such media houses the liberty to provide nothing but the best information possible to cover politics, without fear or favour, and without being forced to reveal the identity of their sponsors or sources.

Many organizations are already making the move towards secure data transfer, as they are already creating blockchain tools that can be used for guarding and monetizing instant messages via Bitcoin digital currency. Such apps are providing a glimpse of what tomorrow holds in the cryptocurrency world. These blockchain-based apps now abound in the market. To complement the efforts of these apps, there is also the distributed immutable ledger. This ledger is different from the traditional ledger and can be used for ensuring the transfer of files, without any authorized person having access to the information contained in the ledger. If this ledger is used for securing information for media houses, it will thus provide a convenient way for the media houses to do what they are good at without the fear of oppression.

Journalists can also purchase the rights to create personal entries on the platform, and these will be available to everyone on the ledger. This technique will prove effective in curbing the excesses of government, especially when it comes to granting the press the freedom they need to feed citizens accurate information. Even where the government sees a piece of information it considers anti-government, it will not be able to remove the content. An example is the content the Chinese government found on Wikipedia. Unlike the Chinese government that deleted this offensive piece, once the information is already stored on the ledger, the government will not have the power to either block, or delete it.

While the government may decide to take court action against a media house that publishes an anti-government content, there is a good chance that the government will lose the case. Even if the government wins, and the judge orders that the entry should be altered to reflect in a government's favor, that can only be done by creating a new entry that will reflect the judge's verdict. However, since the original content that triggered the dispute still cannot be altered, both the new entry and the existing content will remain on the ledger. In that case, it will still always be available for public consumption.

Chapter 25: Challenges of Blockchain Implementation

Blockchain technology, just like any other preceding technologies, has some challenges. While the previous chapters are dedicated to the allure of blockchain technology, this chapter will discuss challenges that the technology faces and the potential impact of those challenges in the future.

Unfamiliar Technology

Blockchain technology is still quite new, and therefore, not many yet have a full knowledge of the technology. Many are still also have little awareness of Bitcoin and cryptocurrency, two other terms related to blockchain technology. The few with adequate knowledge of the technology creates a big challenge, especially during financial crisis. During financial crisis, individuals can turn to digital currency for online transactions and meet their basic needs because digital currencies are not subjected to the local economic conditions. However, that will not happen until there is a greater awareness about digital currencies.

Regulations

Blockchain technology has given rise to the production of new products and services. It is disturbing that an effective regulatory body has not been put in place to address the issues of writing the transactions. It is true that the technology has incorporated transparency into its network, but there is still the need for new regulations to control how the technology is used. It also comes with distributed ledger transactions that have the potential to permanently impacts auditing processes for financial reporting. This also requires a set of regulations to protect information-sharing, and by extension, protect financial and auditing companies, customers, and investors from the evolution of the blockchain technology. Blockchain's smart contracts also have a crucial role to play in the development and application of blockchain in the future. Smart contracts need to be regulated, as well. That is the only way to ensure that the technology is not abused, and to prevent potential negative impact on the industry.

Illiquidity

There are also concerns about the illiquidity of blockchain. Bitcoin, the leading digital currency created from blockchain is finite. It has a cap of just 21 million and a deadline of 2140. The objective of capping the coin is to prevent flooding the economy with it as a preventive measure against inflation. In contrast, fiat currencies are known to be controlled by irrational monetary policies that create unnecessary inflation that may destabilize the economy. This is impossible with the capping of Bitcoin.

Therefore, as more users accept the coin, it experiences a surge in value. This will automatically attract more users as current events have shown. However, while increasing the value of the coin is appealing, there is the possibility of losing all one's coins within a short period of time. If a wallet is lost whatever coins are in it, as well as the subsequent ones that are accidentally sent to it, are lost permanently, especially if the private keys are also lost. This will eventually reduce the number of coins in circulation. If that happens to a certain number of users, the coins will eventually fall far below the projected 21 million

Huge Energy Consumption

In order for a single Bitcoin transaction to be validated, miners will attempt over 450 thousand trillion solutions every second. This consumes a huge amount of computer power and electricity. The proof-of-work has also been used extensively to build people's trust in the blockchain. Although the method has awed many people because it enforces transparency and trustworthiness, it is expensive to run. Many people cannot afford the basic requirements to do so. Therefore, it will be quite challenging for such individuals to take full advantage of the blockchain technology. The power consumption during a transaction validation is estimated to be equal to that of 700 average Americans, or the entire island of Cyprus. That's some 4.5 kilowatt-hours. It is also estimated that it takes over $100 million in electricity annually to process and protect the entire Bitcoin in circulation, about $3 billion worth of the coin. In addition to the high energy needed for mining, power is also needed to cool the mining machines to prevent accidental failure. Obviously, these machines need a huge quantity of electricity to be in operation, and that will also pose a challenge.

High Latency

It usually takes 10 minutes for a transaction to be confirmed on the Bitcoin blockchain network. When compared with some payment mechanisms, this is still a fairly reasonable time. However, while this time is not too long, it may not be ideal for controlling the Internet of Things (IoT) where everything is purely-controlled by blockchain. The devices connected via the Internet of Things must communicate continuously without a break. The time is also too long to conduct financial transactions that are highly dependent on timing. When a need exists to conduct a transaction at a specific time for a specific purpose and the blockchain network is busy with its calculation during that time, this may be frustrating.

The good news is that other digital currencies have addressed this issue by having a latency that is far lower than the ten minutes offered by Bitcoin. For instance, Litecoin has a block time of just 2.5 minutes, while some currencies, such as Ethereum and Ripple, even have a block time of mere seconds.

Opposition from Governments

The problems discussed above are not the only obstacles that blockchain has to contend with. There is also the opposition from governments. This is a disturbing obstacle if one considers how powerful governments are and their natural tendency to stifle the opposition. Blockchain technology is already giving hard currency a fight for relevancy as many countries and organizations are gradually adopting the use of digital currencies as a credible medium of exchange.

Recently, China has given us an inkling of what to expect from governments, if they consider digital currencies as a big threat to their currencies. A number of these governments are concerned about their local currencies, if digital currencies eventually become the globally acceptable medium of exchange. Regulators, legislators, and other stakeholders around the world may push back against it. Courts may rule against blockchain, which would not be surprising, considering their stand on intellectual property. The opposition may be fierce.

Cybersecurity Concerns

Blockchain comes with built-in security measures. For instance, being a distributed and decentralized technology reduces the probability of people taking advantage of the technology and abusing it. A user can count on the technology's strong encryption for security. Nevertheless, there are still cybersecurity concerns about the technology.

These concerns need to be addressed promptly because that is the only way to convince the general public to entrust their personal information or data to blockchain technology.

Behavioral Changes

These are another challenge that may stand in the way of blockchain technology. When some people have issues with their credit card or bank account, they can easily walk up to their bank or the credit card company to lodge a complaint. The ease of doing so has prevented many people from backing up such information. They are convinced that they can always find help whenever they need it, and thus do not bother to have a reliable back up for confidential information.

It is true that blockchain comes fully-armed with its own security system. However, if users do not make effort to ensure the security of their information, they may find it quite challenging to be able to do so in the future. The freedom offered by the blockchain is that it includes stronger security, improved privacy, and autonomy, all of which places more responsibility on the user. A user must ensure that they have a backup for their information and private keys, so they can retrieve these whenever needed. Without the ability to take care of such information, one will have to use third-party services to provide them with backup service.

Integration Concerns

Blockchain technology has been found to be useful in nearly all the sectors of the human economy. As a result, many organizations and industries may consider incorporating it into their businesses or brands. However, this will raise many integration issues. This is because some changes need to be made before the technology can be adapted into an existing system. Sometimes, little changes may need to be made to the system, while there may also be the need for a complete overhaul of the system in some cases. In order to switch to blockchain, companies must consider the cost and other factors, all of which impact the switching to a new system. These integration concerns are some of the most important challenges that must be overcome before the technology can be completely adopted by all.

Inaccessibility

As of the time of this writing, a large percentage of the human population does not have access to blockchain. The available wallet support cannot yet cater to the need of billions of people. Even the existing wallets have user interfaces that are less than ideal. Much still needs to be done if these challenges will be overcome, so that the majority of those interested in blockchain can have easy access to it.

Lack of Legal Recourse

The existence of smart contracts and the irreversibility of blockchain-based transactions are responsible for this challenge. While one is free to make any choice with the technology, the truth is that after making their choice, they are stuck with it. A user cannot withdraw for whatever reason, as is exemplified by smart contracts that will be enforced automatically, regardless of how a user may feel later about an agreement they have previously signed. The global market has never witnessed such certainty. The moment a user signs an agreement or performs a transaction, it is 100% irrevocable. This has greatly improved efficiency and performance. Regardless of how appealing this may be, however, it also has its downside, too. Some may still find a way to renege on their promise, and the judiciary may be needed to settle such disputes.

It is estimated that some 80% of contract breaches are usually ignored instead of being enforced. This is partially due to the high cost of pursuing a court case. Can one expect the situation to improve with the introduction of blockchain technology? Remember that the technology is in absolute control of transactions. What happens when it certifies a transaction as completed? Can it be proven that a breach of agreement has taken place? Does the disgruntled party have enough evidence to pursue the case in court? Even if the case is brought to court, will the court recognize a case that was based on some technology, and not a signed piece of evidence? What about small investors, do they have what it takes to initiate a legal action against big corporations if they feel cheated by such corporations? These are just some of the questions that will need to be answered because of the possible future scenarios they entail.

However, these challenges will never stop the general acceptance of blockchain in the future. Over time, people will gradually begin to trust the technology. Regulations will be put in place to monitor its use. Blockchain will evolve. That's one of the qualities of an emerging technology. Its wide areas of application are reassuring, and its evolution may be faster than previously imagined. Therefore, these challenges can be viewed as only temporary setbacks, and not permanent roadblocks.

Fear of Existing Corporations

Existing corporations are a big threat to blockchains' growth. Just as is customary of these corporations, they may seize the technology for their selfish needs, without using it to meet the growing needs of individuals. The concern over the selfishness of these corporations first came to the forefront during the early days of the Internet. Powerful corporations decided to use their financial power to wrest the Internet's power away from individuals and use it to get the most value for their purposes. They have succeeded in privatizing the digital experience, while shutting out others completely. That's why many corporations now work so secretly, and are also secretive about their plans, information assets, and technology infrastructures.

If they could do that to the Internet, there is the growing concern that blockchain technology may suffer a similar fate. Powerful countries may also feel the need to capture the technology for their selfish interests, without anyone powerful enough to stop them from executing their plans. Even if you have a consensus mechanism for personal use, it can still be sold for the highest bidder, when rich countries and wealthy individuals are ready to use their financial or political powers to get the willingness of people to support their cause, even if that involves selling the mechanism to these people.

Nevertheless, it would be foolish to expect huge organizations and wealthy countries to steer clear of the technology. Blockchain technology is an evolving technology that has a lot to offer. The input of governments and other individuals will eventually assist the developers to maximize the full potentials of the technology. We need these corporations for job and wealth creation, while the government is saddled with the responsibility of providing for other needs. Therefore, both are important and will do well to contribute to the growth of the technology. However, we should be concerned about these organizations and governments taking over the technology completely, without offering any benefit to the people, yet this is preventable, as proven by an incident in the past.

A few years ago, some hackers stole nearly eight million VeriCoins from a reputable exchange, MintPal. Happily, some developers worked to reverse the attack by forking the

VeriCoin blockchain before the hack. This literally means that the developers rolled back time. Thus, VeriCoin was prevented from feeling the huge impact of such a loss. Cryptocurrency experts believe that the same measures can be used to prevent the selfish use of the blockchain technology if some groups of greedy investors, corporations, or governments decide to capture the technology for their personal and selfish use by initiating a fork on the real version of the Bitcoin they decide to capture.

Difficult to Govern

A big challenge that blockchain investors and stakeholders have been struggling with is how to optimize the potentials of this technology. No one can doubt its potential to turn the world around and create endless opportunities for people to make the world a better place, but there is a huge question mark about the most effective way to achieve these goals.

Other technologies, such as the Internet, are governed by a regulatory body that decides how to get the best out of the technology. The Internet has the World Wide Web Consortium and others that work together with the Internet to foresee user's needs and to work towards addressing them. That has led to the unprecedented transformation of the Internet from a simple tool, to a great platform that has been used by people from all walks of life as a research tool, online resource, digital library, and a host of other uses. The absence of such bodies for blockchain technology is another obstacle that may serve as an impediment to its growth.

Another challenge here is the inability of those working towards taking the technology to another level to reach a consensus agreement on the right way to achieve that. They have been unable to agree on a convenient way to ensure the decentralization of the technology, as well as to keep it open without compromising its security. If this problem is not promptly addressed, it is believed that stakeholders may eventually split into warring factions, and this may signal a gradual decline of the technology.

No Adequate Incentives

Miners work behind the scene to keep blockchain technology going. For their efforts, they earn some fractions of a Bitcoin. This serves as an incentive for them to keep working, and thus preserve the technology. What happens if they are not rewarded for their efforts, or if there is network failure? They will lose whatever Bitcoin they have earned and could earn in the future.

The future seems to be gloomy for the miners. As they gradually work towards the pre-determined Bitcoin value, the incentives they get for their efforts also gradually reduce until the cap is reached. What happens then? Most miners will obviously have nothing to show for their efforts and may thus not have any incentive to continue working to ensure the preservation of the blockchain. Some of these miners may shift to another emerging altcoin that offers them the right incentive.

There is also the issue of offering both the miners in the regions where power is cheap and in those with a high cost of power the right incentives to keep working for the overall well-being of the network. The promise of a better incentive by some wealthy individuals for personal gains may lure them away from their obligations, and even assist the wealthy individuals or governments to convert the technology for personal use. In this case, the interested party only need to gain 51% of the nodes and could buy off the remaining 49% to have absolute control of the technology. This scenario may become a reality, with the right incentives from a third-party interested in the blockchain technology.

These are some of the outstanding challenges that the blockchain technology must overcome before it becomes widely accepted. As previously mentioned, they are not insurmountable challenges and should be expected to be overcome in the future.

A Job Killer

Some consider blockchain technology to be a job killer, in respect to the number of areas for which the technology will be deployed in the future. The advocates of this opinion believe that the introduction of the technology will deprive many of employment opportunities, while those in the workforce may lose their jobs to automation that will be supported by smart contracts.

This brings to mind the recent fury that attended the introduction of robots into the workforce. Therefore, the opposition to blockchain always makes reference to the displacement of many people from their works as the robots take over. It may take some years before such individuals are convinced that this technology is not a job killer, but a job creator. The fear of people losing their jobs to the technology was so palpable that, in 2015, it was a topic of consideration at the World Economic Forum held in Davos, Switzerland.

Still Being Watched

Blockchain technology is usually sold to the general public on the basis of its security. It is obviously one of the safest technologies around. The fact that it is a decentralized technology adds to its security because it is never under the control of a single person or organization. Nevertheless, some governments and big companies may decide to still break all protocols and invade individual privacy. This conclusion is drawn from past experiences where such bodies are known for engaging in cyberwarfare or spying on others because of what they stand to gain from it.

A Powerful Tool for Criminals

This was the first challenge blockchain technology had to deal with since the introduction of the technology some years ago. Naysayers hang their pessimism on some of the attributes of blockchain that can make it appealing to criminals to perpetrate their criminal activities. They argued that this is because the technology has an impressive speed, is decentralized, and encourages peer-to-peer transactions.

To further lend credibility to this assumption, there was the unfortunate event that occurred in October 2013, on Silk Road, a site that is notorious for its criminal activities, such as money laundering. When the FBI ransacked the office, they discovered that over 13,000 of the listings were Bitcoin-priced. Products were then secretly mailed to the recipients to evade detection by the law enforcement agencies. This police takeover had an immediate impact on the price of Bitcoin, as the digital currency suffered a drop in price, while many were made to consider digital currencies as the tools of criminals.

Conclusion

When Internet technology was at its early stage, many were skeptical about its potential, but time has proven them wrong. Similarly, both developers and users of the new blockchain technology advocate for it as a technology that not only has immense potential and applications for the future, but that it is also one that can be trusted.

Now that you have read this book and learned all about blockchain and cryptocurrencies, this is the time to start preparing for the future. Invest in cryptocurrency, and you, too, will soon enjoy the significant individual and financial empowerment blockchain technology can offer.

Preview of Cryptocurrency:

Mining, Investing and Trading Bitcoin, Ethereum, Litecoin, Ripple, Dash, Gridcoin, Iota, Digibyte, Dogecoin, Emercoin, Putincoin, Auroracoin and others [3rd edition]

By Abraham K white

AN EXCERPT FROM THE SAMPLE CHAPTER: BITCOIN, ETHEREUM, AND LITECOIN

The anxiety and enthusiasm surrounding Bitcoin can hardly be overshadowed by any other technological invention. Digital currency has been a source of curiosity since it entered the mainstream market approximately in 2011. Currently, interest in Bitcoin is at its highest level: its value has skyrocketed significantly, making millionaires out of those who had previously acquired it in large quantities.

Bitcoin uses decentralized technology for smooth, safe payments and helps store money on its network without any need for real names. As advertised in the mass emails sent out upon its introduction, Bitcoin was produced to liberate money, in ways similar to how the internet provides free information to its users.

Paul Blough (BloughTech) states that the acceptance and adoption of Bitcoin should not be the only subject of focus; rather, emphasis should be placed on the amount of time it will take other virtual currencies to use blockchain technology as well. The earliest user of a type of technology is not always its eventual leader. In addition, while development and research has focused on getting the best from blockchain technology, no specific standard has yet been set.

HOW BITCOIN IS WIRED

Similar to other prominent types of cryptocurrency, Bitcoin operates on a public ledger known as the blockchain.

"Bitcoin's P2P network architecture is much more than a topology choice. Bitcoin is a peer-to-peer digital cash system

by design, and the network architecture is both a reflection and a foundation of that core characteristic. Decentralization of control is a core design principle, and that can only be achieved and maintained by a flat, decentralized P2P consensus network" – Andreas Antonopoulos

As mentioned earlier, blockchain stores decentralized records of transactions held equally by every user of the network, once they have been updated. Bitcoins are created when users manufacture blocks within the system. The computer abilities of users are used to cryptographically create every block. The block is then added to the blockchain, giving users the room to earn, as well as the ability to keep the network in shape. To ensure its value keeps increasing, a restriction on the number of bitcoins that can be created has been embedded into the system. The highest possible number of bitcoins that can be created is around 20 million. Currently, more than 14 million are already in circulation.

UNMASKING THE BITCOIN INVENTOR

As aforementioned, Satoshi Nakamoto is the assumed pseudonym of the creator of Bitcoin and blockchain in general. Numerous efforts to unveil the individual behind this name have proven futile. Recently, a computer scientist from Australia was quoted as saying that he was Satoshi Nakamoto, but he couldn't prove this claim. He subsequently confessed to having made this claim because he wanted the fuss about Satoshi's identity to die down.

THE POPULATION THAT HAS EMBRACED THE BITCOIN

Dieter Huelskamp states that with Bitcoin, there is no certainty regarding the number of Bitcoin users because anyone can use multiple accounts for their exchanges. Also, some accounts can eventually be left idle permanently. However, Huelskamp suggests that one could trace some addresses that were used during transactions within the Bitcoin platform. Better still, one could check the number of addresses that had ever owned bitcoins. The total number in 2014 was about 2.5 million. That information is embedded in the database and introduced during transactions. Another intriguing discovery was that many of the more than two million addresses had not been moved in about three years, which implied that users who are particularly active within the platform are largely minimal, when compared to those who use mostly fiat currencies.

Currently, about six million people around the world have procured cryptocurrencies. A large percentage of them have Bitcoin wallets. In recent times, renowned sites, such as WordPress, Reddit, Namecheap, and Mega, have begun accepting payment in bitcoins for their services.

BITCOIN'S ECONOMIC POWER

In response to a question about Bitcoin's economic implications, Pair (BitPay) states that Bitcoin users can transact internationally without any risk of fraud through credit cards, or related electronic transactions. People occasionally overlook the fact, however, that in some nations around the world, credit card payment is not possible. Such nations therefore cannot participate in internet-based economic transactions. If payment through Bitcoin becomes possible in such countries, and if the United States government accepts the integration of this new and promising sector, the world's economy could receive a significant boost.

The transfer of monies without fees or charges, the investment of traditional currencies, and the funding of companies' activities are among the most common uses of Bitcoin. Bitcoin can also be used to purchase goods on some websites. Some stores in the United Kingdom also accept payments through Bitcoin. Sushi restaurants, pubs, CEX stores and Dell's website, among other vendors, are active traders of Bitcoin. Interestingly, there are several Bitcoin ATMs where bitcoins can also be withdrawn. Other Bitcoin holders hang onto their bitcoins and hope that they will accumulate and earn a significant amount of interest. Electronics, such as cameras, computers, musical instruments, and blood pressure monitors, can be purchased at bitcoinstore.com, using bitcoins as the medium of exchange. There are also Bitcoin-friendly casinos, such as SatoshiBet. Bets of Bitcoin is another prediction market that is based mainly on bitcoins.

Generally, the infrastructure for administering the exchange and storage of bitcoins has grown rapidly. Exchange platforms, in-hand trade facilitators, and Bitcoin debit card dealers have increased in number over the years.

Bitcoin wallets are essentially a set of specially-designed programs that store users' bitcoins, much in the same way a regular wallet stores one's money. They can be used on a computer system or a standard smartphone and can be stored securely on the web, from which they can be accessed anywhere in the world with internet.

Investors can even safely keep *paper wallets* because systems are available for production and printing. There are equally advanced secure e-wallets for users who tend to misplace physical documents.

Casascius coins are already available for purchase. These are compilations and physical illustrations of most Bitcoin stories on the internet. Sold by Mike Caldwell on his website casascius.com, a casascius coin contains a private key on a particular card that has been embedded in the coin. These coins are then sealed with a hologram.

Caldwell lives in Utah and owns a payroll software business. He has about 30 employees and is not affiliated in any way with the Bitcoin Foundation. He is simply a highly-informed and enthusiastic investor in the Bitcoin platform. He believes very strongly in a positive future for the Bitcoin market. He has been a long-time investor, continually investing in the digital currency.

In an interview, Caldwell recalled that chaos and fear erupted when the first Bitcoin crash occurred in 2011. He said news spread that a site had been attacked, which led most to assume that Bitcoin had failed as a cryptocurrency. However, during the crash, Caldwell purchased even more coins, while everyone else was confused over how to proceed.

Those who invested early in Bitcoin are now millionaires. Due to its volatile nature, the exchange rate can rise to unimaginable numbers within days. Since 2013 (the year in which Bitcoin became mainstream), the price of Bitcoin has gone up and down. In fact, that same year, its price rose about 10,000 percent. This trend didn't continue, however, as the breakdown of MT Gox, the biggest Bitcoin exchange platform, caused Bitcoin's price to drop drastically. Soon after, the price began to rise once more, and as of this writing, it is quite high. This success is attributed to the efforts of some regulators that have constantly touted Bitcoin and trade tokens related to Bitcoins. While some pundits have suggested that the recent rise in the price of Bitcoins is just the beginning of greater realizations in the field, others believe it is just another rush period that is ultimately susceptible to yet another crash.

The great increase in Bitcoin value has also been linked to money laundering activities due to the inability to link a wallet to any particular individual.

INVESTING IN BITCOIN

Without a central server or a set of trusted parties, Bitcoin is decentralized. Every transaction is based on cryptographic proof, and not merely on trust.

Investopedia states that Bitcoin is very lucrative at the moment, with individuals, firms and institutions remaining in the system. For a regular individual, there are many ways to acquire and invest in Bitcoin. Sites such as Bitstamp, Local Bitcoin, and Coinbase are well-known for their efforts to promote Bitcoin. Each site has both advantages and disadvantages, so individuals should determine which works best for them.

With traditional currencies, a level of trust is required to make transactions work. For instance, customers must trust their banks to keep their money safe for them. They must also be sure their money will be readily available for use at any point. Banks loan depositor's money in a bid to make a profit. However, with cryptographic proof in the digital currency system, there is no need for a third-party or middleman. Transactions can be safe, fast, and easy, while money can be stored securely.

Moreover, the adoption of bitcoins is bound to increase with time. Its community is expanding rapidly. Chalmers Brown states that he believes if Bitcoin keeps increasing in popularity, and with the inclusion of a stable price, additional organizations and individuals will soon start using it. Brown also believes that because efforts are being made to blend Bitcoin with the standards and regulations in many countries, and more research is being done to discover ways to use Bitcoin on the blockchain, users will eventually become more comfortable with it.

Through decentralization, Bitcoin has proven resistant to theft and fraud. Additionally, it charges no transaction fees. As the price increased from a few dollars, to about $1,100 in 2013, Bitcoin was able to provide massive returns to its investors at the end of that same year. Those who invested more than $1,000 about five years ago are now millionaires.

It is important, however, to note the volatility of bitcoin. In 2016, Bitcoin's price rose significantly, reaching a high of $2,400. However, in May 2016 the price suddenly decreased to only $400 in one day.

Nick Chandi, using the nickname SlickPie, has asserted that cryptocurrency is here to stay, even though mining has become relatively expensive. Perhaps investing in Bitcoin and other cryptocurrencies is still a good idea. However, the Bitcoin evolution may be past its prime, as the digital currency world is still developing. The years during which the platform was similar to gold have passed. Members of the mining pools enjoy more of the currency because of the high number of investors that continued to use human and material resources, as well as a significant number of technological products. Chandi concluded that this type of development would assist the growth of other cryptocurrencies.

Made in the USA
Middletown, DE
03 May 2018